United Nations and Prison Justice

About the Author

James Vadackumchery, Criminologist, M.A. (Crim.), D.Ph., LL.B., Ph.D., First rank holder for B.A. (Crim.) of Karnatak University and M.A. (Crim.) of Saugor University, 2nd rank holder for LL.B (Law) and D.Ph. examinations; Ph.D. in Criminal Justice (Kerala University), Gold Medalist and National Merit Scholarship Winner.

Authentic author of 60 authoritative and research books in the special areas of Police, Crime and Justice and 1000 articles – research and popular-in professional journals, news papers and periodical publications of repute.

Member of many professional organizations; Visiting Professor in universities and institutions of higher learning, research and training including Reserve Bank of India, National Judicial Academy etc.; Member, Board of Studies in Criminology of Karnatak and Saugor Universities and State Advisory Board on Correctional Administration, Member, State Prison Review Committee (Kerala), Consultant to Police Welfare Commission, Public Speaker and Human Rights Activist, Broadcaster over AIR and Telecaster in Indian and International T.V. networks and a constant Consultant to the media (print and electronic) on criminological and human rights issues, Criminologist on the Faculty of the State Police Training College, Thiruvananthapuram for nearly three decades, now a practising lawyer.

Examiner in Universities, Service Commissions and Public Undertakings, Evaluator of research works and theses and supervising teacher for Ph.D. degree in Kerala and Mahatma Gandhi Universities.

A name listed in the International Dictionary of Biographies of the IBC, Cambridge and the winner of the Distinguished International Scholar Award for Life-time Achievement-2003 of the American Society of Criminology, Recepient of the Prestigious Supra Deb Medal of Calcutta University, 2007 and enlisted in Limca Book of Records, 2006 as the one who wrote most books in the special area of crime, police and justice.

United Nations and Prison Justice

The Complete Revision of the Standard Minimum Rules for the Treatment of Prisoners, 1957

JAMES VADACKUMCHERY

CONCEPT PUBLISHING COMPANY PVT. LTD.
NEW DELHI-110059

ISBN-13: 978-81-8069-961-0

First Published 2014

Published and Printed by

Concept
Since 1974

Concept Publishing Company Pvt. Ltd.
A/15-16, Commercial Block, Mohan Garden
New Delhi-110059 (India)
T: 25351460, 25351794, *F*: 091-11-25357109
E: publishing@ccnceptpub.com, W: www.conceptpub.com
Editorial Office: H-13, Bali Nagar, New Delhi-110 015, India.

Cataloging in Publication Data--*Courtesy:* D.K. Agencies (P) Ltd. <docinfo@dkagencies.com>

Vadackumchery, James.
United Nations and prison justice : the complete revision of the Standard Minimum Rules for the Treatment of Prisoners, 1957 / James Vadackumchery.
p. cm.
Includes bibliographical references (p.) and index.
ISBN 9788180699610

1. Prisoners—Legal status, laws, etc.—India. 2. Correctional law—India. 3. United Nations. Standard Minimum Rules for the Treatment of Prisoners, 1957. I. Title.

DDC 344.540356 23

Dedicated to

CHAKKAPPEN [Jacob]
MARIAMMA [Mary]
My parents
and
Anna, George, Ammu
Maria & Ann
My grandchildren
and
Abhilash, Martin
My sons-in-law
and
Neethu, Neethi
My daughters
and
MARY
My wife

Preface

During 1973-75, I was doing my Master's Degree in Criminology and Forensic Science in Saugor University (as the university was then known. It is now renamed as Sir Hari Singh Gour Viswavidyalaya, Sagar, India), we were introduced to the Standard Minimum Rules, 1957 adopted by the United Nations. Even at that time, we raised our objection against the caption of the UN document. The reasons were many, but the most prominent one has been that we knew very well that a Standard could not be prescribed in the treatment of prisoners throughout the world alike. Some countries are well developed while some others are developing. Some are small, some are large. A great variety of conditions, values, customs, religions, faiths, philosophies, traditions and level of living may be seen throughout the world. Nevertheless, a caged bird is a caged bird everywhere. No doubt, the human dignity must be protected everywhere alike, cruelty to the prisoners must be eradicated, inhuman and degrading treatment and punishments must be stopped and in every sense, the effect of isolation/segregation from the family, community and society must be minimized, whatever may be the offence and its nature.

'Standard' means 'anything' as a rule or principle that is used as a basis for judgement. Standard means "an approved model". There cannot be such an approved model which can be applied throughout the world. At the same time, one may think of *Guidelines* for every country. As it is today, the so named Rules are not legally binding. They are considered as *Guidelines*—nothing more, nothing less. The *Guidelines* are fine and they can be implemented *mutatis mutandis* in all countries. *Guidelines* are better than *standard* in every sense.

During the academic course and afterwards, I had many occasions to visit jails and I could observe that the "humans" inside the prisons live in inhuman or sub-human conditions and they have been pointed out by many Prison Reform Committees/Commissions appointed mostly in many parts of the world. Their recommendations remain in papers and in many nations one does not find even "creature comforts" ensured to the caged humans. While the caged birds and animals are provided with good food, medical care, living conditions, cleanliness and hygiene, etc., they are indifferently provided to the people inside the prisons. Prisons are still punitive or better severely punitive in every sense—in spirit and letters. In countries which are underdeveloped, the conditions in prisons are loathsome and sometimes, horrible. Researchers and Reform Committees in many countries attest to the fact that life in prisons is worse than the same in hell.

I started a discussion in *LinkedIn* and the discussion was very active and vibrant for more than four months. Many participated. Nevertheless, I could see that most of the participants in the *LinkedIn* discussion were from a particular country which is economically highly developed. I could see that they could not understand the issues and aching problems faced by prisons, prisoners and officials in other countries. They were under the impression that all was well all over the world-or-all was similar all over the world, exactly as they are in their country. People who eat Pizza do not or cannot know the problems of those under starvation or under semi-starvation. Tapioca is good, but one should get it as a food. Precisely, therefore, let us forget about the *"Standard Minimum"*, rather let us think about *"Guidelines"* for better prisoning and prison-administration. There are countries where custodial staff may be plenty and they manage prison administration. There may be, in some countries a few or no correction staff. If at all one sees a few correction-staff, they receive only a step-motherly attitude/approach from the administration.

There are countries where people die of acute poverty and the photographs of live-skeletons of little children and the aged appear in the media. My God!, they are beyond human conception or imagination! There are prisons in such countries too and a "Standard" prescribed or found good in one country—especially in a well developed country—cannot be applied in another country which is incredibly underdeveloped.

During 1970s and even today, after reading the Standard Minimum Rules, 1955, some of the political party men, police and prison officials, well meaning citizens and concerned prison workers make comments: "It is better to go to a prison than to live in a free society". Yes, they see a lot of disparity in life styles in prisons and outside. Outside the prison, the people are starving while food or prescribed diet may be ensured in jails. Some people say that the jail kitchens are the richest ones in the country as they have budgetary allotment of money for the purchase of food items. Of course, they may be an exaggerated version of what people speak of life in prison and outside, yet the fact remains that there is a lot of truth behind such exaggerations. The life in prisons and the same outside should not conflict each other when "Guidelines" (Not Standard Minimum Rules) are issued and enforced.

Prisons and punishment—both have an unpleasant history. Prisons become a centre for punishment in 1704 and therefore, imprisonment, being a continuation of the punitive policies and corporal punishments became another form of infliction of pain and torments. There is no dearth of literature to show inhuman and subhuman life during imprisonment in the past. Some committed suicide while others became physically and mentally ill. Owing to many humanitarian approaches till date to prisoners, a lot of changes in attitude and approaches came into being—from an utter unconcern to more human rights friendly outlooks. As a result, the personality of prisoners is now taken into account while they undergo incarceration.

Prisoners mean those who suffer imprisonment in a jail or those who stay in a jail as remanded prisoners. The verbal picture of many prisons is horrifying and literature on incarceration is terrifying to anyone having a conscience. In order to effect a change in prison life, prison-management and approach to prisoners, the Standard Minimum Rules for the Treatment of Prisoners was adopted on August 30, 1955 by the First United Nations' Congress on the Prevention of Crime and Treatment of Offenders. At that time, the Science of Correction was not a developed branch in Criminology and therefore, the word 'Prisoner' was used in the Rules. Today, many are of the view that the expression, "Prisoner" is not a "nice to hear" word. Today no one likes to be called a *"Prisoner"* although many look down upon him/her as a "Prisoner after all". The objectives of punishment have travelled a long way from retribution

(*Lex Talionis*) to correction, reformation, rehabilitation, resocialisation, reorientation and reintegration to society back. In other words, a wholistic change for a total transformation in the personality of the crime-doer is the objective of punishment now. The causes of crime have travelled a long way from demonology and innate deprivation to multiple-causation approach, victimology, victim-victimizer relations, victim as a cause of crime, etc.

About 60 years ago or around 1957, a "prisoner" was abhoringly hated and was avoided by many. In my childhood, a prisoner was like an individual who suffered from a deadly and contagious disease and all ran away from him/her as they were afraid of the communicable disease which killed the mankind. Students from schools often visited prisons to see the convicted offenders and those 'humans' inside the bars were only items of curiosity to be seen and enjoyed by the picnic parties. Such pupils saw the gallows in Central Prisons as something not seen or touched till then and the caged convicts were like animals in a zoo. They were feared and, teachers as well as the prison authorities never allowed the picnic students to talk to the prisoners thrown to jail life. They were considered to be "less than human" who needed treatment, advice, admonition and avoidance. Penology was a subject for undergraduate/post graduate courses in criminology in universities during 1970s and the students were told that Penology was the Science or Study of Punishment. Penology was coined from a Latin word *Poena* by Francis Liber, a German Criminologist in 1834. Penology, Poena, Penitentiary, Punishment, Prisoners, Jailor, Warder, hard labour, solitary confinement, death penalty, gallows, chains, handcuffs, cells, capital punishment, imprisonment, etc. were the frequently heard words from the classes of Penology. Today, no student of criminology studies Penology as a subject. Instead, he/she studies the Science of Correction. Who needs 'correction'?—the family?, society?, crime-doer?, culture?, convict?, law enforcement machinery?, criminal justice system?, laws and procedure?, institutions for housing the convicts? There is a growing feeling amidst the people and among the convicts that correction is more needed, perhaps to the prison staff than the same to the prisoners. Certainly, it is an issue which may call for heated debate and in my ***LinkedIn*** discussions, such an observation was violently viewed and attacked by several 'professionals' who worked in a correctional facility. While the convicts' view cannot be dismissed *in limini,* it needs further deliberations. For, some of the prison staff are found to be, perhaps, more criminal in their attitude, approaches and behaviour than many of the convicts inside the prison. When this observation of the researchers was shared in ***LinkedIn*** by me, I was attacked—left and right by the 'professionals' *en masse* working in correctional facility. Most of them were found to be hailing from a well developed country in the West and I consoled myself thinking that they were quite ignorant of the ground realities prevailing in some poor countries of the world. How can the Swans know the sorrows of the Sparrows until they become sparrows themselves? Those divinities in that affluent country could not understand the problems of the mortals and lesser mortals in other nations. Forget about the arguments and counter-arguments for a moment. Now a situation has come into being and the international community loudly thinks of revising the Standard Minimum Rules for the Treatment of Prisoners. The issue is: "Whether or not it is proper to retain the title—i.e., Standard Minimum Rules for the Treatment of Prisoners—as it was in 1957 when the United Nations adopted them?" According to me, the revised Rules—i.e., *Guidelines*—must be applicable to the institution as well as the individuals therein.

Prisons even if the bars are of gold have negative contents pregnant with fear, hatred, contempt, avoidance, stigma, pain, monotony, etc. just like a place to where people hate to go. 'Hell', if it exists, is a place containing only negativities. Prison has been throughout the history a centre of punishment which is nothing but infliction of pain—physical, mental or both. More often than not, life in prison offered physical and mental pain. Doubtlessly, it was a centre of torture where human tears were seen everywhere. The horrible, pathetic and undesirable conditions in many penitentiaries all over the world were sincerely criticized by many who loved humans and humanity. Many jails suffered and have been suffering from corruption and malpractices. There exists laxity of discipline and abundance of abuse of power/misuse of authority. Amidst all these, can the reformatory/correctional exercise be meaningful?

Prisons in many nations are prisons indeed! They are centres of torture where human personality development has little or no scope. An utter unconcern to human personality! Prisons, history reveals, inflicted torture and pain of all types, categories and descriptions to the inmates therein. When the Standard Minimum Rules were adopted, there was a strong inclination to convert prisons from centres of torture to centres of correction. Today, in some countries, still they maintain as Prisons, Jails, Prisons Department, etc. even though some countries have renamed their prisons as Centres of Correction and their Prison Department as Department of Correction signifying nothing very special.

Correction, the word has a negative content too. To call someone "Sinner, Criminal, Crime-doer, Anti-social, Vicious" etc. will not be palatable to him/her whatever may be the ultimate objective. In my view, correction has a negativity, for, it is not good to give a feeling to those who stay in a prison to have or develop a feeling that they are people who need to be corrected for reintegrating to society back. They are people who need development of their personality in an upright way in the right direction. Everyone wants to develop his/her personality and a prisoner is no exception to it. Most of the people who commit crimes are not incarcerated and it is erroneous to think that only those who are in prisons—i.e., just a few of the crime-doers need correction. All others are O.K., and those incarcerated alone are not O.K. There is a feeling that those who are incarcerated are people who are either, as a rule, poor financially or people who are unable to employ learned lawyers to argue their cases in the courts. Whatever that be, everyone needs personality development and therefore, in my considered opinion, the presently used terms 'Institutions of Correction, Correctional Facility, Centres of Correction, etc. for prisons/penitentiaries must be substituted by terms having only positive content and purity of purpose. Why not we call it to be a Centre for Personality Development instead of a Correctional Institution, etc.? Let the Centre for Personality Development be useful to both inmates therein and the officials employed there. Prisons and prisoners are forgotten concepts and therefore, the title, i.e., Standard Minimum Rules for the Treatment of Prisoners must be changed to *"Guidelines for the Management of the Centre of Personality Development"*. The *raison d'etre* for the change from Standard Minimum Rules to Guidelines has already been discussed elsewhere in this book.

Purposefully, I omitted or deleted the words "treatment of prisoners." Why? Again the *raison d'etre* is that the title should not be "person or convict" centred. It must be "institution-individual" centred. An institution, especially a prison like institution, has many areas which need to be evaluated and the *guidelines* must confine to all such areas for a total development of the personality of individuals—both inmates and officials—housed or employed respectively therein. "Treatment" is for sick people and my researches give me enough evidence to show that all those who commit crimes or are confined to prisons are not at all sick people. There are very sane and sober individuals among the "convicts" in a prison. Sometimes, innocent people are convicted. There are short-termers who do not require any treatment at all. There may be recidivists who relapse into crime even after their "treatment" in a prison. There may be hardened offenders, naxalites, terrorists, fanatics, insurgents, fundamentalists, mentally ill and so on. There may be or can be moralists, religious men, civic-minded people, philanthropists, people having very high life values in prisons and they do not require any sort of treatment at all.

Most unfortunately, if at all there are 'sick' convicts, many prisons do not have properly qualified personnel for treating the inmates so much so that the residents stay there as confined humans with ailments. In countries where the general standard of education is poor or very poor, how can they follow the standard minimum rules applied in highly developed nations? There are countries which 'import' educationalists and school teachers for the purpose of imparting primary education to the general public. In such countries too crimes of various categories will be seen and there may be convicts in prisons. Hence, the Standard Minimum in effect in such undeveloped and educationally backward countries may be a luxury for the general public, forget about the convicts in prisons.

"Treatment" is a wrong expression as imprisonment is imprisonment in real life. Don't make a sober dog mad and throw stones at it. They will kill it or will cause serious injury. There is stigma attached to incarceration and the convicted people feel "less" in front of others in society. A person released from a mental hospital after treatment is treated to be a mental patient even after his/her hospitalization. Just like that, a convict released after "treatment" in a penal institution/prison is considered to be a "convicted prisoner/criminal" by his family, kith and kin, neighbours, dear and near, enemies and foes in the community, society at large. On the other hand, if he comes out of the prison—in the new terminology, a Centre for Personality Development—as an individual or person having proper development of his personality (including attitudes and approaches to life realities), he may be able to project out his personality better in social life.

The existing "Standard Minimum Rules for the Treatment of Prisoners" (1957), has two parts, viz., Part I of the Rules covering the general management of institutions and is applicable to all categories of prisoners, criminal or civil, untried or convicted including prisoners subject to 'security measures' or measures ordered by the Judge. Part II of the Rules contains rules applicable only to special categories dealt within each section. Nevertheless, the Rules under Section A, applicable to prisoners under sentence, are equally applicable to categories of prisoners dealt with the Sections B, C and D, provided that they do not conflict with the Rules governing those categories and are for their benefit. O.K., nonetheless there come many objections to such Rules. Prison, in my view, is a place where people convicted for having committed an offence are sent and housed. People remanded to police or judicial custody cannot become a "prisoner". They are detained in police or judicial custody (in a custodial facility) for purposes other than the so-named correction, reformation, reorientation, rehabilitation, resocialisation and reintegration to society back. They are suspected to have committed an offence and are entitled to get bail provided they satisfy certain legal conditions. They have no disqualifications (legally) which are usually attached to convicted offenders released from a prison. Hence, addressing or calling a *suspect* to be a *Prisoner* is indeed unjustifiable. Further, sending suspects to jail custody in the pretext of keeping them under "Judicial Custody" is not proper or legally acceptable. It is just like giving a label (i.e., judicial custody) and sending them to executive custody. There are custodial facilities (judicial) maintained under the administrative control of the judiciary and in my opinion, sending the suspects to judicial custody manned and managed by judicial officers alone can be proper and legally justifiable.

Again, how can a person detained in civil cases be called a 'prisoner'? A prisoner is one, as said above, who is convicted for having committed an offence and therefore, civil prisoner, untried prisoner—both are wrong nomenclatures and must be removed. A person does not become a "Prisoner" just because he stays in a prison. Again, people who are kept in a prison for security purposes should not be called "security prisoners", for, they are not prisoners or they cannot become so. "Corrective measures ordered by the Judge"—what does it mean? The Penal Codes in all countries prescribe punishments including imprisonment as a punishment.

The corrective approaches are introduced not at all by the Penal Codes in any country. The Penal Codes consider imprisonment as a means to a noble end—the end being the development of the convict's personality in an upright way in the right direction. Remember always that the Penal Codes in any country can never become a Code for Personality Development or a Code of Correction. Therefore, the proposed amendment for Part I of the existing Rules is: "Part I of the Guidelines covers the general management of the Centre for Personality Development and is applicable to people who are convicted by a Court of Law for having committed an offence." In my view, there should be separate guidelines for the so-named civil, untried and persons subject to security measures. The purpose of confining them in a custodial facility is different from imprisonment.

The book has the title *"United Nations and Prison Justice"*. I put it so purposefully. *Prison Justice* instead of Correctional Justice as controversies exist about the use of correctional justice. As the objective of incarceration is said to be Development of Personality in an upright way in the right direction *via*, among other things, correction, reformation, reorientation, rehabilitation, resocialisation, reintegration, etc. it is not right or fair to say Correctional Justice. Though there is a move to rename the so-called Centre of Correction to a Centre of Personality Development, the move has not received wide acceptance at the international level as many countries still have Prisons Department, Central Prisons, Sub-Jails, Women's Prisons, etc. Let Prison Justice be retained till a consensus is reached. The book gives a revision of the existing UN Standard Minimum Rules for the Treatment of Prisoners for the international community to discuss and debate. Although, at the international level, the work of revision has been initiated long ago, I am able to publish it now—a time when the United Nations think seriously about the revision, if possible, in 2015 or immediately afterwards.

I must place on record the whole-hearted support rendered by my wife Mary for the revision of the Rules. Also, I place on record my thanks to Abhilash, Martin, Neethu, Neethie, Anna, Maria, George, Ammu (Maria) and Ann for their constant encouragement to bring out this title.

Thiruvananthapuram
17 March, 2013

James Vadackumchery
Criminologist and Advocate

Contents

1

Standard Minimum Rules, 1957

Standard Minimum Rules for the Treatment of Prisoners, 1957 adopted by the United Nations, no doubt, was a landmark advanced towards more humanitarian approach to institutionalized convicts in the penological history. Nearly nine decades of history may be noted since 1926 when the IPPC (International Penal and Penitentiary Commission) made a concrete suggestion to an international body to have a more human approach to those incarcerated by judicial decisions. IPPC congress held at Prague in 1930 accepted a set of 55 Rules allowing minimal "rights" for the convicts. In 1933, the first international draft was prepared and was endorsed by the League of Nations in 1934 (Resolution of September 26, 1934). After the Second World War, in 1949 a revision of the Rules was thought of. It was intended to make Rules up-to-date. In 1957, the First United Nations Congress' on the Prevention of Crime and the Treatment of Offenders held in Geneva adopted a new set of Rules. The Economic and Social Council, by its Resolution 63 C (XXIV) of 31 July, 1957 approved the Standard Minimum Rules for the Treatment of Prisoners. Governments' favourable consideration to the adoption and application of the Rules was invited.

In 1970, the United Nations' Secretariat prepared a working paper about the Standard Minimum Rules for the Treatment of Prisoners in the light of developments then in the penological or better in the correctional field. The paper contained many chapters, namely (1) an introduction, (2) New Development in Correctional Practice, (3) Human Rights and the Principles of Correction, (4) Legal Status of the Rules, (5) The Relevance of the Rules, (6) The Scope and Extent of the Rules, (7) The Modification of the Rules,

(8) Future Prospects of the Rules etc. The paper also contained (a) the balance between rights and correction (b) Rights in the new settings, (c) Authority and Divisibility of the Rules, (d) Rules and Conventions, (e) The effect of status on reception, (f) Extension, relevance and rights, (g) Problems of extension, (h) The background to the Implementation of the Rules, (i) Education, Publicity and Information, (j) Technical assistance, and (k) The issues outstanding etc.

In 1984, the Economic and Social Council, in its Resolution 1984/47 (The procedures were adopted on the basis of the recommendations by the Sixth United Nations' Congress on the Prevention of Crime and Treatment of Offenders and the Committee on Crime Prevention and Control) adopted the procedure for the effective implementation of the Standard Minimum Rules for the Treatment of Prisoners in response to the challenges of translating the Rules into domestic provisions and practices. The procedures had provisions promoting and encouraging the Member States to translate and institutionalize the Rules in their respective systems. The Secretary General of the United Nations asked the Member States to communicate with him every five years the progress in the implementation and application of the Rules in their system. Further, the Secretary General told the Member States to tell him any difficulties faced by them in enforcement of the Rules. Five surveys were conducted during the period 1970-1990.

After the Universal Declaration of Human Rights in 1948 and particularly in 1957 after the adoption of the Standard Minimum Rules for the Treatment of Prisoners, a number of Conventions, Declarations and Principles having reference to the treatment of the incarcerated have been accepted and approved by the United Nations. When the Standard Minimum Rules were drafted, many concepts presently held were not well developed or up-to-date. Hence, later Conventions and Declarations became necessary to clarify the issues, expand on the concepts and general principles which underlined the Rules etc. In 1990, December 14 (by Resolution 45/111), the General Assembly adopted the Basic Principles for the Treatment of Prisoners. Again in 2010, the Rules for the Treatment of Women Prisoners and Non-Custodial Measures for Women Offenders (The Banghok Rules) came into being.

During 1970 and afterwards, I used to think about the revision of the Standard Minimum Rules, 1957. I thought so not only when I studied the Rules at the Post Graduate level at Saugor University or when I taught them to police and prison officials, but also when I worked as a Member of the State Advisory Committee for Correctional Administration in Kerala. Further, I felt the need for a total revision when I was a member of the Sentence Review Committee appointed by the Government of Kerala for the premature release of the life-convicts after 8 years. Hence, I started revising the Rules, but did not get them published as I wanted to publish the revision of the UN Universal Declaration of Human Rights, 1948 prior to the publication of the revised Prison Rules. Now, the book titled *"UN Universal Declaration of Human Rights and Criminal Justice: The Total Revision"* is released for publication by the Concept Publishing Company (P) Ltd., New Delhi. Hence, it is time now to get the revised Rules published for international debate and deliberations. Now, I understand that the General Assembly of the United Nations too has decided to approach the Commission on Crime Prevention and Criminal Justice to establish an open-ended inter-governmental expert group for revision of the existing rules. Fine.

In the meantime, regional human rights treaties and standards-say, European Prison Rules for the Council of Europe—have enhanced the existing Rules. Further, many courts, prison reform committees/commissions appointed in various countries have applied the Rules *mutatis mutandis* while they took decisions or recommendations. In one of the Commissions appointed by Government of Kerala, India, I myself gave an expert advice during nineteen eighties to adopt the principles laid down in the Standard Minimum Rules with necessary changes. In the Americas, the Inter-American Court of Human Rights and in Europe, the European Court of Human Rights contributed a lot in this direction. Human Rights Commissions in India—both National and State—make all attempts to implement international standards on the treatment of prisoners. At this juncture, this revision may be a timely contribution. Besides, the Inter-American Commission, Council of Europe, the African Commission on Human Rights and People's Rights, many concerned individuals are taking special interests in internationalization of prisoners' rights. Further, more regional initiatives like the Permanent Committee of Latin American countries are taking special interest for the revision and updating of the UN Standard Minimum Rules for the Treatment of Prisoners. The issue is under live debate and discussion now. Hence, the next chapter is all about the Background note for an Open-ended Inter-governmental Expert Group Meeting on the United Nation's Standard Minimum Rules for the Treatment of Prisoners.

On November 6, 1967, the Secretary General of the United Nations addressed a *note verbale* to all Member States of the UN asking them to inform how far or how much of the Standard Minimum Rules could be implemented and the difficulties encountered by them during implementation. It was found that only 44 countries replied to his query. Some of them implemented the Rules in an indifferent way while, doubtlessly, a few countries, were influenced or probably influenced by the Rules. Just a handful—i.e., 5 countries only—were found to have enforced partly the Rules in their law and practice.

No fund, no trained or specialist personnel, unsatisfactory physical conditions/facilities, lack of administrative will, legal rigidities, inertia or indifference, antiquated laws, ignorance of prison philosophy, geographical obstacles, unfavourable climatic conditions, etc. hampered many countries to implement the Rules, Doubtlessly, many countries did wish or express their views that the Rules ought to be revised. For, according to them, the 'Standards' which the framers of the 'Standard Minimum Rules, 1957' had could not be accepted as 'Standards' for others who had financial constraints or lack of trained personnel etc. Lack of trained personnel means lack of trained personnel and there is no substitute for it.

In 2012, when I suggested that the "prisons should be renamed as Centres of Personality Development" instead of "Centres of Correction" in the **LinkedIn**, the resistance/objections to such a suggestion was incredible and ununderstandable. Many who raised objections were employed in prison/correction services, yet they objected without making an attempt to appreciate the reasons and the philosophy behind such a suggestion. Some of them even questioned my sincerity in making the suggestion. My researches showed that some of the staff working in the so-named correctional facilities needed more "correction" than the convicts/inmates inside. I could observe corruption and malpractices among some of the custodial and correctional staff in the present prison set-up. The custodial staff who were given police training could not understand the correctional philosophy. They believed only in muscle power and were concerned only about the custody of the inmates—nothing more, nothing less. The inadequate number of the correctional staff was a problem and many of the correctional staff who complained that they got only a step-mortherly attitude from administration was a cry in the wilderness and did not or could not force the administration to initiate any correctional methods. I had to labour a lot and I took several days to convince those who participated in the **LinkedIn** discussion that "correction" was only a means or method for the personality development. "Correction" itself is not or cannot be the end or objective of imprisonment as the end/objective is the development of personality in an upright way in the right direction. Do the Standard Minimum Rules ensure such an end? If not, necessary revision should be made in the Rules so that the personality of the inmates is developed in an upright way in the right direction. For example, take Rule 8 (of the existing Rules) which speaks about separate institutions. Prisons are now overcrowded so much so that a prison which can accommodate less than 1000 people may have double the stated strength and what to do then? The Rules become sterile in such situations and precisely, therefore, cannot be applied.

In many countries, the prisons are antiquated, unsatisfactorily designed and are not good dwelling places with minimum human comforts. A proper and enviable prison architecture is yet to be born. Even newly built prisons have open bathing facilities and everybody can see the convicts taking bath in open spaces. How many prisons have dormitories subdivided into alcoves or having a *camerata* system? Homosexuality is practiced in some prisons by a few inmates. Why? Can two people stay in a single room?—or, should there be a minimum of three people? What about the uniform of the prisoners? Any changes needed in the diet/food in prisons? What or how are the leisure-time activities? Do the people living outside get the facilities which the prisoners enjoy during incarceration?

Rule 31 reads: "Corporal punishment, punishment by placing in a dark cell, and all cruel, inhuman or degrading punishments for disciplinary offences." The UN Secretariat in their working paper prepared in 1970 writes:

"Rule 31: This Rule opposes corporal punishment and the use of dark cells for punishment. Four countries reported that corporal punishment is still used, and three noted the existence of dark cells. However, most of the countries have abandoned these methods entirely; and even the non-observing countries usually note that this kind of punishment is only rarely used."

I give due respect to the Secretariat's note, nevertheless I could learn from my researches that torture used to be the often resorted or applied methods to ensure discipline in prison custody. Though the prison administration may deny the employment of torture in prisons, the fact remains that the prisoners are tortured in reality. Sometimes, administration-favoured prisoners are utilized for torturing other fellow inmates and cases have been reported that the jail authorities shut their eyes to such cruelties. One prisoner told me that sometimes the inmates might be tortured putting a cloth cover on his body so much so that the tortured would not know who tortured him. Thus, the Rules are many and the violations of such Rules inside the four high walls are plenty. No one knows about them or if at all knows them, does not reveal them and the inmates do not speak them out. The media do not report them as most of the violations take place beyond their reach and view. Anyway, the following is the 'Standard Minimum Rules' for a total revision.

Standard Minimum Rules for the Treatment of Prisoners, adopted on August 30, 1957 by the First United Nations Congress on the Prevention of Crime and the Treatment of Offenders, U.N. Doc. A/CONF/611, annex I, E.S.C. res. 663C, 24 U.N. ESCOR Supp. (No. 1) at 11, U.N. Doc. E/3048 (1957), amended E.S.C. res. 2076, 62 U.N. ESCOR Supp. (No. 1) at 35, U.N. Doc. E/5988 (1977).

1. The following rules are not intended to describe in detail a model system of penal institutions. They seek only, on the basis of the general consensus of contemporary thought and the essential elements of the most adequate systems of today, to set out what is generally accepted as being good principle and practice in the treatment of prisoners and the management of institutions.
2. In view of the great variety of legal, social, economic and geographical conditions of the world, it is evident that not all of the rules are capable of application in all places and at all times. They should, however, serve to stimulate a constant endeavour to overcome practical difficulties in the way of their application, in the knowledge that they

represent, as a whole, the minimum conditions which are accepted as suitable by the United Nations.

3. On the other hand, the rules cover a field in which thought is constantly developing. They are not intended to preclude experiment and practices, provided these are in harmony with the principles and seek to further the purposes which derive from the text of the rules as a whole. It will always be justifiable for the central prison administration to authorize departures from the rules in this spirit.

4. (1) Part I of the rules covers the general management of institutions, and is applicable to all categories of prisoners, criminal or civil, untried or convicted, including prisoners subject to "security measures" or corrective measures ordered by the judge.

(2) Part II contains rules applicable only to the special categories dealt with in each section. Nevertheless, the rules under section A, applicable to prisoners under sentence, shall be equally applicable to categories of prisoners dealt with in sections B, C and D, provided they do not conflict with the rules governing those categories and are for their benefit.

5. (1) The rules do not seek to regulate the management of institutions set aside for young persons such as Borstal institutions or correctional schools, but in general part-I would be equally applicable in such institutions.

(2) The category of young prisoners should include at least all young persons who come within the jurisdiction of juvenile courts. As a rule, such young persons should not be sentenced to imprisonment.

PART I
RULES OF GENERAL APPLICATION

Basic Principle

6. (1) The following rules shall be applied impartially. There shall be no discrimination on grounds of race, colour, sex, language, religion, political or other opinion, national or social origin, property, birth or other status.

(2) On the other hand, it is necessary to respect the

religious beliefs and moral precepts of the group to which a prisoner belongs.

Register

7. (1) In every place where persons are imprisoned there shall be kept a bound registration book with numbered pages in which shall be entered in respect of each prisoner received:
   (a) Information concerning his identity;
   (b) The reasons for his commitment and the authority therefor; and
   (c) The day and hour of his admission and release.
   (2) No person shall be received in an institution without a valid commitment order of which the details shall have been previously entered in the register.

Separation of Categories

8. The different categories of prisoners shall be kept in separate institutions or parts of institutions taking account of their sex, age, criminal record, the legal reason for their detention and the necessities of their treatment. Thus,
   (a) Men and women shall so far as possible be detained in separate institutions; in an institution which receives both men and women the whole of the premises allocated to women shall be entirely separate;
   (b) Untried prisoners shall be kept separate from convicted prisoners;
   (c) Persons imprisoned for debt and other civil prisoners shall be kept separate from persons imprisoned by reason of a criminal offence; and
   (d) Young prisoners shall be kept separate from adults.

Accommodation

9. (1) Where sleeping accommodation is in individual cells or rooms, each prisoner shall occupy by night a cell or room by himself. If for special reasons, such as temporary overcrowding, it becomes necessary for the

central prison administration to make an exception to this rule, it is not desirable to have two prisoners in a cell or room.

(2) Where dormitories are used, they shall be occupied by prisoners carefully selected as being suitable to associate with one another in those conditions. There shall be regular supervision by night, in keeping with the nature of the institution.

10. All accommodations provided for the use of prisoners and in particular all sleeping accommodations shall meet all requirements of health, due regard being paid to climatic conditions and particularly to cubic content of air, minimum floor space, lighting, heating and ventilation.

11. In all places where prisoners are required to live or work,

(a) The windows shall be large enough to enable the prisoners to read or work by natural light, and shall be so constructed that they can allow the entrance of fresh air whether or not there is artificial ventilation; and

(b) Artificial light shall be provided sufficient for the prisoners to read or work without injury to eyesight.

12. The sanitary installations shall be adequate to enable every prisoner to comply with the needs of nature when necessary and in a clean and decent manner.

13. Adequate bathing and shower installations shall be provided so that every prisoner may be enabled and required to have a bath or shower, at a temperature suitable to the climate, as frequently as necessary for general hygiene according to season and geographical region, but at least once a week in a temperate climate.

14. All pans of an institution regularly used by prisoners shall be properly maintained and kept scrupulously clean at all times.

Personal Hygiene

15. Prisoners shall be required to keep their persons clean, and to this end they shall be provided with water and with such toilet articles as are necessary for health and cleanliness.

16. In order that prisoners may maintain a good appearance compatible with their self-respect, facilities shall be provided for the proper care of the hair and beard, and men shall be enabled to shave regularly.

Clothing and Bedding

17. (1) Every prisoner who is not allowed to wear his own clothing shall be provided with an outfit of clothing suitable for the climate and adequate to keep him in good health. Such clothing shall in no manner be degrading or humiliating.
(2) All clothing shall be clean and kept in proper condition. Underclothing shall be changed and washed as often as necessary for the maintenance of hygiene.
(3) In exceptional circumstances, whenever a prisoner is removed outside the institution for an authorized purpose, he shall be allowed to wear his own clothing or other inconspicuous clothing.

18. If prisoners are allowed to wear their own clothing, arrangements shall be made on their admission to the institution to ensure that it shall be clean and fit for use.

19. Every prisoner shall, in accordance with local or national standards, be provided with a separate bed, and with separate and sufficient bedding which shall be clean when issued, kept in good order and changed often enough to ensure its cleanliness.

Food

20. (1) Every prisoner shall be provided by the administration at the usual hours with food of nutritional value adequate for health and strength, of wholesome quality and well prepared and served.
(2) Drinking water shall be available to every prisoner whenever he needs it.

Exercise and Sport

21. (1) Every prisoner who is not employed in outdoor work shall have at least one hour of suitable exercise in the open air daily if the weather permits.

(2) Young prisoners, and others of suitable age and physique, shall receive physical and recreational training during the period of exercise. To this end, space, installations and equipment should be provided.

Medical Services

22. (1) At every institution there shall be available the services of at least one qualified medical officer who should have some knowledge of psychiatry. The medical services should be organized in close relationship to the general health administration of the community or nation. They shall include a psychiatric service for the diagnosis and, in proper cases, the treatment of states of mental abnormality.

(2) Sick prisoners who require specialist treatment shall be transferred to specialized institutions or to civil hospitals. Where hospital facilities are provided in an institution, their equipment, furnishings and pharmaceutical supplies shall be proper for the medical care and treatment of sick prisoners, and there shall be a staff of suitably trained officers.

(3) The services of a qualified dental officer shall be available to every prisoner.

23. (1) In women's institutions there shall be special accommodation for all necessary pre-natal and post-natal care and treatment. Arrangements shall be made wherever practicable for children to be born in a hospital outside the institution. If a child is born in prison, this fact shall not be mentioned in the birth certificate.

(2) Where nursing infants are allowed to remain in the institution with their mothers, provision shall be made for a nursery staffed by qualified persons, where the infants shall be placed when they are not in the care of their mothers.

24. The medical officer shall see and examine every prisoner as soon as possible after his admission and thereafter as necessary, with a view particularly to the discovery of physical or mental illness and the taking of all necessary measures; the segregation of prisoners suspected of infectious or contagious conditions; the noting of physical or mental defects which might hamper rehabilitation, and the determination of the physical capacity of every prisoner for work.

25. (1) The medical officer shall have the care of the physical and mental health of the prisoners and should daily see all sick prisoners, all who complain of illness, and any prisoner to whom his attention is specially directed.

(2) The medical officer shall report to the director whenever he considers that a prisoner's physical or mental health has been or will be injuriously affected by continued imprisonment or by any condition of imprisonment.

26. (1) The medical officer shall regularly inspect and advise the director upon:

(a) The quantity, quality, preparation and service of food;

(b) The hygiene and cleanliness of the institution and the prisoners;

(c) The sanitation, heating, lighting and ventilation of the institution;

(d) The suitability and cleanliness of the prisoners' clothing and bedding; and

(e) The observance of the rules concerning physical education and sports, in cases where there is no technical personnel in charge of these activities.

(2) The director shall take into consideration the reports and advice that the medical officer submits according to rules 25(2) and 26 and, in case he concurs with the recommendations made, shall take immediate steps to give effect to those recommendations; if they are not within his competence or if he does not concur with them, he shall immediately submit his own report and the advice of the medical officer to higher authority.

Discipline and Punishment

27. Discipline and order shall be maintained with firmness, but with no more restriction than is necessary for safe custody and well-ordered community life.

28. (1) No prisoner shall be employed, in the service of the institution, in any disciplinary capacity.

(2) This rule shall not, however, impede the proper functioning of systems based on self-government, under which specified social, educational or sports activities or responsibilities are entrusted, under supervision, to prisoners who are formed into groups for the purposes of treatment.

29. The following shall always be determined by the law or by the regulation of the competent administrative authority:

(a) Conduct constituting a disciplinary offence;

(b) The types and duration of punishment which may be inflicted; and

(c) The authority competent to impose such punishment.

30. (1) No prisoner shall be punished except in accordance with the terms of such law or regulation, and never twice for the same offence.

(2) No prisoner shall be punished unless he has been informed of the offence alleged against him and given a proper opportunity of presenting his defence. The competent authority shall conduct a thorough examination of the case.

(3) Where necessary and practicable, the prisoner shall be allowed to make his defence through an interpreter.

31. Corporal punishment, punishment by placing in a dark cell, and all cruel, inhuman or degrading punishments shall be completely prohibited as punishments for disciplinary offences.

32. (1) Punishment by close confinement or reduction of diet shall never be inflicted unless the medical officer has examined the prisoner and certified in writing that he is fit to sustain it.

(2) The same shall apply to any other punishment that may be prejudicial to the physical or mental health of a prisoner. In no case any such punishment be contrary to or depart from the principle stated in Rule 31.

(3) The medical officer shall visit daily prisoners

undergoing such punishments and shall advise the director if he considers the termination or alteration of the punishment necessary on grounds of physical or mental health.

Instruments of Restraint

33. Instruments of restraint, such as handcuffs, chains, irons and strait-jacket, shall never be applied as a punishment. Furthermore, chains or irons shall not be used as restraints. Other instruments of restraint shall not be used except in the following circumstances:

(a) As a precaution against escape during a transfer, provided that they shall be removed when the prisoner appears before a judicial or administrative authority;

(b) On medical grounds by direction of the medical officer; and (c) By order of the director, if other methods of control fail, in order to prevent a prisoner from injuring himself or others or from damaging property; in such instances the director shall at once consult the medical officer and report to the higher administrative authority.

34. The patterns and manner of use of instruments of restraint shall be decided by the central prison administration. Such instruments must not be applied for any longer time than is strictly necessary.

Information to and Complaints by Prisoners

35. (1) Every prisoner on admission shall be provided with written information about the regulations governing the treatment of prisoners of his category, the disciplinary requirements of the institution, the authorized methods of seeking information and making complaints, and all such other matters as are necessary to enable him to understand both his rights and his obligations and to adapt himself to the life of the institution.

(2) If a prisoner is illiterate, the aforesaid information shall be conveyed to him orally.

36. (1) Every prisoner shall have the opportunity each week day of making requests or complaints to the director of the institution or the officer authorized to represent him.

(2) It shall be possible to make requests or complaints to the inspector of prisons during his inspection. The prisoner shall have the opportunity to talk to the inspector or to any other inspecting officer without the director or other members of the staff being present.

(3) Every prisoner shall be allowed to make a request or complaint, without censorship as to substance but in proper form, to the central prison administration, the judicial authority or other proper authorities through approved channels.

(4) Unless it is evidently frivolous or groundless, every request or complaint shall be promptly dealt with and replied to without undue delay.

Contact with the Outside World

37. Prisoners shall be allowed under necessary supervision to communticate with their family and reputable friends at regular intervals, both by correspondence and by receiving visits.

38. (1) Prisoners who are foreign nationals shall be allowed reasonable facilities to communicate with the *diplomatic* and consular representatives of the State to which they belong.

(2) Prisoners who are nationals of States without diplomatic or consular representation in the country and *refugees* or stateless persons shall be allowed similar facilities to communicate with the diplomatic representative of the State which takes charge of their interests or any national or international authority whose task it is to protect such persons.

39. Prisoners shall be kept informed regularly of the more important items of news by the reading of newspapers, periodicals or special institutional publications, by hearing wireless transmissions, by lectures or by any similar means as authorized or controlled by the administration.

Books

40. Every institution shall have a library for the use of all categories of prisoners, adequately stocked with both recreational and instructional books, and prisoners shall be encouraged to make full use of it.

Religion

41. (1) If the institution contains a sufficient number of prisoners of the same religion, a qualified representative of that religion shall be appointed or approved. If the number of prisoners justifies it and conditions permit, the arrangement should be on a full-time basis.

(2) A qualified representative appointed or approved under paragraph (1) shall be allowed to hold regular services and to pay pastoral visits in private to prisoners of his religion at proper times.

(3) Access to a qualified representative of any religion shall not be refused to any prisoner. On the other hand, if any prisoner should object to a visit of any religious representative, his attitude shall be fully respected.

42. So far as practicable, every prisoner shall be allowed to satisfy the needs of his religious life by attending the services provided in the institution and having in his possession the books of religious observance and instruction of his denomination.

Retention of Prisoners' Property

43. (1) All money, valuables, clothing and other effects belonging to a prisoner which under the regulations of the institution he is not allowed to retain shall on his admission to the institution be placed in safe custody. An inventory thereof shall be signed by the prisoner. Steps shall be taken to keep them in good condition.

(2) On the release of the prisoner all such articles and money shall be returned to him except in so far as he has been authorized to spend money or send any such property out of the institution, or it has been found

necessary on hygienic grounds to destroy any article of clothing. The prisoner shall sign a receipt for the articles and money returned to him.

(3) Any money or effects received for a prisoner from outside shall be treated in the same way.

(4) If a prisoner brings in any drugs or medicine, the medical officer shall decide what use shall be made of them.

Notification of Death, Illness, Transfer, etc.

44. (1) Upon the death or serious illness of, or serious injury to a prisoner, or his removal to an institution for the treatment of mental affections, the director shall at once inform the spouse, if the prisoner is married, or the nearest relative and shall in any event inform any other person previously designated by the prisoner.

(2) A prisoner shall be informed at once of the death or serious illness of any near relative. In case of the critical illness of a near relative, the prisoner should be authorized, whenever circumstances allow, to go to his bedside either under escort or alone.

(3) Every prisoner shall have the right to inform at once his family of his imprisonment or his transfer to another institution.

Removal of Prisoners

45. (1) When the prisoners are being removed to or from an institution, they shall be exposed to public view as little as possible, and proper safeguards shall be adopted to protect them from insult, curiosity and publicity in any form.

(2) The transport of prisoners in conveyances with inadequate ventilation or light, or in any way which would subject them to unnecessary physical hardship, shall be prohibited.

(3) The transport of prisoners shall be carried out at the expense of the administration and equal conditions shall obtain for all of them.

Institutional Personnel

46. (1) The prison administration shall provide for the careful selection of every grade of the personnel, since it is on their integrity, humanity, professional capacity and personal suitability for the work that the proper administration of the institutions depends.

(2) The prison administration shall constantly seek to awaken and maintain in the minds both of the personnel and of the public the conviction that this work is a social service of great importance, and to this end all appropriate means of informing the public should be used.

(3) To secure the foregoing ends, personnel shall be appointed on a full-time basis as professional prison officers and have civil service status with security of tenure subject only to good conduct, efficiency and physical fitness. Salaries shall be adequate to attract and retain suitable men and women; employment benefits and conditions of service shall be favourable in view of the exacting nature of the work.

47. (1) The personnel shall possess an adequate standard of education and intelligence.

(2) Before entering on duty, the personnel shall be given a course of training in their general and specific duties and be required to pass theoretical and practical tests.

(3) After entering on duty and during their career, the personnel shall maintain and improve their knowledge and professional capacity by attending courses of in-service training to be organized at suitable intervals.

48. All members of the personnel shall at all times so conduct themselves and perform their duties as to influence the prisoners for good by their example and to command their respect.

49. (1) So far as possible, the personnel shall include a sufficient number of specialists such as psychiatrists, psychologists, social workers, teachers and trade instructors.

(2) The services of social workers, teachers and trade instructors shall be secured on a permanent basis,

without thereby excluding part-time or voluntary workers.

50. (1) The director of an institution should be adequately qualified for his task by character, administrative ability, suitable training and experience.

(2) He shall devote his entire time to his official duties and shall not be appointed on a part-time basis.

(3) He shall reside on the premises of the institution or in its immediate vicinity.

(4) When two or more institutions are under the authority of one director, he shall visit each of them at frequent intervals. A responsible resident official shall be in charge of each of these institutions.

51. (1) The director, his deputy, and the majority of the other personnel of the institution shall be able to speak the language of the greatest number of prisoners, or a language understood by the greatest number of them.

(2) Whenever necessary, the services of an interpreter shall be used.

52. (1) In institutions which are large enough to require the services of one or more full-time medical officers, at least one of them shall reside on the premises of the institution or in its immediate vicinity.

(2) In other institutions the medical officer shall visit daily and shall reside near enough to be able to attend without delay in cases of urgency.

53. (1) In an institution for both men and women, the part of the institution set aside for women shall be under the authority of a responsible woman officer who shall have the custody of the keys of all that part of the institution.

(2) No male member of the staff shall enter the part of the institution set aside for women unless accompanied by a woman officer.

(3) Women prisoners shall be attended and supervised only by women officers. This does not, however, preclude male members of the staff, particularly doctors and teachers, from carrying out their professional duties in institutions or parts of institutions set aside for women.

54. (1) Officers of the institutions shall not, in their relations with the prisoners, use force except in self-defence or in cases of attempted escape, or active or passive physical resistance to an order based on law or regulations. Officers who have recourse to force must use no more than is strictly necessary and must report the incident immediately to the director of the institution.

(2) Prison officers shall be given special physical training to enable them to restrain aggressive prisoners.

(3) Except in special circumstances, staff performing duties which bring them into direct contact with prisoners should not be armed. Furthermore, staff should in no circumstances be provided with arms unless they have been trained in their use.

Inspection

55. There shall be a regular inspection of penal institutions and services by qualified and experienced inspectors appointed by a competent authority. Their task shall be in particular to ensure that these institutions are administered in accordance with existing laws and regulations and with a view to bringing about the objectives of penal and correctional services.

PART II
RULES APPLICABLE TO SPECIAL CATEGORIES

A. PRISONERS UNDER SENTENCE

Guiding Principles

56. The guiding principles hereafter are intended to show the spirit in which penal institutions should be administered and the purposes at which they should aim, in accordance with the declaration made under Preliminary Observation I of the present text.

57. Imprisonment and other measures which result in cutting off an offender from the outside world are afflictive by the very fact of taking from the person the right of self-determination by depriving him of his liberty. Therefore, the prison system shall not, except as incidental to justifiable segregation or the maintenance of discipline, aggravate the suffering inherent in such a situation.

58. The purpose and justification of a sentence of imprisonment or a similar measure deprivative of liberty is ultimately to protect society against crime. This end can only be achieved if the period of imprisonment is used to ensure, so far as possible, that upon his return to society the offender is not only willing but able to lead a law-abiding and self-supporting life.

59. To this end, the institution should utilize all the remedial, educational, moral, spiritual and other forces and forms of assistance which are appropriate and available, and should seek to apply them according to the individual treatment needs of the prisoners.

60. (1) The regime of the institution should seek to minimize any differences between prison life and life at liberty which tend to lessen the responsibility of the prisoners or the respect due to their dignity as human beings.

(2) Before the completion of the sentence, it is desirable that the necessary steps be taken to ensure for the prisoner a gradual return to life in society. This aim may be achieved, depending on the case, by a pre-release regime organized in the same institution or in another appropriate institution, or by release on trial under some kind of supervision which must not be entrusted to the police but should be combined with effective social aid.

61. The treatment of prisoners should emphasize not their exclusion from the community, but their continuing part in it. Community agencies should, therefore, be enlisted wherever possible to assist the staff of the institution in the task of social rehabilitation of the prisoners. There should be in connection with every institution social workers charged with the duty of maintaining and improving all desirable relations of a prisoner with his family and with valuable social agencies. Steps should be taken to safeguard, to the maximum extent compatible with the law and the sentence, the rights relating to civil interests, social security rights and other social benefits of prisoners.

62. The medical services of the institution shall seek to detect and shall treat any physical or mental illnesses or defects which may hamper a prisoner's rehabilitation. All necessary medical, surgical and psychiatric services shall be provided to that end.

63. (1) The fulfilment of these principles requires individualization of treatment and for this purpose a flexible system of classifying prisoners in groups; it is therefore, desirable that such groups should be distributed in separate institutions suitable for the treatment of each group.

(2) These institutions need not provide the same degree of security for every group. It is desirable to provide varying degrees of security according to the needs of different groups. Open institutions, by the very fact that they provide no physical security against escape but rely on the self-discipline of the inmates, provide the conditions most favourable to rehabilitation for carefully selected prisoners.

(3) It is desirable that the number of prisoners in closed institutions should not be so large that the individualization of treatment is hindered. In some countries it is considered that the population of such institutions should not exceed five hundred. In open institutions the population should be as small as possible.

(4) On the other hand, it is undesirable to maintain prisons which are so small that proper facilities cannot be provided.

64. The duty of society does not end with a prisoner's release. There should, therefore, be governmental or private agencies capable of lending the released prisoner efficient after-care directed towards the lessening of prejudice against him and towards his social rehabilitation.

Treatment

65. The treatment of persons sentenced to imprisonment or a similar measure shall have as its purpose, so far as the length of the sentence permits, to establish in them the

will to lead law-abiding and self-supporting lives after their release and to fit them to do so. The treatment shall be such as will encourage their self-respect and develop their sense of responsibility.

66. (1) To these ends, all appropriate means shall be used, including religious care in the countries where this is possible, education, vocational guidance and training, social casework, employment counselling, physical development and strengthening of moral character, in accordance with the individual needs of each prisoner, taking account of his social and criminal history, his physical and mental capacities and aptitudes, his personal temperament, the length of his sentence and his prospects after release.

(2) For every prisoner with a sentence of suitable length, the director shall receive, as soon as possible after his admission, full reports on all the matters referred to in the foregoing paragraph. Such reports shall always include a report by a medical officer, wherever possible qualified in psychiatry, on the physical and mental condition of the prisoner.

(3) The reports and other relevant documents shall be placed in an individual file. This file shall be kept up to date and classified in such a way that it can be consulted by the responsible personnel whenever the need arises.

Classification and Individualization

67. The purposes of classification shall be:

(a) To separate from others those prisoners who, by reason of their criminal records or bad character, are likely to exercise a bad influence; and

(b) To divide the prisoners into classes in order to facilitate their treatment with a view to their social rehabilitation.

68. So far as possible separate institutions or separate sections of an institution shall be used for the treatment of the different classes of prisoners.

69. As soon as possible after admission and after a study of the personality of each prisoner with a sentence of suitable length, a programme of treatment shall be prepared for him in the light of the knowledge obtained about his individual needs, his capacities and dispositions.

Privileges

70. Systems of privileges appropriate for the different classes of prisoners and the different methods of treatment shall be established at every institution, in order to encourage good conduct, develop a sense of responsibility and secure the interest and co-operation of the prisoners in their treatment.

Work

71. (1) Prison labour must not be of an afflictive nature.

(2) All prisoners under sentence shall be required to work, subject to their physical and mental fitness as determined by the medical officer.

(3) Sufficient work of a useful nature shall be provided to keep prisoners actively employed for a normal working day.

(4) So far as possible the work provided shall be such as will maintain or increase the prisoners' ability to earn an honest living after release.

(5) Vocational training in useful trades shall be provided for prisoners able to profit thereby and especially for young prisoners.

(6) Within the limits compatible with proper vocational selection and with the requirements of institutional administration and discipline, the prisoners shall be able to choose the type of work they wish to perform.

72. (1) The organization and methods of work in the institutions shall resemble as closely as possible those of similar work outside institutions, so as to prepare prisoners for the conditions of normal occupational life.

(2) The interests of the prisoners and of their vocational training, however, must not be subordinated to the

purpose of making a financial profit from an industry in the institution.

73. (1) Preferably institutional industries and farms should be operated directly by the administration and not by private contractors.

(2) Where prisoners are employed in work not controlled by the administration, they shall always be under the supervision of the institution's personnel. Unless the work is for other departments of the government the full normal wages for such work shall be paid to the administration by the persons to whom the labour is supplied, account being taken of the output of the prisoners.

74. (1) The precautions laid down to protect the safety and health of free workmen shall be equally observed in institutions.

(2) Provision shall be made to indemnify prisoners against industrial injury, including occupational disease, on terms not less favourable than those extended by law to free workmen.

75. (1) The maximum daily and weekly working hours of the prisoners shall be fixed by law or by administrative regulation, taking into account local rules or custom in regard to the employment of free workmen.

(2) The hours so fixed shall leave one rest day a week and sufficient time for education and other activities required as part of the treatment and rehabilitation of the prisoners.

76. (1) There shall be a system of equitable remuneration of the work of prisoners.

(2) Under the system prisoners shall be allowed to spend at least a part of their earnings on approved articles for their own use and to send a part of their earnings to their family.

(3) The system should also provide that a part of the earnings should be set aside by the administration so as to constitute a savings fund to be handed over to the prisoner on his release.

Education and Recreation

77. (1) Provision shall be made for the further education of all prisoners capable of profiting thereby, including religious instruction in the countries where this is possible. The education of illiterates and young prisoners shall be compulsory and special attention shall be paid to it by the administration.

(2) So far as practicable, the education of prisoners shall be integrated with the educational system of the country so that after their release they may continue their education without difficulty.

78. Recreational and cultural activities shall be provided in all institutions for the benefit of the mental and physical health of prisoners.

Social Relations and After-care

79. Special attention shall be paid to the maintenance and improvement of such relations between a prisoner and his family as are desirable in the best interests of both.

80. From the beginning of a prisoner's sentence consideration shall be given to his future after release and he shall be encouraged and assisted to maintain or establish such relations with persons or agencies outside the institution as may promote the best interests of his family and his own social rehabilitation.

81. (1) Services and agencies, governmental or otherwise, which assist released prisoners to re-establish themselves in society shall ensure, so far as is possible and necessary, that released prisoners be provided with appropriate documents and identification papers, have suitable homes and work to go to, are suitably and adequately clothed having regard to the climate and season, and have sufficient means to reach their destination and maintain themselves in the period immediately following their release.

(2) The approved representatives of such agencies shall have all necessary access to the institution and to prisoners and shall be taken into consultation as to

the future of a prisoner from the beginning of his sentence.

(3) It is desirable that the activities of such agencies shall be centralized or co-ordinated as far as possible in order to secure the best use of their efforts.

B. INSANE AND MENTALLY ABNORMAL PRISONERS

82. (1) Persons who are found to be insane shall not be detained in prisons and arrangements shall be made to remove them to mental institutions as soon as possible.

(2) Prisoners who suffer from other mental diseases or abnormalities shall be observed and treated in specialized institutions under medical management.

(3) During their stay in a prison, such prisoners shall be placed under the special supervision of a medical officer.

(4) The medical or psychiatric service of the penal institutions shall provide for the psychiatric treatment of all other prisoners who are in need of such treatment.

83. It is desirable that steps should be taken, by arrangement with the appropriate agencies, to ensure if necessary the continuation of psychiatric treatment after release and the provision of social-psychiatric after-care.

C. PRISONERS UNDER ARREST OR AWAITING TRIAL

84. (1) Persons arrested or imprisoned by reason of a criminal charge against them, who are detained either in police custody or in prison custody (jail) but have not yet been tried and sentenced, will be referred to as 'untried prisoners,' hereinafter in these rules.

(2) Unconvicted prisoners are presumed to be innocent and shall be treated as such.

(3) Without prejudice to legal rules for the protection of individual liberty or prescribing the procedure to be observed in respect of untried prisoners, these prisoners shall benefit by a special regime which is

described in the following rules in its essential requirements only.

85. (1) Untried prisoners shall be kept separate from convicted prisoners.

(2) Young untried prisoners shall be kept separate from adults and shall in principle be detained in separate institutions.

86. Untried prisoners shall sleep singly in separate rooms, with the reservation of different local custom in respect of the climate.

87. Within the limits compatible with the good order of the institution, untried prisoners may, if they so desire, have their food procured at their own expense from the outside, either through the administration or through their family or friends. Otherwise, the administration shall provide their food.

88. (1) An untried prisoner shall be allowed to wear his own clothing if it is clean and suitable.

(2) If he wears prison dress, it shall be different from that supplied to convicted prisoners.

89. An untried prisoner shall always be offered opportunity to work, but shall not be required to work. If he chooses to work, he shall be paid for it.

90. An untried prisoner shall be allowed to procure at his own expense or at the expense of a third party such books, newspapers, writing materials and other means of occupation as are compatible with the interests of the administration of justice and the security and good order of the institution.

91. An untried prisoner shall be allowed to be visited and treated by his own doctor or dentist if there is reasonable ground for his application and he is able to pay any expenses incurred.

92. An untried prisoner shall be allowed to inform immediately his family of his detention and shall be given all reasonable facilities for communicating with his family and friends, and for receiving visits from them, subject only to restrictions and supervision as are necessary in the interests of the administration of justice and of the security and good order of the institution.

93. For the purposes of his defence, an untried prisoner shall be allowed to apply for free legal aid where such aid is available, and to receive visits from his legal adviser with a view to his defence and to prepare and hand to him confidential instructions. For these purposes, he shall if he so desires be supplied with writing material. Interviews between the prisoner and his legal adviser may be within sight but not within the hearing of a police or institution official.

D. CIVIL PRISONERS

94. In countries where the law permits imprisonment for debt, or by order of a court under any other non-criminal process, persons so imprisoned shall not be subjected to any greater restriction or severity than is necessary to ensure safe custody and good order. Their treatment shall be not less favourable than that of untried prisoners, with the reservation, however, that they may possibly be required to work.

E. PERSONS ARRESTED OR DETAINED WITHOUT CHARGE

95. Without prejudice to the provisions of Article 9 of the International Covenant on Civil and Political Rights, persons arrested or imprisoned without charge shall be accorded the same protection as that accorded under Part I and Part II, Section C. Relevant provisions of Part II, Section A, shall likewise be applicable where their application may be conducive to the benefit of this special group of persons in custody, provided that no measure shall be taken implying that re-education or rehabilitation is in any way appropriate to persons not convicted of any criminal offence.

Legal Status of the Rules

Are these Rules having the status of international law? Of course, they were accepted by the United Nations and approved by the Economic and Social Council. Nevertheless, they are not enough to get the Rules, the status of or force of international law. Yet, they help or serve to lend an international significance to the Rules more than the same enjoyed by international practices and standards.

The Secretary General of the United Nations makes requests to the Member States to inform periodically the progress of implementing the Rules in their respective jurisdictions. It means that the Secretary General wants to get periodical information about the implementation. The periodical reports about the implementation of the Rules will certainly help the Secretary General to communicate with Member States about the status of enlightened correctional practices in the world. The Secretariat of the United Nations in their working paper on the Rules for discussion writes: "It has been widely recognized that the exercise of such a reporting power by the Secretary General amounts, in itself, to a powerful incentive for nations to compete in improving the circumstances of those protected by the Rules."

Opinions emerge demanding that the Rules ought to have stronger authority. They must be adopted by the local, i.e. national or municipal laws. As it is, the Rules have only a mild ethical validity or justification. It must be changed to have a higher moral and international authority. Presently, their implementation is uneven. There exist strong arguments to convert the Rules into a Convention or a series of Conventions which would certainly enhance their international status—converting a set of moral obligations into a set of voluntarily accepted contractual obligations. While discussions and debates are going on everywhere about various aspects of the Rules, nothing very concrete has come out. No revision of the Rules, in my view, worth-noting has come out so far. In the *Background Note*—"Open-ended Inter-governmental expert group meeting on the United Nations' Standard Minimum Rules for the Treatment of Prisoners" (Published at Vienna, 31 January-2 February, 2012), it has been emphatically stated: "Member States would seek substantial review of several of the existing Rules. These might include among others, the scope of the Rules (Rule 4, 94 and 95), the basic principles in Rule 6, separation of categories (Rule 8), accommodation (Rule 9), medical services (Rule 22 to 26 and 82), prohibition of punishing a prisoner twice for the same offence (Rule 30.1), prohibition on corporal punishment (Rule 31), the obligation on the medical officer to visit daily prisoners undergoing certain punishments (Rule 32.3), the use of instruments of restraint (Rules 33 and 34), arrangements for requests and complaints (Rule 36), prisoners' contact with the outside world (Rules 37 to 40), religion (Rule 41), removal of prisoners (Rule 45), institutional personnel (Rules 46 to 54), inspection (Rule 55), the afflictive nature of imprisonment (Rule 57), the purpose and justification of a prison sentence (Rule 58), the regimes for and treatment of prisoners (Rules 59 to 78), social relations and after-care (Rules 79 to 81 and 83), various rules relating to untried prisoners, including the right to sleep singly in separate rooms, to have their food sent in from outside, to wear their own clothes, to be treated by their own doctor (Rules 84 to 93), the rules relating to civil prisoners (Rule 94) and to prisoner detained without charge (Rule 95). The background paper says further that "All Rules would have to be rewritten to make them gender neutral and there would have to be significant updating of terminology. Redrafting would also have to take account of the obligations in the Convention on the Rights of Persons with Disabilities." It is in this context, I revise the entire Rules and place them before international community for debate and discussion.

2

International Move for the Revision of the Standard Minimum Rules for the Treatment of Prisoners

To reiterate what has been said in the previous chapter, "The Standard Minimum Rules for the Treatment of Prisoners" had its birth in 1926 and thus the Rules have a history of development since then with the work of the International Penitentiary Commission. The Commission is now called the International Penal and Penitentiary Commission—i.e., IPPC. The Rules were revised in 1933 and further updated in 1949. Just before its dissolution in 1951, the International Penal and Penitentiary Commission (IPPC) brought out a revised draft of the Rules. The First United Nations' Congress on the Prevention of Crime and the Treatment of Offenders in 1957 adopted the Rules and they were finally approved by the Economic and Social Council in 1957 by Resolution 663 (XXIV) V, UN ESCOR, Supp. No. 1 at 11, U.N. Doc. E/3048 (1957). Many nations accepted the Rules and some accepted them in principle, but did not/could not implement them in reality as they ought to be.

No doubt, the Rules are old now and they must be revised. I had this feeling long ago and I started working on the revision. I am indeed happy now as the U.N. General Assembly on 21 December, 2010 requested the Commission on Crime Prevention and Criminal Justice to establish an open-ended inter-governmental expert group to revise the existing United Nations' Standard Minimum Rules for the Treatment of Prisoners. The revision is to include the latest developments in the science of correction and best practices. As a follow-up action, the UN Secretariat made a request to all Member States to exchange information on best practices and national legislations along with necessary inputs for the revision of the existing United Nations' Standard Minimum Rules for the Treatment of Prisoners. During 2011, there took place a number of consultations with international experts. The twenty-first session of the Commission on Crime Prevention and Criminal Justice in 2012 discussed the issue in more details. In this context, I thought that the publication of the revised Rules by me will be a timely contribution.

Imprisonment: Changes and Development

Imprisonment as a punishment is of recent origin (in 1704 when Catholic Pope Clement XI erected the Papal Prison in Rome) and to begin with, it was very much punitive in nature. The punitive prisons had a notorious past and it took many years to have a shift from the punitiveness to the prisoners' correction, reformation, resocialization, rehabilitation and reintegration to society back. Over the last sixty years since the "Standard Minimum Rules for the Treatment of Prisoners" were adopted by the U.N., the nature and employment of imprisonment have undergone dramatic changes in many respects in some countries. In my view, the very objective of punishment has now changed from Correction to the "Development of Personality in an Upright way in the Right Direction". To me, correction is only one of the several means for the development of a total personality in a holistic way. Such a developed personality will have no difficulties or road blocks to reintegrate himself/herself to the society back. Thus, correction has become only a means to an end, the end being the development of personality in an upright way in the right direction.

The prison population has an incredible increase over the last few decades so much so that, of late, many prisons are being constructed throughout the world. As it is now, it has been reliably estimated that there are over ten million prisoners in the world (May, 2011 according to International Centre for Prison Studies). Overcrowding of the inmates in prisons creates a variety of problems—both administrative and functional. Overcrowding causes deterioration in prison management including inadequate living conditions, accommodation, shortage of educational, medical and leisure time activities and facilities. Occupational training or skill training and work facilities suffer from inadequacies and limited accesses. Many Jail Reforms Commissions/Committees appointed from time to time in many countries have time and again pointed out these limitations. Nevertheless, they are ignored or some administrations show callous indifference to these aching problems which make the prison-life purposeless and incarceration ineffective. In many countries, prisoners are housed in centuries old buildings which are dilapidated. There is no timely maintenance and the prisoners are looked down upon as "criminals after all". Some of these countries have accepted the Standard Minimum Rules in principle but are prepared to implement only those Rules which have no financial implications. What is the use in doing so? There exists an allegation that many of the Rules in the Standard Minimum Rules could be adopted or accepted in developed countries as they have enough fund with them. In a way, these Rules were framed by them without giving due consideration to the situations prevailing in developing or under-developing countries. If the Rules are adopted as they are, the conditions and situations prevailing inside the prisons in those countries will be probably and qualitatively better than the same seen outside the prisons. Whatever that be, the prisoners ought to receive more consideration and concern from the people. Precisely, therefore, the existing Standard Minimum Rules need amendments/ revision at the earliest. For, criminals or crime-doers are human beings "after all".

From 1957 till date, there have been significant changes in the profile of prison population. Women education, women liberation, empowerment of women in many areas of human transactions have, in a way, paved the way for a rise in women criminality. They are seen to involve in many types of crimes, namely human trafficking, sex-work, flesh-trade and drug trafficking, forgery, cheating, white collar crimes, *nexus* criminality, organised racketeering, corruption and malpractices, *Mafia* and forgery, etc. Crimes committed by women alone or along with men/women are certainly on the rise. More and more criminal cases by women are registered, investigated, tried and convicted. Nevertheless, many nations do not have any special facilities and skill training in women's prisons. The situation must be changed and revised Standard Minimum Rules should have special and specific provisions of law for the fair sex in prisons.

In some countries, the juveniles under 18 years of age have their special institutions. But, what about the adolescents and the adults whose involvement in the commission of crimes are unbelievably high. They are found more in number among the terrorists, insurgents, fundamentalists, fanatics and so on. Most of the *goondas* and unprincipled bandits come from them. They involve in easy money making and various forms of crimes in sex industry. There are drug addicts, drug peddlers, traffickers, hootch manufacturers and so on. They involve in the commission of *Mafia* crimes and increasingly commit crimes of violence, murders, highjacking, rapes, relay rapes, organized or syndicate crimes, drinking, frauds, etc. In democratic countries, they commit crimes for politicians or with political interests. Political crimes, attack on policemen, bureaucratic crimes, hoarding and black marketing, pipe money and nefarious money transactions, money chains, multi-money marketings etc. are abnormally high. Some of them are convicted and they are accommodated with simple offenders housed in prisons. No doubt, such intermixing of various sorts of young and adolescent offenders in prisons cause serious rupture in prison management. Some of them turn out to be recidivists. The new Standard Minimum Rules must take into account of these facts and more.

What about the aged and the infirm? At present, in many countries these old people are treated just like an young incarcerated. Some do suffer serious diseases like cancer, trouble in kidney, paralysis or Alzheimer's disease. They are neglected and precisely, therefore, the revised Rules must have special provisions for the old and sick.

There are prisoners who may stay in Minimum Security Institutions. At the same time, there are a few who should house in medium-security institutions. Open prisons or minimum security institutions are plenty in the world. Maximum Security Institutions are needed for accommodating the terrorists, suicide squads, insurgents and so on. What to do with those who suffer AIDs or any such communicable diseases? There are mental patients or inmates with personality disorders—major, minor or borderline. A prison is a microcosm, nevertheless in 1957, the Rules were adopted with predominantly male adult prisoners in mind—with little thoughts given to the different needs of youngsters, women, the aged and the infirm and other vulnerable groups of inmates in prisons.

The educational profile of the prisoners has been poor or very poor in some countries. The economic profile too has been very poor as the affluent get somehow escaped from incarceration. The influential or otherwise privileged are just a few. The jail population often consist of the poor or the handicapped—socially, financially or politically. Resultingly, the health profile of the inmates will be very deplorable or weak. Over the last 60 years, many countries could not achieve much in the areas of health, occupation, skill training, academic education or moral upbringing of the inmates. As such, recidivism continues to be a major problem even today. The Rules did not or could not bring the expected output. They were seen more on papers than in practical reality. The prisons continued to be a sort of punitive centres with little or no correctional or rehabilitative content.

Prisons in some countries have been punitive, in some others have been peno-correctional, in some others have been deterrent-reformative and in a few or very few countries have been correctional. In none of the countries, the prisons achieved the objectives of correction, reformation, resocialization, rehabilitation, reintegration of the prisoner back to society. Perhaps, the Standard Minimum Rules did not have such high aims and objectives when they were adopted by the United Nations. Over the last 60 years, the objectives of the incarceration has travelled a long way and they included the prisoners' resocialisation and reintegration to the society back. Today, the objective of imprisonment is accepted and recognized to be the "Development of Personality in an Upright Way in the Right Direction" so much so that the prisons are now called "Centres of Personality Development" instead of "Centres of Correction" as they were formerly called. When the Rules were framed, the Prisons were called Prisons and therefore, the mindset of the framers was centred on "Prisons" and not on "Centres of Personality Development". Hence, it is high time that the present Rules are revised incorporating the new concepts in personality development of the residents under incarceration.

As a result of inter-national travel, globalization, tourism, business, trade and global movement of people, the problems of prisoners who are not the nationals of the country in which they are imprisoned are many and various. It has been noticed that in some countries, over half of the prisoners are foreign nationals. Prisons are unisex institutions where people affected by sexual problems are found to be many. Under trial prisoners stay in prisons for months together and in some cases for several years. The delay in the disposal of criminal cases is quite inordinate and incredibly high.

In some countries, the strength of the under trial prisoners, is nearly 90 per cent of the inmates' population and in many countries, it goes between 60-80 per cent. The expenditure spent on every inmate is huge indeed and thus the maintenance of the prisons has become a costly affair in many nations. The 'best interest' of the prisoner *via* his/her personality development has become the sole objective of incarceration and certainly, it will bring down recidivism.

Though short-termers are many and they leave the prisons without a long stay, the number of prisoners who serves very long sentences is going up. The age profile of the prisoners becomes a problem in these days. The older they become, the more are their problems which include nursing, medical, hospital and emotional care.

To quote from the Background Note (Open-ended inter-governmental expert group meeting on the United Nations Standard Minimum Rules for the Treatment of Prisoners). "There have also been significant developments in the way that prisons are managed in many countries. One example, in a number of jurisdictions has been the large rise in the number of prisoners held in high security conditions, often either in total isolation or having minimal direct contact with any other person. This is justified on the grounds of the threat which such prisoners would pose were they to escape or the danger that they present to other prisoners or staff, or the influences which they have over other prisoners, or because of the seriousness of the crimes which they have committed." If this is what is the ground reality, one must accept the fact that the UN Standard Minimum Rules already adopted has become obsolete and barren.

Present Situations

Though the Standard Minimum Rules for the Treatment of Prisoners were in existence for nearly six decades, only 80 countries have accepted them. By Resolution 65/230, the UN General Assembly requested the Commission on Crime Prevention and Criminal Justice to establish an open-ended Inter-governmental expert group to exchange information on best practices and national legislations etc. and it was with a purpose of making recommendations to the Commission for a follow-up action. On 9 December, 2011, the Secretariat received only 28 replies to the

Note Verbale of 8 March, 2010 (CU/2011/26) and subsequent reminder (eu. 2011/182 of October 2011).

The countries were Argentina, Austria, Bahrain, Belgium, Brazil, Canada, Chile, China, Denmark, Ecuador, Egypt, Estonia, Finland, Germany, Guatemala, Israel, Italy, Japan, Lebanon, Mauritius, Mexico, New Zealand, South Africa, Switzerland, Thailand, Ukraine, United Kingdom and USA. What happened to other countries? Did they not have any Best Practices?—National Legislations? etc. The countries were requested to provide information on the revision of the existing UN Standard Minimum Rules for the Treatment of Prisoners so that they reflected recent advances in correctional science and best practices with a view to make revision to the existing Rules. Most unfortunately, the UN General Assembly, still has "correctional science" in its mind. From correction, the objective has come to Development of Personality in an upright way in the right direction. Any way, not many countries commented on the revision of the existing UN Rules. Why? No answer or the answer is "no comments". The comments by countries are given below.

Country	*Comments on the Existing Standard Minimum Rules for the Treatment of Prisoners*
Denmark	The national laws had gone beyond the provisions of some of the Rules.
Finland	Revision of the Outdated Rules needed.
New Zealand	Process for a Review of the Rules necessary.
United States of America	Issue of Women should be taken seriously in the revision.
Austria, China, Finland, Japan, Mauritius, Mexico, New Zealand, South Africa, United Kingdom*	National legislation is based or influenced by the Rules.

* See the background Note on open-ended Inter-governmental Expert Group Meeting on the UN Standard Minimum Rules for the Treatment of Prisoners.

The responses received from those few countries were of not much use for the revision of the Rules. Regarding the best practices—

1. Argentina reported that the overcrowding in Federal Prisons controlled through scientific space allocation parameters.
2. Austria introduced programmes—50 different categories—of work for prisoners and they helped them to find out jobs after release.
3. Belgium allowed regular family visits for all prisoners. It helped them to develop strong parental bond with the prisoner's children.
4. Brazil provided a Public Defender for ensuring free legal aid.
5. Canada implemented a new model of training in community supervision. The Day Report Centres provided services to offenders placed under community supervision.
6. Chile introduced the "11 measures to restore dignity" addressing various prisoners' basic needs. They included living conditions, hours spent outside the cell, spiritual assistance, improving care and health services.

The above good practices were seen in the background Note mentioned above. The 'Note' also provided information relating to many other good practices implemented for improving prison life and prisoner's life. Accordingly,

1. China introduced many measures to reduce/prevent torture during incarceration.
2. Ecuador developed many schemes with an objective of improving the quality of life in prisons for social rehabilitation. They helped the incarcerated to integrate well into society after their release.
3. Estonia started a Drug Rehabilitation Unit—ensured the co-operation of non-governmental agencies for group work activities on drug abuse/misuse. HIV testing and medical aid guaranteed very high dividend.
4. Germany started e-learning in prisons.
5. Guatemala has many programmes to offer special care and

concern to the aged and the infirm. Their health requirements are given top priority.

6. Israel provided bed to all prisoners to sleep and recognized that the right to sleep on a bed is a minimum standard of dignity and living.

Of course, many of the good practices seen in prisons as reported by the Background Note are nothing, but the essential minimum standards to be ensured in all prisons everywhere. It is painful to see that prisoners are treated sub-human by administration in some countries. The Background Note continues—

1. Italy conducted a pilot project with an aim to ensure social reintegration of prisoners.
2. Lebanon has some programmes to eradicate illiteracy among prisoners—has a scheme to pursue higher studies in prisons.
3. South Africa introduced conversion of sentence to other non-institutional alternatives. Encouraged community correctional supervision.
4. Switzerland recognized work in prisons and attendance in training courses as of great value for the purpose of rehabilitation.
5. The United Kingdom has special programmes for prevention of suicides, self-harm management and violence reduction.

These Best Practices seen in other parts of the world can be introduced *mutatis mutandis* in all nations of the world. The Standard Minimum Rules should give emphasis to such steps.

Consultation at Santo Domingo, Dominican Republic

A consultation was held from August 3 to August 5, 2011 in Santo Domingo and the Consultation arrived at a decision that nothing should be done to damage or threaten the integrity of the existing Standard Minimum Rules as they were accepted by the world community as O.K. or fine. According to the Consultation, the Rules were neither outdated nor-irrelevant. However, the view was not right as the Rules were framed at a time when the Rules-

Framing Fathers had different concepts/philosophies about jailing or imprisonment or incarceration. Precisely, therefore, some experts who participated in the Consultation held the view that the Rules ought to be revised incorporating the most recent developments and current best practices in prison management.

The World Health Organisation (WHO) on 3 October, 2011 organized a meeting on Health in Prisons at Abano Terme, Italy (4-5 October, 2011), and the technical consultations on the Rules on Health were held. The meeting arrived at the conclusion: "In recognition of the fact that the Rules needed to be interpreted within the context of the development of international law and national legislation relating to imprisonment, and of current understanding of what constituted good practice in the management of prisons, they suggested that interpretative commentaries could be developed" (See, the Background Note for Open-ended Inter-governmental Expert Group Meeting on the United Nations' Standard Minimum Rules for the Treatment of Prisoners).

To quote from the Note:

> "... experts, however, were of the view that the Rules, which in 1957 sought only, on the basis of the general consensus of contemporary thought and the essential elements of the most adequate systems of today, to set out what is generally accepted as being good principle and practice in the treatment of prisoners and the management of institutions, should ideally be reviewed in the light of the numerous developments in human rights and penal science in the past sixty years. They also felt that the language of the Rules was dated and some provisions were insufficient or not acceptable any more. Among those in favour of the revision of the Rules, some preferred a complete revision of the Rules. As a middle way, a number of experts proposed a "targeted" revision of the Rules, focusing on the most urgently required amendments."
> Fine. What I have been thinking for a long time comes to be a reality. I understand that the Thirteenth United Nations' Congress on the Prevention of Crime and Treatment of Offenders which will be held in 2015 will consider a total revision of the Rules as an agenda item.

Again, quoting from the Background Note:

> "Considering that the idea of a Convention on the treatment of prisoners is a recurring one and was last discussed at the Twelfth United Nations' Congress in Salvador de Bahia in 2010, the meeting may wish to consider the option of a binding instrument whereby States parties should be, under the obligation to ensure certain standards in places of detention and to accept inspection visits through a system of mutual evaluation."

Another option would be a complete restructuring and substantive redrafting of the Rules. One model for this option could be the European Prison Rules (2006). According to such a model, a restructured set of Standard Minimum Rules would contain the following main parts:

- A preamble which would refer to all the *human rights standard* listed in the Annex.
- A new section containing basic principles relating to the treatment of prisoners, which might draw on the Basic Principles for the Treatment of Prisoners.
- A section on conditions of imprisonment which would incorporate many of the Rules in the existing Part-1 (Rules of General Application) along with many of the Rules in the existing Part II (Rules Applicable to Special Categories), Section A (Prisoners under Sentence).
- A section on health care.
- A section on good order.
- A section on management and staff.
- A section on inspection and staff.
- A section on the rights of untried prisoners.
- A section on the specific rights of sentenced prisoners.

Of course, the above suggestions can be a good guideline while revising the Standard Minimum Rules of the United Nations. There should be new sections which must be of great use in countries which are outside Europe. As pointed out earlier, there are many other categories of prisoners who need special care and concern and they cannot be treated like or alike the inmates who come under the general categories. This revision contains a total revision of the existing Standard Minimum Rules with a lot of amendments, alterations and additions. Below may be seen an Annex containing the U.N. Instruments dealing with the treatment of prisoners. They come under two categories, namely, (1) UN documents focusing on the Treatment of Prisoners, and (2) UN documents relevant for the Treatment of Prisoners.

ANNEX

International Instruments Dealing with the Treatment of Prisoners

1. UN Instruments

1.1. UN Instruments focusing on the Treatment of Prisoners

- Standard Minimum Rules for the Treatment of Prisoners (1957)
- Principles of Medical Ethics relevant to the Role of Health Personnel, particularly Physicians, in the Protection of Prisoners and Detainees against Torture and Other Cruel, Inhuman or Degrading Treatment or Punishment (1982)
- Procedures for the effective implementation of the Standard Minimum Rules for the Treatment of Offenders (1984)
- Safeguards guaranteeing protection of the rights of those facing the death penalty (1984)
- Model Agreement on the Transfer of Foreign Prisoners and Recommendations for the Treatment of Foreign Prisoners (1985)
- Body of Principles for the Protection of All Persons under any form of Detention or Imprisonment (1988)
- Basic Principles for the Treatment of Prisoners (1990)
- Rules for the Protection of Juveniles Deprived of their Liberty (1990)
- Model Treaty on the Transfer of Supervision of Offenders Conditionally Sentenced or Conditionally Released (1990)
- Kampala Declaration on Prison Conditions in Africa (1996)
- Arusha Declaration on Good Prison Practice (1999)
- Rules for the Treatment of Women Prisoners and Non-custodial Measures for Women Offenders (2010)

1.2. UN Instruments relevant for the Treatment of Prisoners

- Vienna Convention on Consular Relations (1963)
- International Convention on the Elimination of All Forms of Racial Discrimination (1969)
- International Covenant on Civil and Political Rights (1976)
- International Covenant on Economic, Social and Cultural Rights (1976)
- Code of Conduct for Law Enforcement Officials (1979)
- Convention on the Elimination of All Forms of Discrimination against Women (1981)
- Declaration on the Elimination of All Forms of Intolerance and of Discrimination Based on Religion or Belief (1981)
- Declaration of Basic Principles of Justice for Victims of Crime and Abuse of Power (1985)
- Standard Minimum Rules for the Administration of Juvenile Justice (1985)
- Basic Principles on the Independence of the Judiciary (1985)
- Convention against Torture and Other Cruel, Inhuman or Degrading Treatment or Punishment and its Optional Protocol (1987)
- Principles on the Effective Prevention and Investigation of Extra-legal, Arbitrary and Summary Executions (1989)
- Convention on the Rights of the Child (1990)
- Basic Principles on the Use of Force and Firearms by Law Enforcement Officials (1990)
- Basic Principles on the Role of Lawyers (1990)
- Guidelines on the Role of Prosecutors (1990)
- Principles for Older Persons (1991)
- Principles for the protection of persons with mental illness and the improvement of mental health care (1991)
- Declaration on the Rights of Persons Belonging to National or Ethnic, Religious and Linguistic Minorities (1992)
- Declaration on the Protection of All Persons from Enforced Disappearances (1992)
- Declaration on the Elimination of Violence against Women (1993)
- UNHCR Revised Guidelines on Applicable Criteria and

Standards Relating to the Detention of Asylum-Seekers (1999)

- Convention on the Rights of Persons with Disabilities (2006)

2. Regional Instruments

2.1. Regional Instruments focusing on the Treatment of Prisoners

- Recommendation R(98)7 concerning the ethical and organizational aspects of health care in prisons (1998)—Council of Europe, Committee of Ministers
- Recommendation Rec (2003)23 on the management by prison administrators of life sentence and other long-term prisoners—Council of Europe, Committee of Ministers
- European Prison Rules (2006)—Council of Europe
- European Rules on the use of remand in custody, the conditions in which it takes place and the provision of safeguards against abuse (2006)—Council of Europe
- Principles and Best Practices on the Protection of Persons Deprived of Liberty in the Americas (2008)—Inter-American Commission on Human Rights
- European Rules for juvenile offenders subject to sanctions or measures (2009)—Council of Europe

2.2. Regional Instruments relevant for the Treatment of Prisoners

- European Convention on Human Rights (1950)
- American Convention on Human Rights (1978)
- African Charter on Human and People's Rights (1986)
- European Convention for the Prevention of Torture and Inhuman or Degrading Treatment or Punishment (1987)
- Inter-American Convention to Prevent and Punish Torture (1992)
- American Declaration on the Rights and Duties of Man (1998)
- Principles and Guidelines on the Right to a Fair Trial and Legal Assistance in Africa (2001)

3. Other References

- Guidelines for Physicians Concerning Torture and other Cruel, Inhuman or Degrading Treatment or Punishment in Relation to Detention and Imprisonment (1975)— World

Medical Association

- Oath of Athens (1979)—International Council of Prison Medical Services
- Statement on Body Searches of Prisoners (1993)—World Medical Association
- Yogyakarta Principles on the Application of International Human Rights Law in relation to Sexual Orientation and Gender Identity (2006)—International Commission of Jurists.

International Service for Human Rights

- Istanbul Statement on the Use and Effects of Solitary Confinement (2007)—International Psychological Trauma Symposium.
- Basic principles: Religion in Prison (2010)—International Commission of Catholic Prison Pastoral Care.

3

The Sinner and The Saint

One of the objectives of criminal justice administration/punishment is said to be *expiation or atonement.* Fine. For, a man is a moral being with a moral conscience. He has guilt feelings when he violates the moral law—i.e., the law of the conscience. Some are religious and they may make atonement or reparation for the wrong they have committed. If they are neither moral nor religious, they may not expiate or atone. Researches on the incarcerated prove that some do not have any expiation or atonement even if they have committed an offence. They have their justification or rationalization for their acts. Hence, atonement has only limited meaning among the objectives of punishment. Purgatory is a religious concept which means a condition or place in which, according to Roman Catholics and others, the souls of those dying penitent are purified from venial sins, or undergo the remaining temporal punishment for moral sin forgiven on earth. When the Catholic Pope, Clement–XI converted remand prisons to a place of punishment, he thought of the purgatory—i.e., any condition or place of temporary punishment for suffering or expiation. The intention of the Pope for the construction of the Papal Prison in Rome for punishing the offenders was for serving to cleanse, purify or expiate. The concept of **SIN** was transferred to crime and **Purgatory** to the prison. As a result, the Sinner Concept got developed so much so that everyone imprisoned was a **Sinner** and all who were there to look after, advise, counsel, administer etc. were **Saints.** This *Sinner-Saint* approach made many convicts to feel less in front of the prison staff and the prison staff to look down upon the convicts in prisons.

St. Thomas Aquinas (1225?–1274) and his explanation of sin influenced the Catholic Church when the prisons were converted to centres for punishment. In the history of prison-development one might notice that Belgium accepted Pope's outlooks first and later by the British and still later by the international community. Undeniably, the Standard Minimum Rules were drafted with conditions in America, Australia and Europe in mind. Those countries did have the influence of the Christian Church—views so much so that the Saint-and-Sinner approach of the *prison staff-and-the prisoner* got developed. Consequently, the approach was I AM O.K.; You ARE NOT O.K. between the Staff and the prisoner.

The word "Prisoner" used throughout the text (Standard Minimum Rules for the Treatment of Prisoners, 1957) does affect the *Person* in the individual and in all fairness, the unpalatable word must be removed from the text.

Some scholars and researchers in criminology—particulary in prison management—prefer to call "Inmates" of a correctional institution instead of "Prisoners". Some others call them "Residents" of a Correctional institution. Whether or not the prisoners are the "Inmates" or "Residents" is not the question here. Can we say that the prisons are *correctional institutions* or *institution of correction*? Some countries have changed the Prisons Department to Department of Correction. My researches show that the concepts of *Correction* or Correctional Institutions come from the ***Sinner-Saint*** approach in convict-prison staff relations. In my view, the Standard Minimum Rules, 1957 were drafted at a time when the concepts of Correction, Reformation, Rehabilitation of the inmates were not very much in vogue so much so that one smells that the Rules confer some favours (charity) to the Residents. Are the Residents not entitled to get their human rights established?

What is the meaning of Centre For Correction?—or correcting whom? Everyone wants to correct the *sinners* in the institution. The *sinners* are the incarcerated. According to those 'sinners', the prison-staff need sometimes more correction than the residents inside. For, there are criminals among the staff and they put the garb of the correction officer. Offences detected against the prison staff and reported in the media are plenty so much so that let us forget about correctional institutions for a moment and let us call them "Centres of Personality Development". In my **LinkedIn** discussion, I think that many professionals who participated in the discussion ultimately accepted my view to rename the *Correctional Institutions* to be *Centres of Personality Development*.

The question is: "to what extent are the Standard Minimum Rules drafted with conditions prevailed in America, Australia and Europe relevant to conditions in Africa, Asia and Latin America?" Another question is: How far are the Rules prepared in 1950s relevant and suitable during 2013 when the economic, social, technological and crime-conditions have changed a lot? Hence, what is contained in the document drafted in nineteen fifties may not be the *Rules* or may not be the *Standards*. At the most, what is enunciated in the document are just some moral principles or humanitarian concepts to prisons and prisoners. The *Principles and Concepts* can never be Rules, but only *Guidelines*. Precisely, therefore, the Standard Minimum Rules must give way to ***Guidelines***.

***Treatment?*:** What does it mean to the inmates? Who needs treatment? "Treatment" has many meanings in a Dictionary, but in an institution established and maintained under a **Saint-Sinner** concept, treatment means "to deal with (a disease, patient etc.) in order to relieve or cure, as a physician does". Thus, we have suggested to have correctional staff along with the 'custodial staff'. The entire prison philosophy and approach might be derived from the thinking that the inmates/residents needed "Treatment". In this context, it may be of interest to look into what is going on today.

1. Many who are housed in a prison do not require any treatment at all. They are alright otherwise.
2. There exist no programmes worth mentioning for effecting a meaningful *treatment* in majority of prisons, in many parts of the world. Prison management is performed in a ritualistic way giving greater importance to the Custodial Functions than Correctional Functions.
3. Some who are sent to the prisons become recidivists after the 'treatment' and they relapse into the commission of crimes repeatedly. Why? Where is the wrong? No doubt, there take place some problems for the proper development of their personality in an upright way in the right direction. Some become mentally ill during or after incarceration.

Why? Some commit suicide during their life in prisons.
Why? Questions are many and answers are nil.

Nomenclature for the Revised Document

As the *Rules* are no longer needed—**Guidelines** are needed;

As the *Standard* is no more the standard in many countries;

As the word "Treatment" is no more valid or meaningful in the custodial set-up;

As the word "Prisoners" is no longer acceptable;

As the philosophy has been developed from a **Saint-Sinner** Concept, the nomenclature for the revised Draft must be **Guidelines for the Management of a Centre of Personality Development** instead of the ***Standard Minimum Rules for the Treatment of Prisoners.***

4

Experts on the Revision of the Standard Minimum Rules for the Treatment of Prisoners

During the course of 2011, as pointed out earlier, number of consultations with international experts was organized. A high level expert group meeting was held in Santo Domingo from August 3 to August 5 and an expert group meeting was conducted in Vienna on 6th and 7th October. On 4th and 5th October, 2011, the World Health Organization (WHO) held a meeting in Abano Terme, Italy and had technical consultations on some rules (22-26, 32, 52 and 82) of the Standard Minimum Rules for the Treatment of Prisoners. The UN Secretariat asked the member States to give information on the best practices, as well as national legislation and existing international law and on the revision of the present UN Standard Minimum Rules for the Treatment of Prisoners.

It is learnt that the Expert group (The expert group here refers to the meeting of the expert group on the Standard Minimum Rules for the Treatment of prisoners held in Vienna in 2012) had a general agreement that the existing Standard Minimum Rules for the Treatment of Prisoners could withstand the test of time and were globally accepted as the Minimum Standards for the Treatment of Prisoners. How far or how much is the claim by the Expert Group right or acceptable may be a question of dispute as there are many who disagree with their claim. No wonder that the rules framed by developed countries were quite good for them—but were not so for countries which were underdeveloped or undeveloped. Whatever that be, the Expert Group arrived at a consensus that any changes, amendments or revision to the existing Rules should never lower any of the existing Standards. Fine.

The following were the areas which the Expert Group identified in the present Standard Minimum Rules for the Treatment of Prisoners while the Rules were revised. The Expert Group wanted to see that the recent advances in correctional science and best practices were reflected in the revision.

1. Respect for prisoners' inherent dignity and value as human beings;
2. Medical and health services;
3. Disciplinary action and punishment including the role of medical staff, solitary confinement and reduction of diet;
4. Investigation of all deaths in custody as well as any signs or allegations of torture or inhuman or degrading treatment of prisoners;
5. Protection and special needs of vulnerable groups deprived of their liberty, taking into consideration countries in difficult circumstances;
6. The rights of access to legal representation;
7. Complaints and independent inspection;
8. The replacement of outdated terminology; and
9. Training of relevant staff to implement the Standard Minimum Rules.

I had all those points or areas in my mind when I started to revise the rules long ago; I am happy that the Expert Group too identified the same areas which I did earlier.

Reasoned Objections to the Summary of Deliberations by the Expert Group

I went through the report of the meeting of the Expert Group on the Standard Minimum Rules for the Treatment of Prisoners held in Vienna from 31 January to 2 February, 2012. (SCC UNODC/CCPCJ/EG.6/2012/1 dated 16 February, 2012) I have the following strong objections and they are—

A. Exchange of Information on best Practices (Para 21)

"In many countries, prison overcrowding represented a critical challenge to the proper rehabilitation of prisoners and to the implementation of the Standard Minimum Rules." I prefer to call *"Centre of Personality Development"* instead of prisons. For, what is happening in a Centre is not rehabilitation, rather it is the development of the personality *via* correction, reformation, resocialisation, rehabilitation, and reintegration to society back. 'Prisoners' again is not the proper word to be used. In my opinion, it must be the *'inmates'* or *'residents'* of a Centre of Personality Development.

The UNODC/CCPCJ/EG.6/2012 continues "Several speakers underlined the importance of alternatives to imprisonment and shared their experience of various measures ranging from conditional sentencing to early release and electronic monitoring in order to reduce overcrowding in prisons and ensure that imprisonment would only be used as a punishment for the most serious offenders." In my view, imprisonment (i.e., incarceration) is not a punishment at all. It is to be treated as a means or method (always a desirable one) for the development of an inmate's personality in an upright way in the right direction. Viewing punishment from the correct angle is always better than seeing it from the wrong (i.e., punishment) angle.

While talking about the ***Global Prison Crisis,*** it is stated "Generally, not only was the prison population increasing, but its composition was also rapidly changing, with more children..." No, no child shall be in a prison. They are juveniles (children below 18 years of age) and should be housed in special institutions (in extreme cases) intended for their personality development. In fact, the guidelines for the institutions for the children or juveniles are or should be different from the adults. The use of 'Prisons, Prison Crisis, Prison Population, Imprisoned, Older Prisoners, Prison Administration etc., in Para 22 is really iching and irritating to anyone interested in the development of personality of the inmates in a Centre.

The use of the word "Treatment of prisoners" seen in Para 24 of the UNODC/CCPCJ/EG.6/2012/1 is misleading as there takes place no "Treatment" in any Centre of Personality Development. The inmates are not generally sick people and more often than not, they are sane in every respect. "Treatment of prisoners" gives a bad signal and does not convey the real objective of incarceration.

In spite of the existing Standard Minimum Rules for the

Treatment of Prisoners, Para 25 of the UNODC says: "in many countries measures had been introduced to prevent torture and other forms of inhuman and degrading treatment against prisoners." What does it show? Solitary confinement, cases of violence, abuse in prisons—all these show how desperate are we in our attempts to develop the inmates' personality? Who needs personality development?—the inmates in the Centre or the staff in the Centre? To add insult to injury, one sees suicides in the Centre! Who is to be blamed?—the staff or the inmate? What about the occupancy cells? While the Expert Group does not unanimously accept single-occupancy cells, it seems that they favour double occupancy or dormitories. In my view, the double occupancy cells and dormitories have been abused for homosexual relations by the inmates. I have suggested a Camerata System which I think is a set-up in between single-occupancy and dormitory, Yes, the Camerata System provides sufficient space and privacy to the inmates.

B. Revision of the Standard Minimum Rules for the Treatment of Prisoners

The Expert group made four options about the revision of the existing Standard Minimum Rules. Out of the four options, most of the participants expressed their special interest and preference to only two of the options and they were—

1. Restrict the "Substantive redrafting of the Rules to the minimum, identifying changes which were thought to be most essential." (UNODC/CCPCJ/EG.6/2012/1)
2. Recognize the validity of the Rules and then add a Preamble containing relevant human rights and criminal justice instruments, with a commentary to the Rules that would highlight major implications in terms of modern thinking and good practice as well as renewed efforts to more effectively implement the Rules and to monitor their application." (UNODC/CCPCJ/EG.6/2012/1)

I have my strong objections to the option given as (1) above. After all, more than 50 years are over now since the existing Rules were accepted. It needs a total and substantive revision. For, a further revision is not possible in the near future and the incarcerated cannot be or ought not be condemned to suffer the pains even to the extent of sacrificing their human rights. Yes, I have my preference to the option (2) above. Accordingly, in my revision, I have given a Preample. A thorough revision has been done bringing out the rationale behind the revision. I must say that they are only guidelines for every nation to accept and enforce. In my view, the new revision must inspire all to effect reforms in Centres of Personality Development. The revision must throw light on enacting new legislations, policies and practices. They can be the reference points for human rights activists and penal reformers. A complete restructuring and substantive redrafting of the existing Rules may be what is most urgently required. We cannot wait any longer.

According to Para 41 of the UNODC/CCPCJ/EG.6/2012/1, some speakers suggested that the essential updating of the language of selected provisions of the Standard Minimum Rules could deal with the following. I am reproducing the entire text as follows—

(a) Extension of the scope of the Rules to include all persons deprived of their liberty, be it on criminal, civil or administrative grounds (Rules 4, 94 and 95);
(b) Expansion of the general principles in both paragraphs of Rule 6, perhaps drawing on the Basic Principles for the Treatment of Prisoners (General Assembly Resolution 45/111, annex);
(c) Amendment of the Rules relating to medical and health services, including consideration of the issue of confidentiality of medical records, and the role of medical staff in relation to disciplinary action (Rules 22-26, 32 and 82).
(d) Reflection of the duty to investigate all deaths in custody, as well as any signs or allegations of torture or inhuman or degrading treatment against prisoners in Rule 44;
(e) Consideration of Rules 31-33 in respect of close and solitary confinement and the unacceptability of reduction of diet as a punishment;
(f) Expansion of the provisions dealing with the protection and special requirements of vulnerable prisoners, e.g., older prisoners; foreign national prisoners; ethnic and

racial minorities and indigenous people; transgender prisoners etc.;

(g) Addition of the right of access to a lawyer to all prisoners;

(h) Inclusion of the right of access to external means of complaint in Rule 36;

(i) Reinforcement of the importance of monitoring and independent inspection (Rules 36 and 55);

(j) Promotion of the reintegration of offenders into society as one of the main purposes of the provisions on the treatment of prisoners sentenced to imprisonment (Rules 65 and 66), including greater use of temporary exits from prison, parole and early release programmes;

(k) Replacement of outdated terminology, specifically in Rules 82 and 83;

(l) Alignment of the paragraphs with the provisions of the Convention on the Rights of Persons with Disabilities and the Bangkok Rules to avoid inconsistencies, and extension of the provisions of the Bangkok rules on protection from violence and other non-gender-specific issues to cover all prisoners; and

(m) Expansion of training to include correctional and human rights issues for all those working with prisoners in various capacities, including prosecutors, judges and evaluators (Rules 46-54).

I am in full agreement with the Expert Group in matters relating to—

(1) right to safety to the inmates in the Centre;
(2) right to safety and security of the staff in the Centre;
(3) extension of the civil rights to the incarcerated;
(4) inclusion of the provision for judicial review of the inmates' rights; and
(5) role of the civil society in the correction, reformation, resocialization, rehabilitation and reintegration of the inmate back to society.

In addition, I am to bring certain special areas too in the revised text. They may be—

(1) right of the old, the old old, the older old and the oldest old during incarceration, and
(2) role of after-care services in rehabilitation and reintegration of the inmates to society back and many more.

5

UNSMR for the Treatment of Prisoners:
The Critical Analysis

PREAMBLE AND PERSPECTIVES

As said earlier, nearly six decades, the Standard Minimum Rules remained as Guidelines although they were called Rules. Now there is a move to make the Rules a binding instrument whereby States Parties should be under an obligation to ensure certain Standards in Prisons/Centres of Personality Development. Hence, the treatment of prisoners would become or ought to become a binding instrument—a Convention in the near future. In my view, a Preamble is essential—a Preamble stating the reasons and intent of what follows in the *Guidelines*.

Earlier, it was brought out that imprisonment as a method of punishment was of recent origin. Down the millennia, the objective of punishment remained to be an enigma—a riddle for which no answer was available. Deterrence, retribution, incapacitation, atonement, reformation, correction, deterrent-reformation and correction, etc. have been stated as the objectives of punishment; still no one knows what exactly is the "real" objective of punishment. Why should a wrong-doer be punished? How should a wrong-doer be punished? These two questions remain to be questions and no satisfactory or perfect answers are available although many experts say that correction, reformation, rehabilitation, resocialization and reintegration of the crime-doer *via* Personality Development is the ultimate objective of Punishment. Punishment for punishment's sake is not effective as the punishment is or should be only a means to an end—the end being the development of the crime-doer's personality in an upright way in the right direction.

Justice to the juvenile, justice to the adult, justice to the old, justice to women—all differ only in degrees and not in kind. The Preamble may take this fact into serious consideration. Imprisonment has a deterrent value as no one wants to be under the watchful eyes of the prison-staff and living in prisons with controlled food, lack of toilet facilities, accommodation problems, no leisure-time activities, no proper education or religious practices, workshop constraints, etc. provided in restricted conditions. Therefore, it has a deterrent content. By curtailing freedom and by imposing control over the residents in a prison, the society reacts to the crime and criminal's activities. Certainly, it has a retributive content. Imprisonment has incapacitative content and to some extent an atonement content too. Being so, imprisonment is imprisonment, no matter the prisons have heavenly facilities. Amidst the frustrations, conflicts, happiness, pleasures, life under control, etc., the prison staff is said to make attempts to correct, reform, rehabilitate, resocialize and reintegrate every crime-doer to the society back—from where he/she comes to the prison. This is not an easy task as they need a change in the personality of the crime-doers. This is the reason why it is felt that the ultimate aim of imprisonment is the development of personality in an upright way in the right direction.

Once the personality is developed in an upright way in the right direction, there will not be recidivism-or-relapsing into the commission of crimes even after treatment in prisons. In the case of the juveniles, the *Best Interest* of the Child is given paramount importance. Similarly, in the case of women, their *Best Interest* is taken into account: In the case of the old, again the *Best Interest* is taken into serious note of. If so, in the case of the adult too, the Best Interest is to be given preference to all other things. Once, the *Best Interest* is given due importance, correction, reformation, rehabilitation, resocialization, reintegration of the crime-doers will be ensured and thereby recidivism will be reduced. The development of the crime-doer's personality in an upright way in the right direction is a guarantee against recidivism. In the Preamble, the *Best Interest* of the convicts must be given due place and importance.

The Preamble

To consolidate and revise the Standard Minimum Rules for the treatment of Prisoners adopted on 30 August, 1955 by the First United Nations Congress on the Prevention of Crime and the Treatment of Offenders and approved by Economic and Social Council on 31 July, 1957.

To provide proper care, protection, education and training to all inmates incarcerated for the development of their personality in an upright way in the right direction *via* correction, reformation, resocialization, rehabilitation and reintegration back to society.

To make all to ensure a human rights friendly attitude and approach in their interaction with the inmates—in the best interest of the inmates and for their ultimate personality development in an upright way in the right direction through various means and methods resorted to in the Centre of Personality Development—

Whereas, the Universal Declaration of Human Rights has, in several of its Articles, imposes on the Member States of the United Nations a primary responsibility of ensuring that all the needs of the incarcerated are met and their basic human rights are fully protected;

And whereas, the General Assembly of the United Nations has requested the Commission on Crime Prevention and Criminal Justice to establish an open-ended Inter-governmental Expert group on the revision of the existing United Nations Standard Minimum Rules for the Treatment of Prisoners on 21 December, 2010;

And whereas, the UN instruments focusing on the Treatment of Prisoners and the same relevant for the Treatment of Prisoners have prescribed a set of Standards to be adhered to by State Parties in securing the best interests of the inmate incarcerated to a Centre of Personality Development;

And whereas, it is expedient to revise the existing Standard Minimum Rules relating to the treatment of prisoners, be it adopted by the Member States of the United Nations as their guidelines or directives in the management and running of the Centres of Personality Development henceforth."

No doubt, these are the good principles and practices for the development of the personality of the inmates in an upright way in the right direction as well as for the management of the Centres of Personality Development. The directives have been made in the light of very many human rights that have been accepted down the decades. As stated elsewhere these guidelines are aimed at the development of the personality of those inmates who are incarcerated to a Centre of Personality Development. In my view, many who are incarcerated after a long time (sometimes after 4-5 years up to 10-15 years after appeals and appeals) since the commission of the crime do not require any personality development at all. In some cases, they are sent to a Centre only for a short period during which time nothing constructive or meaningful can be done. Some of the incarcerated are too old that they do not need any personality development. They are sick or infirm and not amenable for any personality change *via* correction, reformation, resocialisation, rehabilitation and reintegration to society back. I have seen the old and the infirm inmates aged over 76-80-85, etc., and they need more of medical treatments of their ailments and old age diseases rather than any personality change. Some are affected by incurable diseases like cancer, AIDS, neural problems and they count on their days in prisons and pulling on.

I do not understand the need for incarcerating those who suffer from paralysis, kidney problems, heart diseases, etc. They need very serious medical care and expert treatment more than psychological counselling or personality development. While I was a member of the Sentence Review Committee appointed by Government of Kerala, I could see the futility and uselessness of any measures taken in the case of the aged and infirm, for a change in their personality. It was virtually impossible and I was thinking in terms of granting probation of good conduct instead of incarceration in such cases. The criminal laws in many countries give leniency towards the juveniles below 21 years of age and to women of all age to get probation of good conduct instead of incarceration under certain conditions. Why can't the law take such a lenient or favourable attitude to the old and the infirm? In my view, therefore, there should be a special section in the revised text for the aged and the infirm in the Centre of Personality Development.

"In an upright way in the right direction" means in a human

rights friendly, morally acceptable, socially enviable, ensuring personal happiness, rehabilitation and reintegration to the society back, guaranteeing social welfare, etc., "In the right direction" means "abiding the law and respecting positive values". "The right direction" means that both "means and end" must be good. Instances are there that the end may be good while the means adopted to reach the end may be undesirable/unacceptable. Personality may be developed in the right or wrong way. Those who are in the wrong way become recidivists or hardened criminals. Those who are in the right way become law abiding citizens. The guidelines ought to be to make the inmates law abiding citizens—an asset to the nation. This is an objective.

"*Via* correction, reformation, resocialization, rehabilitation and reintegration to the society back"—what do those concepts mean? Correction is not reformation. "Correct" means " to set or make right; remove the errors or faults from". "Correction" here means correcting the behaviour of the convicts and it must be in accordance with an acknowledged or accepted standard. Psychologists vociferously admit that behaviour modification is possible at any time during the life-span of an individual. Perhaps, prisons as places of atonement, penance, expiation etc., and imprisonment as a method to create such an atonement, penance or expiation are a creation of such a thinking which is not altogether baseless. The correction-staff in the Centre can create such behaviour modification through their commitment and dedication. 'Reformation' is the improvement or amendment of what is wrong or it may be a change to a better form and it is fulfilled by abandoning wrong or evil ways of life or conduct. Certainly, the industries, education, training and the discipline along with the work of the staff should cause reformation in the inmates incarcerated. What is "resocialization"? Socialization is a process by which a neonate is made a social being with values. The socialization may be in the wrong direction and some in the wrong line may commit crimes. Here, they need resocialization which is not that easy. For, the foundation of values is put during the infancy (till 13-14 years) of a child and to resocialize a person from such a foundation is indeed very difficult. Some who come to the Centre need badly resocialization—i.e., associating or mingling sociably with other fellow inmates. Community life in the Centre and the inmates' interaction with other fellow inmates will and certainly help a lot for resocialization provided that they are under the guidance and supervision of the staff in the institution.

Rehabilitation means restoring to a condition of good reputation or standing of as a law abiding citizen. For this, he must have a means of livelihood—should have the ability and willingness to work after his release—should acquire sufficient knowledge and skill during his stay in the Centre of Personality Development—should be accepted by his family, next of kin, kith and kin, friends, neighbours and so on. Finally, he should reintegrate himself with the society back. He must become very much a member of the society—i.e., incorporate himself into the whole. In other words, the inmate must melt with and become part of the culture.

Every incarcerated has all human rights except the rights restricted by law. He does not have the right to movement as his movement is confined within the four walls of the Centre of Personality Development. He has his human rights to life, equality and dignity and his human rights are dealt with by the United Nations under two categories, namely (1) UN documents focusing on the treatment of prisoners, and (2) UN documents relevant for the treatment of prisoners.

The UN documents stated above have prescribed a set of standards to be maintained or clinged to by the State Parties in securing the best interest of the incarcerated. The best interest of the inmates is presumed to be his reintegration to the society back as a citizen who lives in the community by abiding the laws. For this, his personality must be developed in an upright way in the right direction. The personality traits developed in human beings must be most enviable and the values inculcated in them must be most acceptable to the dominant culture in society. Of course, it may not take place one day, too soon. It is a target to be attained by professionals in the science of developing personality through correction, reformation etc. In a **LinkedIn** discussion I initiated, I had received a number of participation—from the professionals who claimed that their endeavour to stop recidivism could find success by their methods. This is called the strategy for the Best Interest of the Incarcerated.

The Best Interest of the incarcerated has on the other side the Best Interest of the society. Though a crime-free society is a myth, a society with reduced number of crimes be a reality.

REGISTER, IDENTITY AND AUTHORITY

Convicts come—convicts go and this necessitates a Register perfect in every sense. About 60 years ago, registration by electronic methods was not in vogue or was unknown. Today, every information is available on the tip of the finger and precisely, therefore, Rule 7 of the prevailing Standard Minimum Rules needs a total revision. As it is, Rule 7(1) reads: "In every place where persons are imprisoned, there shall be kept a bound registration book with numbered pages in which shall be entered in respect of each prisoner received:

(a) Information concerning his identity;
(b) The reasons for his commitment and the authority therefore;
(c) The day and hour of his admission and release; and
(d) No person shall be received in an institution without a valid commitment order of which the details shall have been previously entered in the register."

A casual look into the Rule will tell us that the information which is recorded in the said Register is not enough-or-far away from being adequate/satisfactory. Why?

A bound registration book has very many limitations. A convict to a prison may become a recidivist—may escape from the jail. Hence, maximum identity is essential. Identity can be by photographs, finger printing, identification marks seen on the body of the convict, lip-prints, Iris identification, Portrait Parle and in my considered view, maximum identification should be recorded by making use of computers and electronic technology. This is easy and any information can be searched within no time. For example, Finger-prints including palm prints can provide conclusive evidence to the identity of a person. Today, scientific methods have been developed to take the finger/palm-prints electronically.

Lip prints are the normal lines and fissures in the zone of transition of human lip between labial mucosa and on the outer skin. Lip prints are identifiable as early as the sixth week of intrauterine life, and from that time onwards, the pattern rarely changes—resisting many afflictions such as herpetic lesions—says

Prof. Magda EL. Domiaty. About finger prints, it has been proved that they remain to be the same from womb to tomb in a person. Like the finger prints, the lip-print pattern has proved to be unique (individuality) for an individual—even in twins and siblings.

Iris recognition is the process of recognizing a person by analyzing the random pattern of the Iris. Researchers have proved that although genetically identical, an individual's Irises are unique and structurally distinct, which allow for it to be used for recognition purposes.

Portrait Parle is a French term referring to a picture of an individual in both front and profile views. This can be effectively used for finding convicts who have escaped the prison custody because of the thoroughness of the descriptions. The following gives the key descriptions for a Portrait Parle. The descriptions thus recorded will give a convict's whole personality. Specialists in Portrait Parle have prepared various forms to make a through description of an individual. This can also be used by the authorities.

Portrait Parle: An Overview

Key descriptions for Portrait Parles follow. Notice that the descriptions essentially profile a person's whole personality, not just a physical description.

age	voice	friends	hangouts	piercing	hair length
chin	build	glasses	foot size	residence	hair texture
DNA	blood	habits	eye shape	hair colour	exits scene
ears	teeth	hobbies	lip colour	occupation	accessories
head	height	jewellery	eye colour	background	finger prints
name	family	lip size	eyebrows	automobile	peculiarities
neck	gender	tattoos	lip shape	facial hair	weapon choice
nose	shoes	weight	forehead	ethnicity	complexion
race	scars	—	clothing	lip prints	birthmarks

Photographs of the new convict should invariably be taken and if necessary should be updated as years go by. Hence, the present Rule must be revised accordingly. Rule 7(1)b is about the reasons for the commitment and the authority therefore. The judicial reasons for the commitment should be recorded. Nevertheless, in my view, the commitment is for the development of the convict's personality in an upright way in the right direction *via* correction, reformation, resocialization, rehabilitation and reintegration to society back. Hence, side by side to the judicial causes, the following information too must be recorded. They are—

(1) General information consisting of—(a) brief summary of the offence as narrated by the convict, and (b) Information regarding any situational or environmental factors which contributed to the offence.
(2) Special information collected from the new convict relating to—
    (a) Description and size of the family;
    (b) Nature of the family;
    (c) Attitude, approach and expectation of the convict from incarceration;
    (d) Expectation about other inmates and interaction with them;
    (e) Economic, occupational and other social background;
    (f) Convict's values towards spouse and if they have children, parents and family as a whole, then details about them too;
    (g) Convict's values towards observance of law, obligations, responsibilities, duties, crime, police, court, prison authorities, pleasures, education, friends, people around, life etc.; and
    (h) Any further information found essential for his/her personality development to be recorded.

Rule 7(1)c is about the day and the hour of the admission of the convict and his release from the prison. In other words, it is about the period of his incarceration or period during which the development of his personality in an upright way in the right direction will take place. As far as a short-termer is concerned, the period of his stay in the prison may not be that significant or important as far as his personality development is concerned. Nevertheless, the period spent by the convict after the commission of the crime, during the investigation and trial until the date of incarceration is important from the point of view of his personality development *via* correction, reformation etc. How did the convict adjust with his environment during the pre-incarceration period and how did he manage his relations with his family, kith and kin, friends and other people in the community matters a lot. His attitude and approach towards the people around him, towards the environment, towards the victims of the offence, his/her family too deserve special consideration. His religious life, ethical and social values, leisure-time activities, profession/occupation etc., matter a lot. Anyway or any how he did or could adjust with people and the environment so much so that he did not violate any law during the pre-incarceration days. All these aspects should be taken note of by an expert interviewer at the time of his admission to a prison. The expert can advise the prison staff to prepare the programme and strategies for his personality development on the basis of the data thus collected at the time of his admission. Hence, the Rule (1)c must be amended or revised accordingly.

In my view, Rule 7(1)d is not necessary as no one is received in an institution without a valid commitment order of which the details have been previously entered in the Register. I may suggest that the convict should be given a right to receive a copy of this admission record so that he will have an idea about all parameters recorded therein. He must be given the copy free of cost and should be advised on counselling as to how to behave properly in the prison. Therefore, along with the copy of the Admission Register, every convict ought to be entrusted with a copy of the prison rules in a language understandable to him—which he should observe while he is inside the prison. This will help him a lot to adjust himself well observing the rules of the prison regarding accommodation, work in industries, personal hygiene and conduct, institutional hygiene and food, religious activities and moral training, leisure-time activities and similar matters about which an inmate must have information. Instances are plenty that the new entrants to incarceration are exploited by the prison staff and by other fellow inmates. In my considered view, I may suggest that a pre-entry course lasting for two or three days ought to be conducted and every new comer should be exposed to the prison rules, conduct and interaction with others, inmate-prison staff relations, relations with outside world, recreation facilities, etc., Everything must be done for the *Best Interest* of the inmate and thereby for his rehabilitation and reintegration back to society. A changed personality with a conscience and values formed in an upright way in the right direction is what is desired by incarceration. Hence, the revised guideline/directive will be—

Rule 7—"In every place where persons are housed for the development of personality in an upright way in the right direction by an order of conviction by a competent court of law, there shall be kept a Bound Registration Book with numbered pages in which shall be entered in respect of everyone received—

(1) Information concerning his identity which will further be recorded electronically containing his finger-prints, palm-prints, signature, photographs, Iris ID and Lip-print ID and Portrait Parle.

(2) (a) Judicial reasons for his commitment and the authority, therefore, which will further be recorded in detail electronically containing a brief summary of the offence as narrated by the convict along with a brief summary of any situational or environmental factors which contributed to the offence.

(b) Special information collected from the convict about his family, attitude, approach and expectation in his life in the Centre for Personality Development, economic/occupational and social background, values towards family, observance of law, police, courts, Centre's authorities, duties, works etc., in the Centre and any other information essential for his personality development in an upright way in the right direction.

(3) The day and hour of his admission and release which will further be recorded electronically with details about his life during the pre-incarceration period, during investigation, during trial and the way he managed to live a law abiding life till the date of his admission. His attitude, approach and values towards domestic life, religious life, moral life, social life, leisure-time activities, profession, occupation etc., must be recorded by experts.

(4) Every convict on his admission must be given a copy of the Register so recorded along with a copy of the Centre's Rules which he must observe while he is inside the Centre free of cost and in a language understandable to him.

(5) Every convict on his entry to a Centre has a right to attend

> a pre-entry course to learn the rules of the Centre along with the conduct norms, rules for the staff-inmate interaction, etiquette in community living and such other matters found necessary for the best interest of the inmate and the institution."

Ignorance of the inmates about the rules and the illiteracy/semi-literacy of the convicts create a lot of problems for their harmonious co-existence in the Centre. This can be remedied to a great extent by the exposure to a short term course to teach them about the essentials in community life.

SEPARATION OF CATEGORIES

The present Standard Minimum Rules under Rule 8 reads: "The different categories of prisoners shall be kept in separate institutions or parts of institutions taking into account of their sex, age, criminal record, the legal reason for their detention and the necessities of their treatment." Thus,

Rule 8(a) "Men and women shall so far as possible be detained in separate institutions, in an institution which receives both men and women, the whole of premises allocated to women shall be entirely separate;

(b) Untried prisoners shall be kept separate from convicted prisoners;

(c) Persons imprisoned for debt and other civil prisoners shall be kept separate from persons imprisoned by reason of a criminal offence; and

(d) Young prisoners shall be kept separate from adults."

First of all, let us take away the repeated use of the words *prisoners, imprisoned,* etc. from the text. For obvious reasons, the expressions are not human rights friendly. They affect the very dignity of the persons. There may be any number of expressions which can be used. Some use "*Residents*" while others say "*inmates*"—both do not have any stigma attached. 'Prison' again is *not a "nice-to-hear"* word. Instead, a Centre of Personality Development may be substituted.

Different Categories of Prisoners—the expression is vague and not couched in clarity. One and the same person can come under different categories. What is meant by *"criminal record"*? Does the Rule mean a first offender or a repeater?—or—an offender against human body or an offender against property? Again, what is the real meaning of "the legal reason for their detention". The *"legal reason"* means the judicial cause/s or reason/s for conviction and everyone knows that the cause/s may be well defined under the existing penal laws of the country. If one's behaviour has been in violation of the ingredients of the definition of a given penal law, he becomes judicially or legally liable to punishment—nothing more and nothing less. "Necessities of their treatment"—what does it mean? What type of treatment do they need? To consider that everyone convicted by a court of law is sick may be against facts as there may be any number of inmates who are not sick at all. Psychological explanation of the causes of crime is only one of the many explanations about the causes or factors leading to criminality. Criminal is a sick person—is one of the several explanations about the causes of crime. Some of the psychological approaches or explanations of the causes of crime are rejected on the basis of research evidence. What type of treatment is required for short termers? Nothing is clear and the Rule causes confusion. Obscurity is seen and when one reads the Rule repeatedly, he goes from obscurity to obscurities.

'Untried Prisoner' (under Rule 8(b)) is understandable when the expression is read within the meaning given in a dictionary—namely, *Prisoner* means *"a person who is confined in a prison or kept in custody, esp. as a result of legal process."* In that sense, the expression "untried prisoner" has some sense/meaning. A person who is suspected to have committed a crime may be remanded to police or judicial custody. It means that he should be detained in a custodial facility and not in a prison. Judicial custody means *detention* in a custodial facility manned and managed by the judiciary. In some countries, the detainees are kept in the prisons—i.e., under an executive custody with a label called judicial custody. There exists strong objection in doing so. Those who protest the existing procedure insist that judicial custody ought to be "Judicial Custody" and *"not executive custody"* under a judicial order.

Just because a suspect is kept in a prison, he does not become a prisoner. If a person in police custody is not called a *prisoner*, then any person who is in judicial custody should never be called a prisoner. He is a detainee under a judicial order and not a prisoner as the expression is understood now. A person in police or judicial custody does not need any treatment and to put such people under the "Standard Minimum Rules for the Treatment of Prisoners" may be ethically and otherwise wrong. Nothing should be mentioned about such people who are remanded under police or judicial custody. Forgetting the meaning given in the dictionary, a prisoner means, for all practical purposes, a prisoner convicted for an offence—nothing more and nothing less.

"Persons imprisoned for debt and other civil prisoners shall be kept separate from persons imprisoned by reason of a criminal offence"—[Rule 8(c) of the existing Standard Minimum Rules]. Such people do not have any scope to come under the purview of the Standard Minimum Rules. For, they do not come under *treatment of prisoners* in any way. It is not fair or morally justifiable to send them to prisons where convicts in criminal cases are housed.

According to Rule 8(d) of the present Standard Minimum Rules, young prisoners shall be kept separate from adults. If young prisoners (youth) are considered to be those who come in the group of 18-35 years of age, then adults should be limited to those who are in the range of 35-60 years of age. 60 years and above are treated to be senior citizens in many countries and therefore, the old, the older old, the oldest old must be kept separate from adults. For, their attitude, approach, problems and difficulties are certainly different from the same of the young or adults. This is a time when the old people are given special consideration and anything done to the aged, to the aged infirm and so on is treated to be their right and not a charity shown to them.

In my view there is the immediate need or urgency for a total rehauling of the Rule 8(a-d) of the existing Standard Minimum Rules. I propose that Rule 8(b, c and d) may be deleted and the Rule must be redrafted as follows:

Rule 8(a) The different categories of residents in a Centre of Personality Development shall be housed in separate Institutions or parts of the Institution *(Cameratae)* taking into account of their (1) sex, (2) age, (3) crime record, (4) marital status, (5) professional or occupational status, (6) economic background, (7) length of stay, (8) necessities of treatment after diagnosis or any other special ground as may be found necessary.

(b) Men and women shall be housed in separate institutions which are located in different places geographically.

Why do I make such a revision adding or deleting Rule 8 (a-d)? The reasons are—

(1) Sex is biological and work very strongly in man and woman. It is an animal instinct which works very powerfully in human beings. There is no need for any stronger arguments to keep the inmates in separate institutions basing on sex particularly when everyone in a Centre is suffering from sexual starvation. I do not and cannot recommend parts of the institution for housing male and female inmates separately within the same Centre for the simple reason that the locational or geographical nearness of two institutions is likely to have undesirable impacts on both sexes. I suggest, therefore, that the male and female institutions must be geographically separated and situated in two places separated by physical distance. Even the sounds heard from the female institution has caused disturbance in the nearby male institution separated by a wall—this is a research evidence in my hand and in such a situation, the two Centres, for males and females should be geographically distant.

(2) No doubt, the juvenile (those under 18 years of age) have their Centres—adequately or inadequately constructed in many countries. Of course, administration of juvenile justice is not given due importance in some countries. This is of bad taste, for a control of juvenile offences (delinquencies) is a control of young and adult criminality. The young are those who come in the age group of 18-35 years of age. Among the young, there may be *Young Young* (18-25 years of age), the *middle young* (26-30 years of age), and the *old young* (31-35 years of age), who must be separated by *cameratae* accommodation. Among the adults, again there will be the young adult (36-45 years of age), the *middle adult* (46-55 years of age), and the *old adult* (56-60 years of age).

They should be separated by *cameratae* accommodation. Of course, their dormitory accommodation alone should be in *cameratae* which must contain toilet and bathing facilities as well. The rest of their works and activities may be common. With this in view, the Centre of Personality Development must be constructed.

(3) The old inmates have their problems different from the young or adult inmates. It has been found that the older residents, particularly if they have stayed longer in a Centre, misuse, abuse or exploit the younger ones in many ways and particularly in sexuality. Homosexuality may be practiced on a new comer especially if he is young/very young. It is a good proposition that the old or aged inmates (60 years or above) are housed in a separate Centre away from the young inmates. Physical ailments, old-age diseases, psychological problems of the old are many and various. There is research evidence to show that the aged and the infirm under incarceration have many miseries and problems. It is, therefore, felt that the *young old* (60-65 years of age), the *middle old* (66-70 years of age), the *old old* (71-75 years of age), the older old (76-80 years of old), the oldest old (81 years and above) are to be housed in separate *cameratae* having toilet and bathing facilities. There is a view that the oldest old should not be convicted for imprisonment. This will be discussed further later. Excepting their sleeping, toilet, bathing facilities in the *cameratae,* everything must be common and all must participate in the community life of the Centre.

(4) Crime-record is important for the simple reason that the first offenders should not mingle and mix with recidivists. The recidivists teach and the new entrants learn many methods of committing various types of crimes—thereby, their personality may be shaped in a wrong way. In my view, the Centres must be classified on the basis of the category of offenders. There may be hardened inmates, residents who need tight security (e.g., terrorists, fundamentalists, insurgents, fanatics and so on), long termers and short termers, inmates who require psychological and therapeutic assistance etc. Presently, there are institutions which accommodate large number of

inmates. In my opinion, construction of such large institutions is an old concept which has not proved to be beneficial for the development of the personality of the residents housed therein. Researches prove that large institutions which accommodate different categories of inmates on the basis of their criminal record are not seen to be successful in reforming or reshaping their personality.

(5) Marital status is to be considered when inmates are housed. Birds of the same feather flock together. People who are married will have many problems and matters common for talk and certainly, they can share their experiences. They may talk about their children, their future, family etc. "Sorrows are lessened when shared"—is an accepted fact in human life. Let the married stay separate from the unmarried, divorced, separated or deserted. This will help to reduce sexual aberrations and abnormalities which may creep into their life in the Centres.

(6) Educational, professional or occupational status is of paramount significance when separation of inmates is thought of. The illiterate, semi-literate, moderately educated, highly educated inmates find it extremely difficult to stay together and communicate. They have communication problems whereas the inmates of the same educational, professional and occupational background have common topics of interest for discussion. This will help them to talk of subjects which are not crime-centred.

(7) Economic background is another factor to be considered. The rich and the affluent may feel difficulties to stay with the poor who have different style of living, thinking and behaving. Today the number of the inmates having affluent background goes up and people having economic motives behind the commission of their crimes may not have anything to share with the residents having different motives.

(8) Length of stay in a Centre means whether or not an inmate is a long termer or a short termer. Short termers have days/weeks/months to go whereas the long termers have years/many years to stay before they are released pre-maturely or on completion of the prison sentence. No meaningful programme for personality development can be planned

or thought of for very short termers. On the other hand, constructive—objective oriented—plans/programmes are designed and implemented in the case of long termers provided there are well trained staff. This is more applicable in the case of lifers in the Centre. Most unfortunately many countries have dearth of qualified personnel in their Centres, inadequate or insufficient funds, lack of interest, innertia to implement any worthwhile programmes, etc.

(9) Necessities of their treatment after a proper diagnosis are another parameter on the basis of which the inmates are housed. The diagnosis must be done by a team of qualified personnel. There may be moral wrecks, psychopaths, sociopaths, people suffering from psychoneuroses, manias etc. They need professional care and sometimes therapeutic treatment. They should not stay with others who do not have any such problems.

The classification and separation of the inmates is indeed a difficult task, but must be done with earnestness. Development of personality in an upright way in the right direction is what is intended by staying in a Centre. It is for the "*Best Interest*" of the inmate and of the society. I have formulated a theory of Crime-Causution and I call it *Push-Pull Ego Factor Theory*. Accordingly, all energies that activate a man or energize a person to behave in a particular way may be put under *Push Factors*. All situational or environmental factors which pull him to behave in a particular way may be put under *Pull Factors*. If the Centre of Personality Development provides conducive atmosphere to shape one's *Ego* in an upright way in the right direction, then he/she is corrected, reformed, resocialized, rehabilitated and reintegrated to the society back. This is what is desired by classification and separation and as such a value centred environment in every respect ought to be created. The Ego is then modified and reshaped so much so that he/she leaves the Centre with a changed Ego or Personality.

SLEEPING ACCOMMODATIONS

Rule 9(1&2) and Rule 10 speak about sleeping accommodation. To reproduce Rule 9(1), "Where sleeping accommodation is in individual cells or rooms, each prisoner shall occupy by night a cell or room by himself. If for special reasons, such as temporary over-crowding, it becomes necessary for the central prison administration to make an exception to this rule, it is not desirable to have two persons in a cell or room." According to Rule 9(2), "Where dormitories are used, they shall be occupied by prisoners carefully selected as being suitable to associate with one another in those conditions. There shall be regular supervision by night in keeping with the nature of the institution."

As a rule, I am not inclined to suggest accommodation in individual cells or rooms. For, staying alone in a room is really killing and that too in a room which does have only creature—comforts or less than that. One feels lonely and forsaken and solitary life in a room with no human comforts is likely to produce negative/unnecessary thoughts. He may feel depressed. If the food in the prison is far away from being satisfactory, the depression may be doubled or tribled—moving towards committing suicides. There is a common saying that an idle mind is the devil's worshop and precisely, therefore, he is likely to have all sorts of destructive thoughts. Development of personality in such an atmosphere is not possible—rather development of desperate thoughts is quite possible. What is more? He may start to have a feeling of self-contempt or contempt to everyone. He may hate the world around including the laws, legal system and law enforcement machinery. He may curse all who made his life miserable and my researches give me enough proof to show that the theory of expiation or atonement rarely works hopefully with the inmates who are in solitude. Instead, he develops anger, vengeance and revenge towards many. Man is a social being and he wants people around. Hence, I disfavour sleeping accommodation in individual rooms or cells during night hours. It must be generally resorted to only in the rarest of rare cases or in special circumstances.

The expression 'Cell' is penal and has its roots attached to the punitive cell. Some mental patients are chained in cells and look at their faces. They are very gloomy or become angry, expressing their frustration. If this is what is seen in mental patients, the same will be seen in crime-doers or in inmates. I fail to understand why one must say "condemned cell" to mean that it is meant for those convicted for capital punishment. If development of human personality in an upright way in the right direction is desired, then avoid all those terms, words, phrases and expressions which look down upon the inmates. A "Prisoner after all" should not be the attitude/approach of anyone towards the inmates.

Talk with dignity and use the word "cubicle" in a *Camerata* which is known after a beautiful flower or after a river, mountain or anything that will evoke pleasant feelings. A *Camerata* may be called "Surya" which means "Sun" or flower "Rose" which has a nice scent. The names so given must have positive contents and future. A rising Sun means a lot or a scenting flower produces fragrance around. Use of the "Room" should be avoided, if possible. No two persons in a single room—it is quite acceptable in a sexually starved atmosphere like the one existing in prisons. In *Camerata* accommodation, the question of two people staying in a single room does not arise. By *Cameratae* accommodation, I mean 16-20 inmates living together in separate cubicles in a hall having its own toilet and bathing facilities. Each cubicle in the *Camerata* provides sufficient cubic content of air and privacy for every inmate. There is a central path running through the middle of the hall. The cubicles are on two sides of the central path and they have only clothe curtains in front which ensure sufficient privacy and safety for the inmates. The two sides of the cubicle will have half walls having a height of five or six feet. At one end of the hall, there should be a room constructed with walls having five or six feet height above which there should be only bars to see, observe and supervise the dangerous inmates by a member of the custodial staff/correctional staff as the case may be. Hence, I wish to redraft the Rule 9(1) as under—

"(1) Sleeping accommodation shall be provided in cubicles in *Cameratae* for 16-20 inmates to enable them to develop community life.

(2) Sleeping accommodation in individual rooms shall be allowed only in rarest of rare cases, or in special circumstances if possible.

(3) Sleeping accommodation in individual cubicles having safety walls with bars and security doors in *cameratae* shall be allowed in all cases where Rule 9(2) is not applied."

Since *Camerata* is a dormitory-type accommodation, Rule 9(2) of the present Standard Minimum Rules is not necessary. Preparing an inmate to live a community life by associating with others should be one of the objectives of developing personality through resocialization and reintegration to society back after one's release. I suggest to delete Rule 9(2) from the present text.

Rule 10 of the existing Standard Minimum Rules reads: "All accommodation provided for the use of prisoners and in particular all sleeping accommodations shall meet all requirements of health, due regard being paid to climatic conditions and particularly to cubic content of air, minimum floor space, lighting, heating and ventilation." The entire Rule can be retained although the proposed *Cameratae* accommodations will have all the facilities enumerated above such as cubic content of air, minimum floor space, lighting, ventilation etc. Every *Camerata* will have facilities for toilets, bathing and washing.

Rule 11 of the present Rules relates to places where the inmates are required to live or work and reads:

"In all places where prisoners are required to live or work,

(a) The windows shall be large enough to enable the prisoners to read or work by natural light, and shall be so constructed that they can allow the entrance of fresh air whether or not there is artificial ventilation.
(b) Artificial light shall be provided sufficient for the prisoners to read or work without injury to eye-sight."

A casual reading of Rule 11 may show that the prisoners are a special category of human beings who can live and survive in any conditions or situations in which ordinary people cannot live or survive. As they have committed a crime, they are condemned to suffer anything. If they get any human comforts, they are given at the mercy of others or as a result of charity shown to them. I have a question. 'Are they subhuman beings who do not deserve any human comforts or should not enjoy any human rights?' As a concession shown to the prisoners, the Rule 11 says 'that the windows shall be large enough to enable prisoners to read or work by natural light'. In my view, there are or there should not be any special windows especially manufactured for the prisoners. Every country has its own construction styles and the use of windows and doors. Suppose one says that the "door shall be large enough for the people to go into and come out of the house", it means that there are doors which do not allow the people to go into or come out of the house. If the doors do not provide the facility they must to the people, then they are not doors. Everything has a purpose.

In the present case, I may suggest to forget the description of the windows and their utility as given in Rule 11(a). If the so-named windows do not allow the prisoners to read or work by natural light, they are no more 'windows' or they cannot be called so. If the windows do not permit the entrance of fresh air, then they are not windows. What is the real meaning of injury to eye-sight? Are the prisoners to live and work in the jails to make them blind? Are they incarcerated to develop their personality *via* correction, reformation, resocialization etc.?-or- are they incarcerated to become sick and die? 'Becoming sick' in prisons cannot or should not be called 'personality development'. Here, an amendment of Rule 11(a & b) is required. Hence,

(a) "In all places where the inmates are required to work, there shall be *sufficient* natural light for them to read and work. If it is not possible, the artificial lights provided should be pleasant enough for their eyes to read or work."

If natural lights are available for the inmates to read and work, it means that the windows are good enough and they permit free flow of fresh air. If only artificial ventilation is available, then a provision should be made in the Rules to have the flow of fresh air. Hence, the amendment.

(b) "There shall be free flow of fresh air whether or not there is artificial ventilation."

Prisons constructed with a punitive mind or retributive spirit may make human life miserable by providing discomforts. At present, the only purpose is to provide all facilities to the inmates to develop their personality so that they do not relapse into the commission of crime after their incarceration.

SANITARY AND BATHING INSTALLATIONS

Many who are convicted and incarcerated may not have got proper toilet training. Some of them do not have used even good latrines and bathrooms. I know a country where many people answer their nature's call in public and the domestic animals like buffaloes, pigs, or birds like chicken, etc., clean the area. The municipality of that area decided to construct public latrines for the people's use. Most unfortunately, none of the people knew how to use latrines and bathrooms. They found it extremely difficult to answer their nature's call in a closed room and they refused to make use of the facility. Ultimately the authorities had to ask the policemen to force the people to make use of the public latrines. After a few day's use, the municipality had to close the public latrines and bathrooms. Even today, some people do not know how to use the latrines and bathrooms.

Rule 12 of the present Rules says: "The sanitary installations shall be adequate to enable every prisoner to comply with the needs of nature when necessary and in a clean and decent manner."

Honestly saying, it is horrible, sometimes, to see the sanitary installations in some prisons. Animals in the zoo are provided with better sanitary facilities. Many become sick from the latrines which are not clean. In some prisons, there is no privacy for the prisoners to bath and as a result, they bath publicly in groups. A horrible sight indeed!—a sort of crowd bathing. In prisons, everything is to be finished in time as there is a time-table followed. Overcrowding in prisons make the latrines a place of verbal abuses and heated exchange of foul words. Even prison riots had their start in latrines and bathrooms. How many inmates should use a latrine/bathroom within the time allotted for the same in the time table? Can they use them with a mental peace?

The Rule 12 speaks about the 'adequacy' of the sanitary installations. This is interpreted by the administration in a manner which may please only the interpreters and not the inmates. Open bathing is "adequate" for them. How can the inmates clean their body including their private parts in public? The inmates should be provided with facilities to comply with the needs of nature in a clean and decent manner. What is meant by "clean and decent manner"? What is the position in women's prisons? Less number of latrines and inadequate facilities for bathing means definite quarrels—either openly or secretly. Some prisoners make use of the facility forgetting their sense of dignity. "A prisoner after all" approach is seen and "the prisoner needs only this much" attitude is shown. In older days, life in a prison was worse than life in a hell; but—now things have improved a lot to the better. Therefore, Rule 12 must be redrafted to read:

> "There should be sufficient number of latrines and bathrooms not only in the *camerata* where the inmates stay, but also outside to enable the residents to comply with the needs of nature when necessary and to use them keeping their privacy and human decency attached to such use."
>
> Rule 13 is about bathing and shower installations and says:
>
> "Adequate bathing and shower installations shall be provided so that every prisoner may be enabled and required to have a bath or shower, at a temperature suitable to the climate, as frequently as necessary for general hygiene according to season and geographical region, but at least once a week in a temperate climate."

'General hygiene' is something to be decided by a medical team attached to the prison (Centre for Personality Development) and is not something that should be entrusted to the individual decision of the inmates. If the inmates have to work as per the judgement of the courts, then they ought to have a bath or shower daily. Therefore, the proposed revision is—

> "Every inmate shall be compulsorily required to have a bath or shower, at a temperature suitable to the climate as frequently as necessary for the general hygiene according to season and geographical region decided by the medical doctor attached to the institution:
>
> Provided that the inmates who work as per the judgements of the courts ought to have the bath or shower at least once a day:
>
> Provided further that taking a bath or shower in public or in the visibility of other inmates is degrading and should be avoided at any cost."

Many poor people are incarcerated and precisely, therefore, they may not feel any shame or they may not have any feeling of degrading if at all they are asked to take a bath in the visibility of other inmates having a short loin cloth. Some of the inmates are homeless or are having no settled place of abode so much so that they may feel at home even if they do not have a bath or shower even for weeks together. This should never happen in a community where the hygiene of the individuals and the institution affect a lot the general health/hygiene of a Centre of Personality Development.

Rule 14 of the present Standard Minimum Rules is retained as it is—i.e. "All parts of an institution regularly used by prisoners shall be properly maintained and kept scrupulously clean at all times." For, it goes without saying that the entire atmosphere—not only those areas regularly used by the inmates—of an institution of personality development ought to be maintained and kept scrupulously clean at all times. The caged human beings have a right to have such a dirt-free atmosphere inside the institution. For, it is next to food for the inmates.

Personally, I am not in favour of large compounds for prisons. There are open-air prisons having several hectares of land. Many walled prisons too have large compounds and they accommodate work industries, agricultural lands, place for cultivation of vegetables etc., I suggest that the inmates should stay in a building away from their work area. Of course, the living accommodation can have their prayer halls, recreation facility, facility for reading and indoor games, library, *yoga* centre, auditorium, dining hall, kitchen, etc., and they must be scrupulously clean at all times. Other areas of inmates' activities may consist of work industries, agricultural land, playgrounds, hospitals, educational buildings etc. They can be or should be located geographically at a distance from the living accommodation of the inmates.

PERSONAL HYGIENE

Many people incarcerated do not understand the meaning of personal hygiene. They lack education and information about how hygienic their body should be. Hygiene or hygienic is the science that deals with the preservation of health. It also means a condition or practice conducive to the preservation of health, as cleanliness. Rule 15 and Rule 16 are reproduced below:

Rule 15: "Prisoners shall be required to keep their persons clean, and to this end they shall be provided with water and with such other toilet articles as are necessary for health and cleanliness."

Rule 16: "In order that prisoners may maintain a good appearance compatible with their self-respect, facilities shall be provided for the proper care of the hair and beard and men shall be enabled to shave regularly."

Personal hygiene to me means a lot. It is much more than taking bath and going to a water closet or cutting the hair and shaving regularly. In order to have a condition or practice conducive to the preservation of health, as cleanliness, one must be clean not only physically but also psychologically.

Time is an important aspect in an inmate's life. In a life with a strict time-table, the question is: Is an inmate given enough time to keep his person clean? One has to perform the cleaning function within the allotted time and if the Centre is overcrowded, keeping his person clean becomes really difficult. Another question is: Does he get sufficient privacy to keep his person clean? The inmates in some Centres take bath in open air and precisely, therefore, cleaning every part of the body, especially the private, becomes difficult. Instances have been reported that some homosexuals enjoy the sight of others taking open bath. This is bad indeed.

Psychologically, inmates taking bath openly causes pain to many. This is more so among the women who have special needs. Personal appearance is reflected on the face and some in the Centre, even though they appear clean externally, are depressed and gloomy. Sometimes, one may listen to verbal abuses when they take open bath and at other times, they have to take bath in the presence of the staff of the Centre. Such situations are bad and in order to give a psychological satisfaction while the inmates clean their body, they must have sufficient privacy. The proposed *Camerata* accommodation will provide the needed privacy for the residents to keep their body clean. A third question is: Does an inmate get enough toilet articles to keep his person clean? The toilet articles are given free of cost and therefore, there is rationing in the supply of toilet articles.

Taking any number of bath during a day may be fine to keep one's body clean. But, this is not possible in a Centre. There are people who do not take a bath once in a day. Such people should be encouraged to make it a habit to have a bath daily and see to it that they do it so. For, they live in a community where bodily cleanliness of everyone is very important. Inmates who suffer from any skin diseases must be isolated and should stay separately so that they do not communicate their skin diseases to other fellow inmates. Hence, in my view, the inmates must be given toilet articles along with disinfectants too—i.e., any chemical agent that destroys harmful organisms. Hence, the Rule 15 may be redrafted as:

(a) "Inmates shall keep their person clean in a psychologically conducive atmosphere and to this end, they shall be provided with sufficient time, water and with such other toilet articles along with disinfectants without too much rationing and free of cost as are necessary for maintaining health and cleanliness."

In my view, each inmate must be periodically examined medically by experts with an aim to give to each one of them advice and counselling as may become necessary. When men are considered in Rule 16 for their maintenance of good appearance, nothing is specially said about women and old men/women. Some men shave regularly and certainly they need to be attended to with shaving materials. At the same time, women have their special needs of nature and they must be specially attended to. Hence, sanitary napkins and more toilet articles are required for women on those monthly days of special needs. Old inmates need warm water and sometimes, they need assistance to keep their body clean. The revised text of Rule 16 may be—

(a) "In order that the inmates may maintain a good appearance compatible with their self-respect, facilities shall be provided for the proper care of hair, beard and their private parts. Men shall be enabled to shave regularly and old men shall be provided with assistance/assistants to shave regularly, if needed. Women shall be provided with necessary sanitary articles free of cost for attending their special needs of nature every month. Old men and women should be given every assistance and assistants to keep their body clean taking into account of their physical disabilities to perform the functions related to hygiene."

Apparel makes a man/women—yes, it is. Psychologically, one's apparel makes him/her to feel high, low, humiliated, down, depressed, less, etc. Prisons have prescribed uniform for the prisoners, especially the convicts. I think that a prescribed uniform in the Centre is fine for everyone convicted and housed there. I am of the view that the uniform given in some prisons is humiliating or degrading. They deserve better uniforms, better colour and better stitching. Personal hygiene means good appearance in clean uniforms which is neat, tidy and pleasing to the human eye. Hence, the revised Rule 17 will be—

(b) "Every inmate shall be required to wear clean uniform which is neat and tidy. They must change their uniform everyday after the cleaning of their body by bath or otherwise or as and when the change of shabby uniform is necessary."

Facilities to wash the uniform must be provided and the washing should be by using washing machines. Washing by hand and washing the clothes by beating on a hard stone or cemented floor etc. is unheard of in many countries. They must be, if they exist, stopped forthwith. Hence, in the amended text, there should be a new provision:

(e) "Every Centre should have facilities for washing clothes by the use of washing machines and the facility should be provided with sufficient washing materials to keep the inmates' uniform and other personal belongings clean, neat and tidy."

It is really cruel and inhuman to address the inmates every time and repeatedly in every sentence by "Prisoner, Prisoner, Prisoner". This is what is seen in the next Rule of the existing text. What is this? It is not a word palatable to anyone and especially to a person convicted for an offence. If an ugly or unpalatable word is used repeatedly, it irritates all and the affected person may become violent. Be good and noble in the use of the words even against one's enemy, for, everyone has a right for dignity. The aim of incarceration is the development of one's personality in an upright way in the right direction. But, the use of the word "Prisoner, Prisoner, Prisoner" everywhere will be counter-productive ensuring only negativity in personality development. Avoid such human rights unfriendly words even in the talks and conversation.

CLOTHING, UNIFORM AND SLEEP

In the previous paragraph, the need for avoiding the use of the word 'Prisoner, Prisoner, Prisoner' everywhere has been discussed. The word is psychologically harmful for the development of the inmates' personality in an upright way in the right direction. Look at Rule 17(1, 2 & 3) of the present text—

Rule 17 (1, 2 & 3) reads:

17(1) "Every prisoner who is not allowed to wear his own clothing shall be provided with an outfit of clothing suitable for the climate and adequate to keep him in good health. Such clothing shall in no manner be degrading or humiliating.

(2) All clothing shall be clean and kept in proper condition. Underclothing shall be changed and washed as often as necessary for the maintenance of hygiene.

(3) In exceptional circumstances, whenever a prisoner is removed outside the institution for an authorized purpose, he shall be allowed to wear his own clothing or other inconspicuous clothing."

In my view, every inmate in a Centre of Personality Development should be in uniform and no one shall be allowed to wear his own clothing. What is the meaning of telling "Shall be provided with an outfit of clothing suitable for the climate?". Giving or providing with an outfit of clothing is not a charity, rather is the right of the inmate. The outfit of clothing should be decided by a team of medical experts and such an outfit will be adequate to keep the inmate in good health. In my view, it should not be only to keep him in 'good health' alone rather should be "adequate for the well being of the inmate." "Well being" means both physical and psychological including health as stated in the existing Rule 17(1). Hence, the amended text can be—

17(1) "Every inmate shall be provided with an outfit of clothing prescribed by a medical team of experts and such an outfit shall ensure the well-being of the inmate in every aspect."

The question of "degrading or humiliating" does not arise when the outfit of clothing is prescribed by a medical team which has nothing other than the "well-being" of the inmates in mind. Everything is done for the best interest of the inmates and that too is for the development of their personality in an upright way in the right direction. "All clothing shall be clean and kept in proper condition"—this has been brought out in the last guideline and therefore, there is no need to repeat it here. Hence, the revised text will be—

17(2) (a) "Underclothing shall be changed and washed as often as necessary and in any case once in every day."

I say so because the convicts who come from low or very low social or economic background may not use underclothings. Some use only minimum underclothing as they may be poor or because it may be the usual underclothing among them. Some feel irritated or feel discomfort to wear any underclothing. Therefore, the underclothing of the inmates must be prescribed by a medical team of experts and they must be educated and introduced into the necessity and use of underclothing in daily life. The women should have their underclothing prescribed by the medical team of experts and likewise, the old and the infirm should have their underclothing prescribed by the medical team.

17(2)(b) "The underclothing for the inmates in general and for the women or the aged and infirm in particular shall be prescribed by a medical team of experts and everyone shall be educated and introduced to the use of underclothing in daily life."

Rule 17(3) may be revised as—

17(3) "Whenever an inmate goes outside the Centre for an authorized purpose, he shall be allowed to wear a clothing which does not reveal his identity as an inmate of a Centre."

One should be positive when he looks at the inmate and that is the reason why I do not wish to say anything negatively to express positive ideas. Avoid the use of degrading, humiliating, inconspicuous clothing etc., if possible in the revised text. What is the meaning of "inconspicuous clothing?" Of course, the idea is clear from the context, but the language of writing hurts anyone who reads the Rule. The text should be couched in clarity. In my view an inmate must wear a dress which does not reveal his identity to be an inmate in a Centre of Personality Development. If that is the intention, express it in simple language. "Such clothing shall in no manner be degrading or humiliating"—the same idea can be better expressed by "Such clothing should be dignified" or better can be well avoided as I have done it under Rule 17 (1) of the revised text.

Rule 18 of the existing Standard Minimum Rules for the Treatment of Prisoners reads:

> "If prisoners are allowed to wear their own clothing, arrangements shall be made on their admission to the institution to ensure that it shall be clean and fit for use."

This rule is not to be included in the revised text as the institution which is meant to admit only convicts—all of them are in the uniform prescribed by the medical team. The uniform given to every inmate must be tailor-cut and not mass produced. Presently, some inmates wear uniforms which are not stitched for them. Such uniforms will be humiliating or degrading. Hence, the uniforms issued to every inmate should be dignified and tailor cut. A uniform used by an inmate must be destroyed when he leaves the Centre. The used uniforms washed again and reissuing them to a new comer is to be discouraged at any cost. Some inmates feel that the used uniform transfers all the evils which the earlier user had and therefore, they may not be mentally happy to wear an already used uniform. Hence, the revised text should be—

> 18. "Every new inmate has a right to get new uniforms issued and they shall be tailor-cut and not mass-produced."

In the *Camerata* model of institution, every inmate should have a right to get a coat along with bed and separate and sufficient bedding which shall be clean when issued and throughout his stay in the Centre. The revised text, therefore, should be—

19. "Every inmate has a right to get a coat issued along with a separate bed, pillow or bedding which shall be clean when issued and throughout his stay in the Centre, kept in good order and changed often to ensure the cleanliness."

Presently, some prisons do not provide any coats to the inmates so much so that the residents sleep on the floor with difficulties. This is found to be not conducive for the development of their personality in an upright way in the right direction. They sleep on the floor cursing everyone and at times, some do not sleep at all. When they lie on the floor without getting sleep, devils work in their mind. Some may become homosexuals or may masturbate to sleep well. The old and the infirm people may find it extremely difficult to sleep on the floor which may result in becoming sick. In any case, the aged inmates deserve special consideration and they ought to sleep well. If the inmates sleep well, then they are likely to behave properly when awake. Sleepless nights or disturbed sleep will make some to behave in an unbecoming way afterwards. A "Criminal after all" attitude or approach to the facilities provided for sleeping will be counter-productive as far as development of personality is concerned. Life in a Centre is a community life which necessitates a certain amount of human dignity. 'Creature-Comforts'—this is a concept used even in the case of animals and birds. If creature-comforts are not guaranteed, animals and birds react violently. If so, human beings are no exception. Coat, bed, beddings etc. are the creature-comforts for human beings and certainly they are so for the inmates in a Centre of Personality Development.

Remember always that "Muddy water does not make a mirror." Likewise, muddy atmosphere, living conditions, environments and treatment do not make any inmate law abiding.

FOOD AND WATER

Food is a cause of fight even among the animals and birds. " Two dogs and a bone" is an example. If the kitchen in a home is fine, many things are finer. Hence, kitchen, food, quality of food, quantity given, preparation of food, misappropriation of food materials etc. become issues of dispute and quarrels in many prisons. The edibles in the kitchen are taken away, are lost, misused or unduly enjoyed by some inmates with the connivance or approval of the officials who are in good terms with them. The relationship is established on considerations which are mutually beneficial for the officials and the preferred inmates of the Centre equally. In every country, there will be special and specific rules about the diet in prisons. The problem is in the abuse of the rules or in the misuse of authority. For example, Rule 20 (1) of the existing Standard Minimum Rules says:

> 20(1) "Every prisoner shall be provided by the administration at the usual hours with food of nutritional value adequate for health and strength, of wholesome quantity and well prepared and served."

Beautiful indeed on paper, but in practice? Let us take one after the other.

(1) *Well prepared*: About the kitchen, Dr. M.Z. Khan writes, "In the square-shaped high ceilinged and tile-thatched smallish room, food is cooked to serve three meals a day to some four hundred residents. The kitchen uses firewood in open hearths, large aluminium pots for preparing gravy, and large *tawas* outsized iron-plates, for baking *chapattis*....... Despite ventilators, the kitchen remains almost throughout the day filled with smoke, vapours and heat......... even during summer, when the mercury touches about 46°C, they have to brave the heat often for six hours a day." This is about the place where the food is prepared.

(2) *Well served*: It is disturbing to the human eye to see the inmates in a queue receiving food and eating it. There is no dining halls in many prisons and the inmates get food as the *refugees* in a refugee camp receive it and eat it as animals eat in sheds. Even animals in a zoo are given food better than what is seen in some jails. In my view, there must be special dining halls arranged with dining tables and chairs (benches) for the inmates to eat their food in dignity. How is the food served is more important than what is served in prisons. The intention of serving food is not only to keep them healthy but also to develop their personality in an upright way in the right direction. Humiliate them to the maximum everywhere should not be the aim during incarceration. A crime-doer or a convict is fed not to make him a recidivist or a hardened criminal. He is fed to make a law abiding citizen.

(3) *Food of nutritional value*: Yes, they are given food of nutritional value. The nutrition alone is not everything in food. The quality of food is important. Sometimes fights, quarrels, disputes and conflicts result on heated talks about the quality of the food. Everything is available to make the food tasty or qualitatively good; but the way it is prepared is of a questionable nature. For example, too much of salt put, too much of oil poured or no oil is poured, preparing the food with no care or lack of interest, half-boiled food, etc., can make the food inferior in quality and taste. Again the quantity of food can be an issue. Some favoured inmates get enough food and all depends upon the server of the food. The plates given to the inmates are of poor quality so much so that even beggars have better plates to receive food in a beggar's camp. In any case, this is an area which must receive special attention from authorities and precisely, therefore, the revised text must be—

20(1) "Every inmate shall be provided with enough food of nutritional value well prepared qualitatively at the usual hours and shall be served in a dining hall having tables and seats to eat it in dignity. The food shall be of wholesome quality adequate for health and strength."

There was a time drinking water had restriction in punitive prisons. Resultingly, many became kidney patients. Drinking water is a human right and more required than food for human existence. If at all food is denied to a person, drinking water must not be denied. For, with drinking water, a man survives for days together even without any food. Therefore, the revised text should be—

20(2) "Drinking water shall be made available to all inmates who may drink it lavishly whenever he needs it."

Drinking water means water without germs and bacteria. It should be purified and disease-free. What is given in some prisons is the pipe-water supplied by the water authority. Sometimes, the quality is of a questionable nature and causes diseases. As many diseases are transmitted through water, I may recommend boiled water to the inmates for drinking as a precaution against communicable diseases through water.

EXERCISE AND SPORTS

Exercise of body is important to keep the body fit. A person spends his time in a Centre and works till his official release. However, there are convicts who need not work during the period of their incarceration in a Centre. As a result, they spend their time in an idle way without any body exercise. Those who work have some exercise which may keep their body fit during and after their life in a Centre. It is very desirable to advise those who do not work in the Centre to opt for a work in the Centre. Rule 21(1) reads: "Every prisoner who is not employed in outdoor work shall have at least one hour of suitable exercise in the open air daily if the weather permits." Why can't an indoor facility be made for the inmates to do body exercise even if the weather does not permit? Again, how can the aged (sometimes, infirm too) have at least one hour of suitable exercise in the open air? In my view, every prison should have sufficient open space to do the exercise, a body fitness centre for those who want to do the exercise making use of the indoor facility. The aged (infirm) can have a Yoga Centre to keep their body fit. What about the exercise of women in a Centre? The existing Rule 20(1) & (2) is:

21 (1) "Every prisoner who is not employed in outdoor work shall have at least one hour of suitable exercise in open air daily if the weather permits.

(2) Young prisoners and others of suitable age and physique, shall receive physical and recreational training during the period of exercise. To this end, space, installation and equipment should be provided."

The revised text may be—

21 (1) "Every inmate who is not employed, i.e., those who are incarcerated with simple imprisonment—shall be persuaded and encouraged to engage in a work of his interest available in the Centre. If he is unwilling to

do a work, he shall have one hour of suitable exercise—indoor or outdoor—daily as decided by the medical officer in consultation with the instructor of physical training.

(2) Inmates who are aged and unable to work in spite of a sentence of rigorous imprisonment shall have one hour (more or less) of suitable exercise—indoor or outdoor—daily as decided by the medical officer in consultation with the instructor of physical training. If no exercise is advised, he shall do Yoga daily as decided and controlled by an instructor of yogic culture.

(3) Women inmates undergoing simple imprisonment, if not employed at her option, pregnant women, aged women, sick or unhealthy women shall have physical exercise or *Yoga* as the case may be utilizing the indoor or outdoor facility, daily as decided by the medical officer in consultation with a lady instructor of physical training/Yogic culture.

(4) Physical exercise or *Yoga* shall be done only under the supervision of a qualified instructor who shall be a man for the male inmates and a woman for the female inmates separately.

(5). Any inmate who does not belong to any of the categories stated above wants to do physical exercise/ *Yoga* along with those mentioned above, facilities shall be provided for the fulfilment of his/her decision.

(6) Every Centre shall have indoor and outdoor facility to do the physical exercise, to receive physical training and to do *Yoga*. To this end, space, installations and equipments shall be provided. The inmates shall be given special physical exercise dress/*Yoga* dress free of cost for the purpose. After the physical exercise/ *Yoga*, they must have a bath and washing of the dress for which facilities shall be provided and washing materials given free of cost."

Physical exercise/*Yoga* gives a mental relaxation for the inmates and certainly it will develop their personality. Fitness of the body is a *sine qua non* for the rehabilitation of the inmate and his reintegration to the society back after his release. Every inmate has many stresses and frustrations in his life in the Centre. The physical exercise/*Yoga* is a mental shock-absorber for anyone who is incarcerated. A good exercise gives good sleep and makes the inmates feel fresh after the sleep. Sports are as important or more important than physical exercise/*Yoga*. Every Centre should have facilities for indoor and outdoor games. Hence, the revised text will have—

21 (7) "Facilities for indoor and outdoor games shall be provided in every Centre and every inmate may be encouraged to make use of the facility. Every inmate shall be provided with sports dress free of cost. Outdoor games shall be played by the inmates under the guidance and supervision of an instructor of physical education and training. The instructor shall be male for male inmates and female for female inmates.

(8) Facilities for playing indoor games shall be provided. Every Centre should have a recreation hall and the kinds of indoor games shall be decided by the instructor of physical training in consultation with the director of the Centre."

Both indoor and outdoor games give mental relaxation for the inmates. They forget many things while they play and they mix with other fellow inmates. This will help them to develop interpersonnel relations and thereby reintegrate themselves with environments of the Centre. Even competitions can be arranged and thus a spirit of community life can be developed. The exercise, *Yoga* and games help them to forget their past and to have positive thoughts pregnant with hopes, expectations and values. In my opinion, everything done outside the prison for the development of one's personality can work well with the inmates inside the prison as well. For, there is no much difference between a man in the prison and a man outside. The only difference is that the man inside the prison is convicted whereas the man outside is not.

MEDICAL OFFICERS AND TREATMENT

As far as various diseases are concerned, the prison is a cross-section of the society. Jails have patients with AIDS and other venereal diseases. Inmates with communicable diseases may be many, nevertheless many will not speak it out. They keep their diseases as secret and some with an evil mind to contaminate the small community with the ailments they suffer. The present Rule 22 of the Standard Minimum Rules for the Treatment of Prisoners reads:

> 22(1) "At every institution there shall be available the services of at least one qualified medical officer who should have some knowledge in psychiatry. The medical services should be organized in close relationship to the general health administration of the community or nation. They shall include a psychiatric service for the diagnosis and in proper cases,the treatment of states of mental abnormality."

In the above Rule 22(1), the services of at least one qualified medical officer who should have some knowledge in psychiatry were suggested. In my view, it is not enough for the simple reason that many of the diseases are psychosomatic and especially when the patients are inmates in a Centre. They live in a tightly controlled environment where they have nothing much to do. Though their food, dress, accommodation etc., are guaranteed, many of them are not found to be happy. Some are very much depressed and feel fish out of water. The environment is quite suffocating to many. They do not like to stay under the watchful eyes of the custodial staff in the Centre where everything is abnormal to many. Some become sick and many diseases have their causative roots on the abnormality of the environments in the Centre. Moreover, there is a school of thought that the crime-doers are sick people and they need treatment. The psychological treatment, counselling etc., are given to the inmates to develop their personality in the right direction. Hence, while the appointment of a qualified medical officer who has some knowledge in psychiatry is a welcome rule, the services of a fully qualified psychiatrist plus the services of a clinical psychologist and the same of a psychiatric social worker may be very much needed. Though the services of a medical officer qualified in allopathy may be really fine and necessary, many of the diseases of the aged may require the services of a qualified medical officer in Ayurveda/Homeo etc. As there are many systems of medicine offering treatment to patients, I am of the view that the medical services in the Centre should make use of at least the services of qualified medical officers of two systems of medicine. Hence, the revised Rule will be—

22 (1) "At every Institution there shall be available the services of at least one qualified medical officer from at least two systems of medicine. As many diseases are psychosomatic in origin, the qualified medical officers thus appointed should have good knowledge of Psychiatry.

The medical services should be organized in close relationship with the services rendered by a qualified Psychiatrist, Clinical Psychologist and a Psychiatric Social Worker who are on the medical team of the Centre.

The medical services should be organized further in close relationship to the general health administration of the community or nation. They shall include the services of all systems of medicine for the proper diagnosis and treatment of physical, mental or psychosomatic diseases."

Rule 22(2) says:

"Sick persons who require specialist treatment shall be transferred to specialized institutions or to civil hospitals. Where hospital facilities are provided in an institution, their equipment, furnishings and pharmaceutical supplies shall be proper for the medical care and treatment of sick persons, and there shall be a nursing staff of suitably trained officers."

Rule 22(3) reads: "The services of a qualified dental officer shall be available to every prisoner."

As some specialized institutions are not owned by the Government, it becomes necessary to transfer the inmates to institutions owned and operated by wealthy individuals/ organizations and they will be very costly and in which cases expenditure from the public exchequer cannot be justified. In such instances, the services of specialist doctors may be made available to the hospitals run by the Government or to the hospitals attached to the Centre.

Some Government hospitals or civil hospitals will not have wards or facilities for the accommodation of the inmates. In such situations, the services of the specialist doctors may be made available to the hospitals attached to the Centre.

Instances are reported that the services of specialist doctors available in specialist hospitals cannot be given to Government owned hospitals or civil hospitals. In such instances, the sick inmates may be treated in such specialist hospitals for which the expenditure incurred must be borne by the inmates themselves. This will avoid many criticisms from the people as well as the tendency of the affluent inmates to misuse the provision of extending services of specialist hospitals to their favour. In such instances, the ward or room where the sick inmate is housed shall be declared as an extension of the Centre where the rules of the Centre alone will be in operation. Therefore, the revised text will be—

Rule 22(3) "The specialist institutions or civil hospitals to which a sick inmate is transferred does not have facilities to accommodate the inmate with safety and security, then the services of the specialist medical officers available in such institution/ hospital is to be made available to the hospital attached to the Centre."

22 (4) "The services of specialist hospitals owned and operated by private individuals or organizations shall be made available, if needed, to the sick inmate who is in the hospital attached to the Centre. If the services of such doctors cannot be made available to the hospital attached to the Centre, then the sick inmate may be transferred to such private institution on condition that—

(a) The expenditure necessary for such treatment shall be borne by the inmate.

(b) The private institution or the ward/room

where the inmate is accommodated shall be declared as an extension of the hospital attached to the Centre.

(c) The institution/ward/room shall have all the necessary requirements to have the safety and security of the inmate accommodated there. The rules and conduct norms applicable to the Centre will be strictly made applicable to such extension of the Centre."

What about the equipments, furnishings and pharmaceutical supplies? The revised text must be—

22(5) "Where hospital facilities are provided in an institution, their equipment, furnishings and pharmaceutical supplies shall be proper for the medical care and treatment of sick persons, and there shall be staff of suitable trained persons who shall be male in men's institutions and female in women's institutions. The nursing staff in the Centre's institution should be adequate to provide proper nursing care to the inpatients if facilities for treating the inmates as inpatients is provided. The nursing staff shall be male in Men's Centres and female in Women's Centres."

Rule 22(3) in the present Standard Minimum Rules may be retained as 22(6) in the revised text. i.e. "The Services of a qualified dental officer shall be available to every prisoner".

MEDICAL SERVICES IN WOMEN'S INSTITUTIONS

There are prisons exclusively constructed and managed for women. There are women's prison annexed to a prison constructed for men. In my view, the latter category is not conducive for personality development and, therefore, is not favoured by me. Any way, many women, especially feminists, demand that there should be women police officials, women prosecutors, women judges and women jailors to look into and deal with women's cases. Though I may not fully agree with their views during investigation, prosecution and adjudication, I have no difficulty or objection to accept that women-convicts (inmates) should be housed in a Centre manned and managed only by women officials. The reason is that the convicts live in strictly controlled conditions and mud may stick, with or without cause, if male officials manage the institutions for women. The women convicts may advance to the male officials with their suppressed or surcharged sexual desires/energy. Again, mud may stick. The men officials may misuse or abuse their interaction with the helpless female inmates.

Rule 23(1) of the existing Standard Minimum Rules says:

> "In women's institutions there shall be special accommodation for all necessary pre-natal and post-natal care and treatment. Arrangements shall be made wherever practicable for children to be born in a hospital outside the institution. If a child is born in prison, this fact shall not be mentioned in the birth certificate."

Before such a Rule it is necessary to have another rule on the basis of the discussion that has been held above—that is to say that the Rule 23(1) should be split into 23(1)(a) and (b). Accordingly the Guideline 23(1) (a) must read:

> 23(1)(a) "At every women's institution or part of the institution where female inmates are housed, there shall be the services of at least one lady medical officer who should be solely responsible for making arrangements for specialist treatment, if that is needed for women-inmates in accordance with the guidelines given under Rule 22."

In my considered view, the sentence of incarceration should be stayed till a pregnant women delivers the baby. If that is not possible, then she must be accommodated in an institution other than a prison and it can be a Government hospital where accommodation for the convicts is available. Hence, Rule 23 (1)(b) may be—

> "The sentence of conviction to imprisonment may be stayed in the case of pregnant women until her delivery. If that is not possible, the pregnant women shall be accommodated in a facility available in Government

hospitals until her delivery for pre-natal care and treatment. After the delivery of a baby, she shall be admitted in a women's institution where all facilities to provide post-natal care and treatment are available."

23(2) of the existing Rule is—"Where nursing infants are allowed to remain in the institution with their mothers, provision shall be made for a nursery staffed by qualified persons, where infants shall be placed when they are not in the care of their parents."

I do not favour female inmates who have to breast-feed their children staying with other women who do not have such needs. I suggest that all mothers who breast feed their children may stay in a *camerata* where they have all facilities to look after the special needs of the babies and their mothers. Hence the revised text will be—

23(2)(a) "Where babies who are breast-fed are in the institution with their mothers, provision shall be made for accommodating the mothers and babies in a *camerata* physically separated from other *camerata*e."

23(2)(b) "Where nursing infants are allowed to remain in the institution with their mothers, provision shall be made for a nursery separated physically from the institution by a wall in a different compound staffed by qualified persons, where the infants shall spend their time when their mothers are away for work or similar activities."

Infants and babies should stay with their mothers during their early infancy. For, it is found out that the mother is their "first teacher." Even if the infants and babies have their father still, it is better in every sense that they spend their time with the mother. Nevertheless, they must see their father for which facility should be provided by the institution to meet and mingle with the father. Hence, the revised text should have—

23(2)(c) "Where infants stay with their mothers in the institution, provision shall be made for the infants to meet and mingle with their father as often as found necessary and in any case at least once in a month."

If the growing children do not get the love and care of both their parents—father and mother, it is likely that they develop a personality which may be defective in every sense.

More and more women are found to involve in the commission of crimes. More and more women are seen convicted to imprisonment. Resultantly, there comes the necessity to construct more and more Centres for Personality Development for women convicts. Presently, prisons for women are constructed as attachments to the prisons for men so that the officials including the medical team are one and the same. Experiences show that it is better to construct prisons for women geographically away from the prisons for men. Experience shows that it is better to have medical facilities exclusively for women and they are examined and treated by a medical team consisting of women doctors, nurses, pharmacists and so on.

MEDICAL OFFICERS AND EXAMINATION OF THE NEW ENTRANTS

The existing Rule 24 reads:

> "The medical officer shall see and examine every prisoner as soon as possible after his admission and thereafter as necessary, with a view particularly to the discovery of physical or mental illness and the taking of all necessary measures; the segregation of prisoners suspected of infectious or contagious conditions; the noting of physical and mental defects which might hamper rehabilitation, and the determination of the physical capacity of every prisoner for work."

The above rule seems to treat a medical officer to be an "all knowing individual" which is far away from being real. In my view, the examination must be done by a team which consists of a medical officer too. There should be the medical officer, the psychiatrist, the clinical psychologist, the psychiatric social worker, the workshop chief, the chief of the teaching staff, the welfare officer of the Centre and so on and they should individually examine the new entrant to the Centre and jointly take a decision as to his/her stay, labour, education, leisure-time activities etc., needed for his personality development *via* correction, reformation, resocialization, rehabilitation and finally to the reintegration to the society back.

The medical doctor shall, on admission of a convict, examine him/her with a view particularly to the discovery of any physical illness, infectious or contagious diseases or diseases which need prolonged treatment or treatment by specialists or in specialist institutions. Hence, the Rule 24 may be rewritten as:

24 (1) "The medical officer shall examine every new entrant as soon as possible after his/her admission with a view particularly to the discovery of any physical illness, infectious or contagious diseases, diseases which need prolonged treatment or treatment by specialists or in specialist institutions. The medical officer shall see that all necessary measures are taken for the segregation/isolation of inmates suffering from any infectious or contagious or communicable diseases."

(2) "The Psychiatrist, Psychiatric social worker, Clinical Psychologist, the workshop chief, the chief of the teaching staff, the welfare officer shall examine every inmate immediately after his/her admission and they shall together with the medical officer jointly take a decision for the total development of his/her personality in a upright way in the right direction."

The decision will consist of the work, education, moral training, counselling, religious life, leisure-time activities, hygiene and other diet/food habits, etiquette and community life and anything which will accelerate his/her correction, reformation, resocialization, rehabilitation after release and reintegration to society back. There should be a holistic development of the personality and it is or should be a community work and not an individual endeavour. At a time only the services of medical officers only were available, the existing Rule 24 was drafted. But, today, the officials who make attempts to develop the personality of the inmates in an upright way in the right direction are many and, therefore, the responsibility should be of a team consisting of a psychiatrist, psychiatric social worker, clinical psychologist, welfare officer and so on. In many Centres, there exist no such experts so much so that the development of the personality of the inmates in an upright way in the right direction does not take place in an enviable way.

What does the Rule 25 say? It reads:

> 25 (1) "The medical officer shall have the care of the physical and mental health of the prisoners and should daily see all sick prisoners, all who complain of illness and any prisoner to whom his attention is specially directed.
>
> (2) The medical officer shall report to the director whenever he considers that a prisoner's physical and mental health has been or will be injuriously affected by continued imprisonment or by any condition of imprisonment."

I am not inclined to entrust fully the physical and mental health of the inmates only to the medical officer. As said earlier, there is a psychiatrist, a clinical psychologist and a psychiatric social worker, welfare officer and so on in every Centre. Hence, the physical and mental health of the inmates shall be the joint responsibility of all of them. Everyone put together will be called the health-care and welfare team.

Every member of the health-care and welfare team ought to see, talk, understand daily all sick persons—i.e., physical, psychologically disturbed or psychosomatic,—all who complain of illness and any inmate to whom their–individually or jointly-attention is specially directed. The director of the Centre shall be the coordinator of the advice and activities of the medical team.

The revised text will be—

> 25 (1) "A health-care and welfare team consisting of the medical officer, psychiatrist, clinical psychologist, psychiatric social worker and the welfare officer shall have the care of the physical and psychological health of the inmates.
>
> (2) Any member of the health-care and welfare team or all of them shall be free to see, talk and understand all sick persons—i.e., physical, psychologically disturbed or psychosomatic—all who complain of illness and any inmate to their—individually or jointly—attention

is specially directed. The director of the Centre will be the coordinator of the advice and activities of the medical team.

(3) Any member of the health-care and welfare team is free to report to the director whenever he considers that an inmate's physical, psychological (or both) health has been or will be injuriously affected by continued imprisonment or any condition of imprisonment. The director, on receipt of such an information, shall act positively keeping in mind the development of the personality of the inmate in an upright way in the right direction.

(4) Any inmate who is diagnosed to be affected by insanity proper shall be transferred to the Government hospital for such patients for free treatment or to any specialist hospitals for treating them at their expense. The director of the Centre shall be free to make arrangements to have the services of the specialists in specialist hospitals to the Government hospitals, if that is needed-all with the sole purpose of developing the personality of the inmates in an upright way in the right direction."

HEALTH-CARE AND WELFARE TEAM AND THEIR ADVICE

Rule 26(1&2) of the present Standard Minimum Rules for the Treatment of Prisoners is—

26 (1) "The medical officer shall regularly inspect and advise the director upon:

(a) The quality, quantity, preparation and service of food;

(b) The hygiene and cleanliness of the institution and the prisoners;

(c) The sanitation, heating, lighting and ventilation of the institution;

(d) The suitability and cleanliness of the prisoners' clothing and bedding; and

(e) The observance of the rules concerning physical education and sports, in cases where there is no technical personnel in charge of these activities.

(2) The director shall take into consideration the reports and advice that the medical officer submits according to Rule 25(2) and Rule 26 and, in case he concurs shall take immediate steps to give effect to those recommendations; if they are not within his competence, if he does not concur with them, his own report and the advice of the medical officer be sent to higher authority."

The above Rule was drafted and accepted at a time the prisons had no health-care and welfare team. During 1950s, there was only a medical officer and as a rule, he would be from the allopathic system of treatment. Today, different systems of medicine and treatment are available and a medical officer in a single system of medicine alone cannot give advice on many areas of the inmates' life in prisons. What advice can be given by a medical officer about the quality or preparation of food? In my view, any member in the healthcare and welfare team shall have the authority to collect the feed-back of the inmates to make recommendations to the director of the Centre. Hence, the revised text ought to be—

26 (1) "Any member of the health-care and welfare team shall regularly inspect, get the feedback from the inmates and advise the director upon:

(a) The quality, quantity, preparation and service of the food;

(b) The hygiene and cleanliness of the toilet, bathing and washing facilities provided in the institution;

(c) The personal hygiene of the inmates and the cleanliness of the inmates' clothings, undergarments, beds and bedding;

(d) The hygiene and cleanliness of the institution, waste management, hygiene in the workshops, hospital, schools, *cameratae*, recreation hall, canteen etc.;

(e) The sanitation, heating, lighting, ventilation, air-flow of every building in the Centre;

(f) The purity, purification and quality of the drinking water, food-materials given, vegetables and anything purchased from outside or produced inside the Centre;

(g) Suitability, dignity and neatness of the inmates' uniform and the uniform (dress) of the officials employed in the service of the institution; and

(h) Observance of the rules concerning physical education and sports, work in the Centre, leisure-time activities in cases where there is no technical personnel in charge of these activities.

(2) The director shall take into consideration the reports and advice that any member of the health-care and welfare team presents before him in accordance to Rules 25(3) and 26 and in case he concurs with the recommendations made, shall take immediate steps to rectify the defects or to give effect to those recommendations *mutatis mutandis*; if they are not within his competence or if he does not concur with them, he shall immediately submit his own report justifying his position and the advice of the member of the health-care and welfare team to his higher authority."

Why do I say so? The reasons are—

If the authority to inspect, advise etc., is given only to the medical officer, there is all likelihood that he misuses/abuses his authority. Instances have been reported that some medical officers are bribed or otherwise influenced to do special favours. They are found to yield to such influences and temptations. The medical officer in a prison is not an attractive posting compared to other medical postings in health services in many countries. The medical officers, therefore, suffer from relative deprivation which makes them to yield to some temptations or become susceptible to corrupt practices. The fact that the authority is shared or executed concurrently by all members in the health-care and welfare team means that corruption, malpractices and misuse/abuse of authority by medical officers can be reduced considerably.

The ego-clashes that may exist between the medical officers and the director may result in the rejection of the advice/ recommendations given by the medical officer to the latter. This can be brought down if all members in the team is empowered to give advice or make recommendations. Further, medical officers, as they are, may be good in making recommendations about the physical ailments or health hazards etc. Here, many other areas like ventilation, lighting, service of the food, preparation of the food, etc., are seen. No doubt, there are experts who are better to make advice or recommendations in such aspects. In my view, each member of the team can consult with experts in the concerned area before they make a recommendation or give advice to the director. The director can, if needed, consult with the experts before he accepts the recommendation/advice or before he sends up his report to the higher authority. It is good that many look at the issue from very many angles and their advice/recommendations will be better or more conducive for the development of the inmates' personality in an upright way in the right direction.

DISCIPLINE AND PUNISHMENT

Discipline and Punishment put together under Rule 27 of the existing Standard Minimum Rules give a bad or wrong signal. *Discipline* means (1) behaviour in accordance to rules of conduct; (2) training to act in accordance with rule; (3) instruction and exercise designed to train to proper conduct or action. Fine. Discipline during the early years of childhood is found to be very effective to make children to act in accordance to rules. As one grows older in age, it is not that easy to make one disciplined. Anyway, a Centre is an institution where community life is seen. Anyone who lives in such a community ought to behave in accordance to rules of conduct for harmonious living and peaceful coexistence. Discipline is inculcated to the members of a community by or through very many means and methods. Punishment is one of the methods or is the least preferred method to discipline a human being. Punishment is not found to be the best method to develop the inmate's personality in an upright way in the right direction.

Rule 27 of the present Standard Minimum Rules for the Treatment of Prisoners reads:

> 27. "Discipline and order shall be maintained with firmness, but with no more restriction than is necessary for safe custody and well ordered community life."

Discipline and order must be maintained with firmness not

only among the inmates but also among the staff working in the Centre. Allegations are plenty against the staff and some studies show that criminality is seen among the staff as well. An exaggerated version of the research findings may be that some of the officials in the Centre are more criminal or criminal minded than the convicts inside(!). There is a school of thought which argues that discipline and order must be enforced both among the staff as well as among the inmates. There may be unholy nexus found between the inmates and the staff. Court conviction means, either rightly or wrongly, that the convict needs some self-discipline. Research studies attest to the view that some of the members among the staff in the Centre too need self-discipline.

There may be a number of violations of the prison rules and there is punishment for each violation. The violations may be connected with (1) the work—i.e., omitting to report, loss, breakage or injury caused to Centre's properties, making of some articles without the knowledge or permission of the authorities of the Centre, performing any work or portion of the work allotted to another inmate, etc., (2) quarrellings, assaults and mutiny—i.e., doing or omitting to do some act with intent to cause to himself any illness, injury or disability, taking part in any attack against the fellow inmates or the Centre's staff, causing or omitting to assist in suppressing violence or insubordination of any kind, etc. (3) the possession of contraband articles—i.e., eating or appropriating any food not assigned to the inmate, keeping any weapon, clothing or eatables which are not permitted; (4) miscellaneous—i.e., omitting or refusing to keep the Centre clean, removing, defacing or altering any distinctive marks or badge, committing any nuisance in any part of the Centre, spitting on the floor or wall etc. The punishment to the inmates for the violation of the rules vary depending upon the nature of the offence. Minor punishments may include a formal warning, change of labour for a stated period to some irksome or severe form, forfeiture of the remission earned by the inmate, privileges in the Centre, separate confinement for a fixed period etc. Instances are not rare that some inmates violate the rules with the connivance and the approval/full knowledge of the staff. In some cases, unholy nexus may be seen between the two.

What about the corporal punishments? There exists no record in many Centres to show that corporal punishments are inflicted.

My personal interviews with ex-convicts released from the Centres give me ample evidence to assert that the inmates are tortured physically under some cause or another. The blinding episode in India and many such cruel treatments in prisons outside India shown in the media are proofs to prove that torture is resorted to in some Centres. I cannot say that the torture thus seen in the Centres is resorted to as a method of punishment or for any other purposes. Hence, the revised version of the text shall be—

27(1) "Discipline and order shall be maintained with firmness both among the staff and among the inmates. No unholy nexus between the staff and the inmates shall be allowed and any violation of the rule owing to the unholy nexus between the staff and the inmates shall be treated as an offence under the criminal laws.

(2) No corporal punishment shall be inflicted on inmates in disciplinary cases. Any torture in any capacity from the staff to an inmate or by an inmate at the instigation of any member/s of the staff shall be treated as an offence against the criminal laws.

(3) No inmate shall be punished without holding an inquiry in the matter keeping all principles of natural justice."

Forfeiture of the remission marks is found to be a good punishment for the violation of the rules. Likewise, the withholding of the inmates' privileges may work as a good tool to maintain discipline among the inmates. *Ticket to leave system* by which the prisoners showing good conduct may be extended more liberally to those who show good behaviour in the Centre. It can be an incentive. Therefore, the revised text shall have:

> Rule 27(4)—"Forfeiture of the remission marks, withholding of the privilege enjoyed by the inmate, refusal to grand *ticket to leave* for the inmates may be included as punishments in diciplinary cases. Discipline and order shall be maintained with no more restriction than is necessary for the safe custody, well-ordered community life and the development of the personality of the inmate in an upright way in the right direction."

It may be remembered that every member of the staff in the

Centre is a role model for any inmate. Hence, the discipline and order maintained by the staff may have a very powerful influence upon the inmates in the Centre. There is a common saying "One mistake by the role model will cause fifty one mistakes in the followers." Hence, be careful.

DISCIPLINE AND PERSONALITY DEVELOPMENT

See the Rule 28 in the existing Standard Minimum Rules. It reads:

(1) "No prisoner shall be employed in the service of the institution in any disciplinary capacity.

(2) This rule shall not, however, impede the proper functioning of systems based on self-Government, under which specified social, educational or sports activities or responsibilities are entrusted, under supervision, to prisoners who are formed into groups for the purposes of treatment."

Anything done in the Centre is or ought to be for the personality development of the inmates and the discipline or the punishment for the violation of the disciplinary rules too has no other objective than the development of the personality of the punished. At the time the Standard Minimum Rules were accepted, the objective of imprisonment/punishment for violating the rule has been treatment of the inmates and thereby correction of the convicts. I have no objection in retaining the above rule as it is, but I want to make a change to Rule 28 (2) as follows:

28 (2) "This rule shall not, however, impede the proper functioning of the systems based on self-government, under which specified social, educational or sports activities or responsibilities are entrusted under supervision, to inmates who are formed into groups for the purposes of personality development in an upright way in the right direction."

Treatment of the prisoners is not a *nice to hear* expression as treatment is not the objective or purpose of the present day imprisonment. The treatment approach and programmes in prisons have travelled a long distance from the "Houses of Correction" organized at the close of the sixteenth century in England. Incarceration, hard labour, punishments for violating prison rules, loathsome cells, penitential conditions in jails, living conditions everywhere in the prisons were appalling and resultantly no treatment could be thought of. Nevertheless, the penitentiary movement in the half of the nineteenth century did little or something in the direction of treatment. The Eastern Penitentiary in Philadelphia, the congregate system tried in New York at Auburn State prison and at the Sing Sing Prison could be mentioned in this context. Studies showed that the programmes and systems prevailed even in developed countries had hardly any scope for treatment. The Elmira Reformatory (1879) was a turning point. It laid down the foundation for a variety of treatment programmes including general education, vocational training, religious education, recreation and the like. Nevertheless, these programmes, though were called treatment programmes did not produce the desired effects. Recidivism continued to be a problem and still continues to be an aching problem even today. Many relapse into crimes even after incarceration and some become hardened criminals even after the 'so named treatment' in prisons. The treatment is no treatment and that is the main reason the objective has been changed from "treatment" to "personality development in an upright way in the right direction."

DISCIPLINARY OFFENCE, PUNISHMENT AND AUTHORITY

My interviews with many inmates tell me that most of the inmates do not know many of the disciplinary rules or offences. They are kept secret for reasons unknown to many. Some commit an act most innocently and they are shocked to know that they committed a disciplinary offence. The seniors in prison do not tell anything about the prison offences to the new comers. The staff in the prison keep them a secret. There is no information boards kept anywhere in prisons so that the new entrants may know the commissions/ omissions which constitute offences in the prison life. What a misfortune!

Rule 29 of the existing Standard Minimum Rules for the Treatment of Prisoners says:

Rule 29 "The following shall always be determined by the law or by the regulation of the competent administrative authority:

(a) Conduct constituting a disciplinary offence;
(b) The types and duration of punishment which may be inflicted; and
(c) The authority competent to impose such punishment.

The conduct may be commissions or omissions. They must be clearly spelt out. The procedure for conducting the disciplinary inquiry must be keeping the principles of natural justice. The evidence that may be collected and the type, intensity, nature and duration of punishment which may be inflicted should be specifically specified. Finally, the authority competent to impose such punishment should be clearly spelt out.

There may be illiterate, semi-literate, moderately educated, not educated inmates. Some inmates may be able to read, but not in a position to write. Therefore, special classes may be arranged to enlighten every new entrant to know the commissions and omissions which may constitute a disciplinary offence. Many who violate the disciplinary rules may not know the procedure to conduct the inquiry in which case they need to know how to defend their case. There is nothing wrong in offering assistance to defend one's case and it can be done by an official of his choice or a fellow inmate willing to help him. Every opportunity should be offered to prove his innocence, if that is needed. The type, intensity, nature and duration of punishments may be told to him in advance and everything is to be done not to put him in further mental tension and depression. Every step shall be initiated and executed with an objective of developing his personality in an upright way in the right direction. Taking everything into consideration, the revised text may be—

Rule 29. There shall be written laws, rules or regulations—

(a) Defining a violation-commission or omission—to be a disciplinary misconduct;
(b) Prescribing the procedure for the conduct of the inquiry and the evidence to be taken;
(c) Clearly specifying the type, intensity, nature and duration of the punishment which may be inflicted;

(d) Specifying the authority competent to impose such punishment;

(e) Stating the procedure for making appeals and the authority to decide on the appeal and pronounce a judgment; and

(f) All steps must be initiated and executed with an objective of developing the personality of the inmate in an upright way in the right direction.

Even in inflicting a punishment or penalty, the best interest of the inmate must be given prime importance. Any person, who lives in a prison in tightly controlled conditions, may behave in an undesirable manner. Hence, interpreting everything as an offence is not the way to deal with it. A misconduct is a misconduct and it needs not necessarily be an offence always. Humanitarian treatment to those who commit misconduct will give rich dividend. The purpose of punishing a delinquent inmate should not be negative in any sense. Remember always that a prison is not a pleasant place to stay. It imposes rigid discipline, provides only bare necessities and minimum creature-comforts, offers only monotonous/boring routine life. At the same time, many prisoners are well conscious of their rights and obligations of the prison staff towards them. Some of them may get every chance to communicate to the media and their contact with the outside world provides them opportunities bringing their problems to the notice of the general public. Therefore, the punishment inflicted on the erring inmates should not be a cause for further indiscipline in the Centre—even leading to a prison riot. The complaint often heard from the inmates is that the officials in the Centre are often very rough and rude in their behaviour towards them. The reciprocation to such rough and tough behaviour will be rough and tough from the inmates. Some of the staff in the Centre are corrupt and susceptible to corrupt practices. They may show special favours to favoured inmates and certainly they cause displeasure among the inmates who may exhibit their dissatisfaction by way of misconduct. Hence, remember that the cause of misconduct of the inmate may be the misbehaviour of the officials of the Centre. Hence, everything must be taken into account when judgements are passed in disciplinary matters. The one who judges the inmate in disciplinary case has an upper hand

and it must not be a cause for causing displeasure among the inmates.

CONDUCT OF DISCIPLINARY CASES

Disciplinary justice is a special area and the conduct of the inquiry is quasi-judicial. Quasi-judicial inquiry means that the inquiry must be conducted only in accordance with the principles of natural justice. A convict under disciplinary inquiry has all the rights which any other person facing a disciplinary inquiry outside the prison is entitled to. The fact that an individual is incarcerated at the time when the disciplinary inquiry is conducted does not make him not eligible to get the rights which the law permits. Rule 30 of the present Standard Minimum Rules, it appears, does not take into account of this principle when it says—

Rule 30 (1) "No prisoner shall be punished except in accordance with the terms of such law or regulation, and never twice for the same offence.

(2) No prisoner shall be punished unless he has been informed of the offence alleged against him and given a proper opportunity of presenting his defence. The competent authority shall conduct a thorough examination of the case.

(3) When necessary and practicable, the prisoner shall be allowed to make his defence through an interpreter."

The Rule 30 (1,2&3) is not couched in clarity. First of all, let us admit the fact that disciplinary inquiries are fact finding investigations by administrative authorities who have an upper hand over the incarcerated under inquiry. It is a principle of natural justice that all acts done and decisions taken must be in good faith. In many instances, the inquiry is conducted by officials who are known to the incarcerated under inquiry. As a result, prejudice, partiality, displeasure with the incarcerated, parochialism, self-interest, partiality, illegal influence etc., are likely to creep into so much so that an officer who works in the same Centre is found to be incapable, often, to take decisions in good faith. The interviews with the incarcerated under inquiry give me enough evidence to argue that a disciplinary proceedings against an incarcerated should be entrusted to an officer who works outside the Centre where the delinquent is accommodated. Hence, the revised text shall be—

Rule 30 (1) "No inmate under a disciplinary inquiry shall be punished unless he has been issued with charges which must be specific and precise and should convey to the delinquent in the clearest possible terms the act of misconduct under law or regulation levelled against him.

(2) No inmate under a disciplinary inquiry shall be punished unless he is given a reasonable opportunity to defend his case.

(3) Every incarcerated under disciplinary inquiry has a right to—

(a) adduce all relevant and material evidence on which he relies his defence;

(b) have the evidence of the witnesses against him taken in his presence and to cross-examine such witness/es; and

(c) See all relevant documents to which he is entitled to have accessibility.

(4) All the acts done and decisions taken must be done in good faith.

(5) No incarcerated under inquiry shall be punished twice for the same offence and no one shall be punished without giving him an opportunity to make representations as to why the proposed punishment should not be inflicted on him and get his representation to make a through examination of the case under inquiry.

(6) No incarcerated under inquiry shall be punished unless the delinquent is allowed to be represented by a fellow associate or by himself or by an official employee of the Centre on whom he has trust. Under no circumstances, a lawyer shall be allowed to represent the incarcerated under inquiry in disciplinary matters. Where necessary, the incarcerated under inquiry shall be allowed to make his defence through an interpreter."

Rule 30(6) becomes necessary and sometimes a *sine qua non* for the simple reason that some of the convicts are illiterate or are from tribes or communities which are educationally backward. They have little or no information about their rights, natural justice, conduct of the inquiry or anything which rule or law stipulates. Ignorance is a serious factor and precisely, therefore, the incarcerated under inquiry should be provided with assistance to defend their case before the inquiry authority. However, the services of a lawyer or a practicing advocate are not desirable as they may complicate the issue. The purpose of disciplinary justice is not at all to punish the guilty in any way or any how. The purpose is to develop his personality in an upright way so that he reintegrates himself to the society back when released. More disciplinary inquiries mean more indiscipline in the Centre. The administration is guilty for such a situation. The entire blame for indiscipline cannot be put on the incarcerated alone. Hence, when more and more indiscipline is reported, the underlying causes should be identified and remedial steps taken. This is what is seen in the history of jails. Correcting the evils in the Centre's administration will be reducing the number of evil-doers in the Centre. Correcting the evil-doers in the Centre means reducing indiscipline in the Centre. Punishment alone is not a solution. Of course, it can if done in good faith and for the best interest of the inmate under inquiry.

PUNISHMENTS IN DISCIPLINARY INQUIRIES

Punishments upon punishment and it is not an enviable policy in any type of justice administration. If a person having punished and incarcerated for violating a law by a court continues to violate the conduct norms/Centre's regulations/rules and thereby he challenges the very purpose of incarceration, no correction is effected or no change in personality or values takes place. What is wrong here? -or- where is the defect? Can a punishment solve the issue under discussion? Rule 31 of the present Standard Minimum Rules for the Treatment of Prisoners reads:

Rule 31: "Corporal punishments, punishment by placing in a dark cell, and all cruel inhuman or degrading punishments shall be completely prohibited as punishments for disciplinary offences."

Fine. The Rule says many things, but does not say anything about what type of punishments must be given to those who violate the prison rules or exhibit conduct disorder. The rule ought to have stated about what type of penalty or punishments must be given. Be positive and state how are the disciplinary cases disposed of after the conduct of the inquiry. Here is the revised text—

Rule 31 (1): "Where a disciplinary authority is satisfied on the conduct of a disciplinary inquiry that an incarcerated has committed a misconduct or violated a conduct norm/Centre's rule/regulation etc., the disciplinary authority may if it thinks so fit.

(a) allow the incarcerated delinquent to abide by the norms/rules/regulations after an advice or admonition with or without attending special counselling session arranged by the authorities for developing his personality and values in an upright way;

(b) direct the incarcerated delinquent to participate in group counselling and similar activities for a period of time regularly arranged by authorities for similar inmates;

(c) order the incarcerated delinquent to perform some community services inside the prison as chosen by him from a list prepared by the authorities for a period of time;

(d) order the incarcerated delinquent to pay a fine if he works in the prison;

(e) direct the incarcerated inmate to be under the special care, watch and surveillance of a specified officer of the Centre for a period of time provided that the officer so entrusted takes the responsibility for his good behaviour for a period of time as fixed by the disciplinary authority;

(f) direct the incarcerated delinquent to do some extra work in addition to the normal hours of work, if he works or to do some extra work for fixed hours, if he does not work;

(g) order for the forfeiture of the remission marks earned by him during his stay;

(h) order for delaying the consideration for premature release (Parole) for a specified period of time as decided by the authority;

(i) order for refusing the grant of "ticket to leave" or home visit for a period of time as decided by the authority;

(j) order for the withholding of the privileges enjoyed by the inmate for a period of time; and

(k) order for a change of labour for a stated period to some irksome or severe form.

(2) Corporal punishments, punishments by placing in a dark cell, separate or solitary confinement for a prolonged period exceeding 14 days, reduction of diet and all cruel, inhuman, sub-human or degrading punishments for disciplinary offences shall be completely prohibited."

Corporal punishments brutalizes the inmates and the Centre's authorities alike. It breeds hatred and bitterness, uproots personal dignity, eradicates the very objective of imprisonment, frustrates any attempt for the development of the inmate's personality in an upright way in the right direction. Corporal punishments for all sorts of crimes and crime-doers are disfavoured throughout the world so much so that such brutal methods should be abolished in institutions where the convicts are confined. All said and done, instances are reported from many prisons that the prisoners are brutally manhandled.

In some cases, video pictures are telecasted and the world community expresses its resentment and objection to inhuman treatments. In spite of all restrictions and prohibitions, reports appear in the media and the Human Rights Commission receive complaints of torture and brutal treatment from the incarcerated. They may not be the end result of an order of disciplinary authority; but may be the result of a silent approval from the disciplinary authority.

MEDICAL OFFICERS AND PUNISHMENTS

I am not in favour of the use of the term punishment in relation to disciplinary proceedings. Yet, I have used that word in the revised text and it implies only a strategy, means or methods for developing the personality of the erring inmate in an upright way. In my liberal or special view, the misconducts or the violations of the Centre's rules/regulations are not misconducts or violations rather are the ways or means by which the personality of the inmates may be developed. Perhaps or better, certainly the personality of an inmate will not be or cannot be developed in a desirable manner in the absence of such misconducts or violations of Centre's norms, rules or regulations. In my opinion, misconducts/violations of the norms, regulations and rules of the Centre are the *sine-que-non* or *the condition without which* one's personality cannot be developed. In the existing Rule 32 of the Standard Minimum Rules for the treatment of Prisoners, one may see—

Rule 32 (1) "Punishments by close confinement or reduction of diet shall never be inflicted unless the medical officer has examined the prisoner and certified in writing that he is fit to sustain it.

(2) The same shall apply to any other punishment that may be prejudicial to the physical or mental health of a prisoner. In no case may such punishment be contrary to or depart from the principle stated in Rule 31.

(3) The medical officer shall visit daily prisoners undergoing such punishments and shall advise the director if he considers the termination or alteration of the punishment necessary on grounds of physical or mental health."

I cannot or I do not agree with the Rule 32 (1, 2 & 3), as I have reasoned objections to many wrongly or ill-conceived concepts contained in the said rule. First of all, a medical officer is one of the several professionals employed in a Centre for developing the personality of the inmates—they may be erring inmates—in an upright way in the right direction. There may be the psychiatrist, the welfare officer, the psychiatric social worker, the clinical psychologist, the chief of the workshop, the teachers or anyone devotedly or religiously committed to perform duties for the welfare of the inmates including the erring ones. Hence, the disciplinary authority needs to consult anyone or more of them before he takes a decision on the type, nature, intensity etc., of the punishment. Hence, the suggested revision will be—

Rule 32 (1) "The disciplinary authority shall obtain an investigation—medical, social, clinical—psychological, psychiatric, welfare, educational, professional/occupational/work—report on the inmate through anyone or more of the professional staff in the Centre and shall take into consideration the findings of such report before passing the order.

(2) No incarcerated inmate who violates the norms rules or regulations shall be punished to close confinement unless it is certified by the health-care and welfare team that he is fit to sustain it and is not detrimental to the development of the personality of the inmate. In cases, the professionals in the health-care and welfare team are not in a position to file a consensus report jointly, the disciplinary authority may take a decision evaluating the majority opinion. If that too is not possible, the disciplinary authority shall take a decision in goodwill or faith for the best interest of the incarcerated inmate.

(3) The same principle shall apply to any other punishment that may be prejudicial to the physical or psychological health of the inmate. In any case, the order shall be passed in goodwill, in fairness, equity and good conscience for the best interest of the inmate—for the development of his personality in an upright way in the right direction.

(4) Any or all members of the health care and welfare team shall allow the inmates undergoing punishments to visit him/them as and when necessary for obtaining advice. The medical officer along with the psychiatrist shall visit daily inmates undergoing close confinement or such other punishment that may be prejudicial to the physical or psychological health of the inmate and

> shall advise the director if he considers the termination or alteration of the punishment necessary on grounds of physical or psychological health."

Even a mini form of parole—i.e., pre-mature release from the punishment can be allowed. In other words, the director can reduce the intensity of the punishment, change the type or nature of punishment or a lesser one even cancelling his order punishing the inmate in case he is satisfied with the behaviour and conduct of the inmate after the order of punishment has been passed. Nevertheless, he must not enjoy any authority to enhance the type or nature of punishment or extend the period under any circumstances. No punishments twice for the same delinquency is the principle to be followed in disciplinary cases. Therefore, I suggest the following provision to be added to the revised text as Rule 32 (5).

> "The director of the Centre may if he is satisfied having regard to the nature of the misconduct or violation of the rule and the circumstances of the case and the good behaviour shown by the inmate after the order of punishment has been passed, it is expedient to do, for reasons to be recorded, reduce the intensity of the punishment, change the type or nature of the punishment to a lesser one or to cancel the order of punishment of the disciplinary authority in goodwill for the best interest of the inmate and for developing his personality in an upright way in the right direction."

Rules 32(6) may be a reproduction of the Rule 57 of the existing Standard Minimum Rules-1957. Hence, Rule 32(6):

> "Imprisonment and other measures which result in cutting of an offender from the outside world are afflictive by the very fact of taking from the person the right of self-determination by depriving him of his liberty. Therefore, the system shall not, except as incidental or justifiable segregation or the maintainance of discipline, aggravate the suffering inherent in such a situation."

INSTRUMENTS OF RESTRAINT

Any instrument of restraint is an instrument of humiliation. Mad men are chained at home and the family members do not want it to be known by people outside. Women who argue for their freedom from patriarchy always complain of the restraints on them. Many of them want to get out from such social restraints. While the under-trial prisoners are taken out for production before a court, instruments of restraints are used in some countries by the escorting police party only if the under-trial prisoners are likely to break out of police custody or play the vanishing trick. No doubt, when the people look at anybody in handcuffs, they look down upon him. The handcuffed people feel desperate and sometimes, they become dangerous too. Hence, some countries have special guidelines about handcuffing the under-trial prisoners and they are—

(1) Increasing in the number of policemen in the escort team.
(2) Arming the escort party, if necessary.
(3) Giving special training to the escorting team.
(4) Transporting the under-trial prisoners/other prisoners in protected vehicles.

Even when such measures are taken, the prisoners escape not only from the prisons but also while they move out under escort. For, restraining a person by any means—physical or psychological—is disliked and vehemently resisted. The imprisoned convicts are desperate even if the bars of the prison are made of gold. They react to such restraints several times a day in their mind, but a few of them may express their anger out. Anyway, Rule 33 of the existing Standard Minimum Rules for the Treatment of Prisoners says:

Rule 33: "Instruments of restraint, such as handcuffs, chains, irons and strait-jacket, shall never be applied as punishment. Further more, chains or irons shall not be used as restraints. Other instruments of restraint shall not be used except in the following circumstances:

(a) As a precaution against escape during a transfer provided that they shall be removed when the prisoner appears before a judicial or administrative authority;

(b) On medical ground by direction of the medical officer; and

(c) By order of the director if other methods of control fail in order to prevent a prisoner from injuring himself or others or from damaging property; in such instances, the director shall at once consult the medical officer and report to the higher administrative authority."

Doubtlessly, there exists a general disliking for instruments of restraints among the inmates. No one, except the film makers likes the old and conspicuous types of handcuffs or instruments of restraints. I have seen such inmate's in handcuffs, chains, irons and strait jacket in films. The intention of the film makers is business and the objective is to make money. In reality, the intention is and should be the development of the inmates' personality in an upright way in the right direction. Hence, there should be restrictions on the use/misuse of such instruments of restraint. The prison administration has the power, strength and authority to restrain an inmate, if that is needed. Nevertheless, there is the simultaneous restraint by law on the authorities of the Centre to exercise their power with caution, discretion and necessity. The first principle and the principal policy of any Centre of Personality Development (prison or correctional institutional as the Centre is now known) is and should be that the instruments of restraints should not be employed as instruments of restraints in a routine manner. The convict in a Centre has only minimum freedom of movement within the four walls of the institution and precisely, therefore, no one should make unnecessary or unwarranted attempts to put down that 'little' freedom by application of any instruments of restraint or loops.

It is a truth to be accepted that a person or an authority who has more strength will have a tendency to misuse/abuse his strength/authority. The authorities of the Centre have an upper hand always over the inmates and therefore, there is a likelihood or tendency for the officials to abuse/misuse their power and authority. An inmate comes to a Centre because he is convicted for having committed an offence or violated the rules of the institution. It makes him eligible for punishment. The questions that need answers are many, but a few may be—

(1) Why does he show misconduct?
(2) Why does he violate the rule?
(3) What is the role played by the officials in the Centre, other fellow convicts, environment etc., to make him a violator of prison rules?

No one generally looks into those aspects. The complaints of the inmates are not patiently heard and solutions sought out. Yes, those condemned lot do not deserve any special consideration! Anyway, there is an allegation against some of the prison officials that they lavishly employ the use of restraints arbitrarily or without any justifiable cause. Their misuse/abuse of power pleases them most. My view is that the violation of a prison rule is no valid ground for the use of the instruments of restrains. It will irritate them a lot and the use of physical restraints will be counter-productive in developing one's personality.

It has been observed that some inmates violate the prison rules because they do not know the rules—they are not told or taught. If anyone violates the prison rules out of his ignorance, he must not be punitively dealt with. Never multiply the punishments. Multiplication of punishments will be violently reacted against. The existing Rule 33 permits the use of handcuffs and strait jacket as a precaution against escape during a transfer. What are the situations in which the inmates go out of the prison? As under-trial prisoners, they go out for production before a court of law. If an under-trial prisoner is dangerous or desperate or likely to break out of custody or play the vanishing trick, he can very well be transported in protected vehicles. This is a time of video-presentation of the under-trial prisoners. Why not the video-presentation be introduced to avoid the transport? There is a school of thought which argues that the criminal courts should be constructed in the vicinity of the prisons so that transporting of many under-trails can be avoided. There is yet another school which advocates a three-tier (3-tire) system of justice administration. In other words, one tier consists of the police and the other tiers are of the prison and the court. The "lift" operating in the system will make everything easy.

Rule 33 allows the use of certain type of restraints on medical grounds by the direction of the medical officer. What are those medical grounds? A medical ground can easily be found out if the administration decides so. Allegations are heard that the medical officers are forced to give such directions if the prison administration demands so. Hence, my suggestion is to refer the matter to the health-care and welfare team or a medical board which will be free from any sort of influence from the prison administration. Even if the health-care and welfare team/medical board recommends the use of the instruments of restraint, I am not inclined to accept it as it is always counter productive to the development of one's personality and will defeat the very purpose of incarceration. The use of restraints will not be as a rule to the best interest of the inmate.

The third situation in which the use of certain types of instruments of restraints is permitted when other methods of control do not work with the inmates. What does it mean? Here, the authority is given to the director of the Centre and the purpose is to prevent him from injuring himself or others or from damaging property. The question is: "Why do other methods fail"? Is it because he is a psychic problem? If so, he needs psychiatric treatment more than instruments of restraints. Hence, the revised text will be—

Rule 33 "Instruments of restrains, such as handcuffs, chains, irons and strait jacket shall never be applied as a punishment.

(1) Instruments of restrains shall not be used as a precaution against escape during a transfer as the transport must be done in a protected vehicle with the help of adequate number of trained personnel (with arms, if necessary) or as the transport may be avoided by video-presentation, a three-tier system of justice administration or the authority situated in the vicinity of the Centre or any other ways by virtue of which the escape of the inmate can be prevented.

(2) Instruments of restrains shall not be used on medical grounds without obtaining the direction from the health-care and welfare team or a medical board which shall give such directions only for the best interest of the inmate without jeopardizing the objective of incarceration which is the development of the inmates' personality in an upright way in the right direction."

I am in favour of deleting everything expressed under Rule 33 (a & b) in the existing document. Rule 34 of the present text becomes irrelevant. The central prison administration has no role except to implement the decision and direction of the health-care and welfare team/medical board. Hence the Rule 34 shall be:

> "The patterns and manner of instruments of restraint, if needed, shall be decided by the health-care and welfare team/medical board. Such instruments shall be approved by the central administration of the Centres of Personality Development and such instruments shall not be applied for any longer time than is strictly necessary for the development of the inmates' personality in an upright way in the right direction."

INFORMATION TO AND COMPLAINTS BY PRISONERS

People outside the prison have very many strange or unrealistic ideas of prisons. Many of them have not even seen the inside of a prison. Much of their information depends upon the media reportings, films, T.V. serials, books and people's or convicts'/ex-convicts' conversation about the prisons. Some have wrong impressions as well about the prisons, prison rules, life in prison, prison labour, prison education, prison discipline etc. The changes that are brought to prisons periodically are not told to people outside so much so that most of the people are still ignorant of what is going on inside the prisons. The bad things happening in prisons come out through the media and people discuss them everywhere. The good things seen in the prisons do not go out and precisely, therefore, in my opinion, the new entrants to a Centre ought to be informed of–

(1) What are rules of the prison?
(2) What is the time-table?
(3) What are the rights of the inmates?
(4) What are the duties of the inmates?
(5) What are the facilities in the Centre?
(6) What are the duties, responsibilities and obligations of the inmates to the Centre's staff and *vice versa*?
(7) How should be the community life inside the Centre?

(8) What is the noble purpose of incarceration and tell the new entrants to the Centre that the prime and the only objective of incarceration is development of personality in an upright way in the right direction *via* correction, reformation, resocilization, rehabilitation and reintegration to the society back as a responsible citizen. Most unfortunately, in many countries, nothing is told to the new inmates. The ignorance of the inmates on those aspects is their weakness and the Centre's staff as well as other fellow inmates cash on their ignorance.

Rule 35(1&2) is very clear and says:

Rule 35 (1) "Every prisoner on admission shall be provided with written information about the regulations governing the treatment of prisoners of his category, the disciplinary requirements of the institution, the authorized methods of seeking information and making complaints, and all such other matters as are necessary to enable him to understand both his rights and his obligations and to adapt to the life of the institution.

(2) If a prisoner is illiterate, the above said information shall be conveyed to him orally."

"Treatment of prisoners" — what does it convey? Though the word 'treatment' has many meanings [to act or behave towards (a person) in some specified way; to deal with in speech or writing etc., [any person thinks about dealing with (a disease, patient, etc.)] in order to relieve or cure as a physician does. Such a feeling is found more in a convict as there is a school of thought that the crime-doers are sick persons who need *treatment* badly. The approach is not accepted as many who commit crimes are not sick or psychiatric patients. In 'treatment of prisoners', the approach is negative although the outcome may be positive. Hence, and owing to many other reasons I suggest to substitute the words "for developing the personality in an upright way in the right direction" in the place of "treatment of prisoners."

"All such other matters" — is again vague and therefore, must be specific or couched in clarity. Rewrite Rule 35(1) as under:

Rule 35 (1) "Every new entrant admitted to a Centre shall be provided with written information about—

(a) time-table of the Centre;

(b) disciplinary rules;

(c) misconduct and violations of rules including punishments;

(d) purpose of incarceration for personality development and the need for co-operation;

(e) rules relating to labour, education, leisure-time activities, religious performances, workshop, neatness, hygiene, cleanliness, behaviour in the dining hall and *camerata,* interpersonnel relations, interaction with the Centre's staff etc.;

(f) rights, duties, responsibilities and obligations of the inmates;

(g) rules of remission, privileges, canteen and correspondence with family and outside world;

(h) authorized methods of seeking information and making complaints;

(i) authorized methods to get counselling, moral training, use of library and reading rooms, etiquette, manners and good behaviour; and

(j) facilities in the Centre and the behavioural principles, values and traits for the development of personality in an upright way in the right direction.

(2) If an inmate is illiterate, semi-literate or moderately educated, the aforesaid information shall be conveyed to him orally through an orientation course lasting at least two days. Those who attend the orientation course on admission shall be asked to attend a refresher course at least once in an year.

(3) Boards containing the information shall be displayed in a conspicuous manner in the Centre. Audio-visual gadgets may be used for the purpose."

An inmate in the Centre is under the State care and protection. Anything done to him by the State is not to be considered as a charity shown to him. They have a right to demand and the State has an obligation to provide with all information needed for the development of the inmates' personality. Some among the staff in the Centre may feel that they are a blessed lot and the inmates are their servants who live and survive because they get considerations. Some among the staff employ the inmates as domestic servants to wash their clothes, to clean their houses, to maintain their garden, to do menial jobs and occasionally such reports appear in the media. On interviewing the inmates/ex-inmates, one may understand that they are exploited because they are ignorant of the rules, regulations, duties, responsibilities and obligations, etc., which they have while they undergo incarceration. This can be avoided if the guidelines given above are enforced or implemented properly or meaningfully.

REQUESTS AND COMPLAINTS

Prisons contain a community of disgruntled people who generally curse their fate, horoscope, environments, birth and what not? And my studies on such prisoners show that they suffer from a high degree of dissatisfaction expressing anger showing violence and aggression. They have or will have many requests as they come from very many backgrounds and environments. There is a common saying that *what is food to one may be poison to another* and accordingly, each one may have his own requests and special requests which the authorities cannot always entertain. They may have complaints against other fellow inmates or officials working amidst them. The complaints originate from many sources which are known or unknown to the complainants. Some may have psychological problems which may be expressed in the form of requests or complaints. If adequate opportunities are not provided, the stress may be multiplied and fresh problems created. He may convert his own and others' lives in the Centre miserable. It may result in disciplinary actions or registration of fresh cases after cases. Therefore, Rule 36 (1, 2, 3 & 4) is about making requests and complains. It says:

Rule 36 (1) "Every prisoner shall have opportunity each week day of making requests or complaints to the director of the institution or the officer authorized to represent him.

(2) It shall be possible to make requests or complaints to the inspector of prisons during his inspection. The

prisoner shall have the opportunity to talk to the inspector or to any other inspecting officer without the director or other members of the staff being present.

(3) Every prisoner shall be allowed to make a request or complaint, without censorship as to substance but in proper form, to the central prison administration, the judicial authority or other proper authorities through approved channels.

(4) Unless it is evidently frivolous or groundless, every request or complaint shall be promptly dealt with and relied to without undue delay."

Rule 36 (1) is fine, nevertheless, seldom many inmates come forward to make requests and especially complaints. Those who make requests or complaints become 'noted' inmates and they may be subjected to several kinds of hardships and mental harassments including disciplinary action or loss of remission. The prison rules are so comprehensive that any behaviour of an inmate can be interpreted as a violation of some rules with some justifications. The staff in the institution can make them or 'in a way' force them to violate the prison rules and see that they have a miserable life inside the prison-walls. That is, what the ex-inmates speak loudly or inmates themselves tell in silent language. In spite of it, the authorities must know what is going on in the Centre and therefore, it is desirable to keep a "Request-cum-Complaint Box" in every Centre. The facts in each request or complaint may be more important than the inmate who makes it. Hence, anonymity in making requests/complaints may be accepted/encouraged. For everything, solutions are to be sought out. Under no circumstances, a request or complaint shall become a cause of persecution for the inmates. Hence, the amended text will be—

Rule 36 (1) "Every inmate, orally or in writing, shall have the opportunity each week day of making requests or complaints to the director of the Centre or the officer authorized to represent him. A box with a lock and key to receive the requests/complaints should be kept in every institution and its key should be kept in the personal custody of the director. Requests and

> complaints made in an anonymous way shall be accepted for making inquiries to find out remedial solutions, if that is needed. No action, disciplinary or otherwise, shall be initiated against an inmate making requests and/or complaints. No request or complaint shall be made to be a cause of persecution for the inmates individually or for the institution generally."

Rule 36(2) is good as it enables the inmates to make requests and complaints to the head of the Prisons Department. But, it is not enough. In many countries, the Centres are visited by the Minister in charge of the prison administration, Judicial officers of various ranks, Members of the Human Rights Commission, members of the Legislature, members of the Legislative sub-committee, members of the Women Commission and thus a number of authorities makes periodical visits to the Centre. No doubt, such visits should be encouraged and the inmates should have the opportunity to make requests or complaints to each such authorities.

Rule 36(2) says that the inspector of prisons or any officer inspecting may be approached with requests and complaints. Who is the inspector of prisons? Is he the Head of the Prisons Department? Who is this "any other inspecting officer"? The idea is not clear and the designation of the post is not universally known or accepted. Hence, make it to be the "Head of the Prison Department." As said above, the idea is good, but will it work to the advantage of the inmate/s? My findings from my researches show that the prison staff as a whole in many institutions makes a community and the Head of the Department is, more often than not, a part of it. He cannot be separate from the staff who together feel that there should be no problems in the administration. If anything bad is reported in the media, it affects the reputation of the institution and the authorities alike. Hence, they want to cover any defects if at all they are brought to their notice. During the inspection of the Head of the Department, it is often virtually difficult for the inmates to make requests or complaints to him directly. There may not be enough time or if at all there is time, the inmates are reluctant to approach him for making requests or complaints as they are afraid of being "*noted*" by the prison staff. Doubtlessly, he can expect evil consequences and misinterpretations so much so that Rule 36(2), sometimes becomes sterile in practical prison administration. Hence, the amended text will be—

36(2)(a) "It shall be possible for the inmates to make requests and complaints to the Head of the Department during his inspection. The inmates shall have the opportunity to talk to the Head of the Department *in camera* without anyone of the staff being present;

(b) The Head of the Department shall convene a general meeting of the inmates during his inspection to receive requests and complaints so that solutions to the common problems of the inmates can be solved instantly or otherwise; and

(c) The Guideline 36(2)(a) is applicable to all authorities like the Human Rights Commission, Sub-committees of the Legislature, Minister of the State empowered to inspect and hold discussions with the inmates and the staff. All such authorities empowered shall make attempts to solve the problems and settle the issues and complaints which have a common interest in consultation with or without the Head of the Department."

I remember a real incident in a prison. The prison had kept a complaint/request box with lock and key. The key was to be kept by the senior most officer of the judiciary in the district and he made periodical inspection of the prison. He never received any requests or complaints from any of the inmates. Initially, he thought that "all is well that ends well." Later, he developed suspicion and on a close inspection of the box, it was found out that the box could be opened without key kept by the judicial officer. The prison authorities made use of a hidden/secret facility for their advantage. With this in mind, the Rule 36(3) may be read. In that Rule, it is mentioned about an "Approved Channel." The "Approved Channel" makes everything difficult. No one, usually, will be volunteering to do so as he may become a noted 'inmate' and "a......" in the eyes of the prison staff. Here, anonymity should be maintained and secrecy ensured. The caged inmates are persecuted and I have first hand information from the mouth of the released prisoners about such harassments and miseries, persecutions and sleepless nights. Hence, I suggest the revision to be:

Rule 36 (3) "Every inmate shall have the freedom to make a request or complaint, without censorship as to substance but in proper form, to the Head of the Department, the judicial authority and other proper authorities like the Minister in charge of the Centres of Personality Development, Human Rights Commissions, Sub-committee of the Legislature empowered to inspect the Centre through means and methods ensuring to protect the secrecy and even anonymity."

I have no objections or difficulties to accept Rule 36(4) in the existing Standard Minimum Rules, 1957. Nevertheless, the question is: "Who will deal with the requests and complaints?" Presently, some individual prison official will be entrusted with the task of dealing with the requests and complaints. Sometimes, it so happens that he takes his own time and takes a decision. Sometimes, he is influenced by some extraneous factors not conducive for the development of inmates' personality or institution's well-being. Hence, I suggest that there should be an Inquiry Board/Committee to look into the requests or complaints of the inmates so that the justness and objectivity may be established and ensured. The inmates are a voiceless mass or a soundless folk whose complaints may remain there as complaints written on waters or on the shores of a sea. Justice should be done and it should appear that justice has been done. What is this undue day? Delay may be days, months or years and, therefore, it is of importance to specify the period. There may be anonymous complaints/requests of the cowards in the Centre. They also must be inquired into and the decisions taken at the earliest. The revised text will be—

Rule 36 (4) "Unless it is evidently frivolous or groundless, every request or complaint—anonymous or otherwise—shall be promply dealt with by an Inquiry Board/ Committee with its investigating team and replied to the inmates if their identity is revealed or otherwise

> informed to the inmates in a common way, if it is anonymous, by methods and means adopted in each Centre for the information of the inmates in general within 30 days or earlier after the request or complaint has been received."

Remember always that every request has some merit and every complaint has a grain of truth, no matter it is filed with the identity of the inmates or without revealing the identity in an anonymous way. Great changes have been brought in some jails after conducting an honest inquiry in anonymous requests/complaints. Hence, never discard the requests/complaints of a community of people whose energy is very intense, but sound or voice is very feeble. The energy created by neglecting the request or by discarding the complaints may be converted to prison riots, prison-escapes or serious violation of the prison rules or the State's penal laws.

CONTACT WITH THE OUTSIDE WORLD

No convict except those convicted for capital punishment goes to a prison for his/her burial. Everyone wants to come back to society. Everyone sent to a prison is a son/daughter of his/her parents. Some may be sons/daughters-in-law. Some may be the father/mother. Some may be the husbands/wives and thus everyone has very many contacts outside the prison. There is nothing wrong in having such innocent and needed contacts. Nevertheless, there may be dangerous contacts—contacts with terrorists, fundamentalists, fanatics or the enemies of the State. A few instances of such objectionable contacts were detected from some prisons and the information was shocking. After the extensive misuse of mobile phones had come into being, some contacts went beyond any boundaries which were dangerous and suspicious. Hundreds of mobile phones were found out after a raid being conducted in a prison notoriously occupied by the adherents of certain political parties, 'isms' or 'logies'. Such misuse/abuse of the outside world contacts may be dangerous. Otherwise, there is no harm in having contacts with the outside world. Rule 37 of the existing Standard Minimum Rules for the Treatment of Prisoners reads:

Rule 37: "Prisoners shall be allowed under necessary supervision to communicate with their family and reputable friends at regular intervals, both by correspondence and by receiving visits."

"Under necessary supervision" and "communicate"—both need explanation. Supervision becomes very necessary in view of the nature of crimes committed. Do the contents of communication relate to Terrorism, Naxalism, Anti-Government activities, *Mafia* or similar organized crimes, prison riots or escape from the prison? Recent episodes in some countries give ample evidence to become suspicious of many prisoners who exhibit very good conduct and behaviour during their stay in the Centre. Some of the inmates have linkages with the media and political hierarchy. The staff in the Centre become suspicious of every prisoner as they do not want to see that the inner secrets in the life of the inmate inside the Centre are leaked out. In spite of the supervision, some secrets are leaked out through many routes including certain unscrupulous staff who have unholy nexus, contacts and transactions with the inmates.

As the staff in the Centre are honestly afraid of the human rights activists, media, pressmen, politicians of the opposition political party, etc., they take extra care and caution while the inmates make visits. The visitors may be carriers of secrets, drug traffickers, gang men, organized racketeers, terrorists, insurgents and so on. Hence, they allow prison visits under supervision. How? Generally, they ensure their presence at the time of visits. Often they remain there with the inmates in such a way that they hear their conversation, as well as they see everything they do. Certainly, it irritates most of the inmates and my considered view is that the unnecessary supervision' should be substituted by "Under Camera Surveillance" (CCTV) which will certainly deter the inmates to do what is expected from them. Camera Surveillance ensures audio-recording too. The physical presence of the staff gives an itching experience to many inmates and their visitors. It can be reduced or removed by the video recording of the visits and such a record will be a permanent record that can be kept by the authorities.

What is meant by "reputed friends"? Every friend is reputed for the inmate or at least expected to be reputed or reputable and on admission of a convict, he/she must be asked to give a list of their friends who are to be permitted to see him/her on regular basis. Once the names of the reputed friends are available with the authorities, the character, antecedents and reputation of each one can be verified by the officials immediately. If some one other than those enlisted as "reputable" friends comes to visit an inmate, certainly his reputation and purpose can be checked by means found suitable for the prison authorities. The inmates should be told earlier that they are not expected to communicate with their relatives and friends anything that is detrimental to his personality development and the well-being of the institution. Hence, the revised text shall be—

Rule 37 (a) "Inmates shall be allowed under necessary 'camera surveillance' (CCTV) to communicate with their family and reputable friends enlisted by them, at the time of admission, at regular intervals, both by correspondence and by receiving visits;

(b) The authorities of the Centre shall verify the character, antecedents and reputation of the family members and friends enlisted by them immediately after the admission. Persons other than those enlisted by them as members of their family or friends come to visit them, the authority may refuse permission if they fail to or refuse to prove their identity and reputation.

(c) The correspondence of the inmates to outside the Centre shall be screened for the purpose of security and welfare of the society in general and institution in particular. The correspondence may be *via* letters or land line telephones (Under Camera Surveillance) and under no circumstances shall be through internet or other electronic means of communication. No mobile phones will be permitted to communicate between an inmate and the people outside."

Why are the mobile phones prohibited? Instances are plenty to show that some inmates having unholy nexus with notorious criminals or terrorists communicate by using mobile phones which they keep in a clandestine way inside the Centre. Raids conducted to find out mobile phones in the Centres in some countries bring out incredibly large number of mobile phones with very many SIM cards. Government put jammers to stop communication *via* mobile phones. Later investigation proved that the telephone providers (i.e., the company) used to manipulate the frequency so much so that the jammers become ineffective or useless. This points to a fact that some of the inmates are highly affluent and influential so much so that they can do many undesirable things by misusing the mobile phones. Now mobile phones with internet facilities are available—even very small electronic gadgets with internet connections are available in the market and under no circumstances, the use of such communication equipments must be allowed in a Centre.

According to Rule 38 (1 &2) of the existing Standard Minimum Rules for the Treatment of Prisons:

Rule 38 (1) "Prisoners who are foreign nationals shall be allowed reasonable facilities to communicate with the diplomatic and consular representatives of the State to which they belong.

(2) Prisoners who are nationals of States without diplomatic or consular representation in the country and refugees or Stateless persons shall be allowed similar facilities to communicate with the diplomatic representative of the State which takes charge of their interest or any national or international authority whose task is to protect such persons."

There is or there cannot be any difficulty to allow communication for foreign nationals incarcerated with diplomatic and consular representatives. But such communications must be with the consent of the Centre's authority 'Under Camera Surveillance' (CCTV). This is a time of terrorism and insurgency and some countries speak about cross-border terrorism. The situation is not bright and therefore, it is to the interest of any country that the inmates communicate with the diplomatic and consular representatives under camera surveillance. The revised text will be:

Rule 38 (1) "Inmates who are foreign nationals shall be allowed reasonable facilities to communicate with the diplomatic and consular representatives of the State to which they belong.

(2) Inmates who are nationals of States without diplomatic or consular representation in the country and refugees or Stateless persons shall be allowed similar facilities to communicate with the diplomatic representative of the State which takes charge of their interests or any national or international authority whose task it is to protect such persons:

Provided that (a) the communication allowed under Rule 38 (1 & 2) shall be with the consent of the Centre's authorities for a fixed time decided by the authorities;

(b) the communication shall be under camera surveillance and the video of the communication shall be kept under the custody of authorities; and

(c) The expenditure shall be met by the inmate who communicates with the diplomatic/ consular/others in all cases stated under Rule 38 (1 & 2)."

LIBRARY AND READING ROOM

Rule 39 of the present Standard Minimum Rules for the Treatment of Prisoners says:

Rule 39: "Prisoners shall be kept informed regularly of the more important items of news by the reading of news papers, periodicals or special institutional publications, by hearing wireless transmissions, by lectures or by any similar means as authorized or controlled by the administration."

The above Rule 39 is about the need for Reading Rooms in every Centre. This is not a charity or favour, rather is the right of the inmates. It is not a desirable consideration but an unavoidable necessity. If the citizens of a nation has the right to information and education, the inmates in the Centre too have it. No one can or should deny it to an inmate just because he is involved in the commission of a crime. Confinement and denial of the freedom of movement outside the Centre under a court order do not mean that the inmate is denied to enjoy his freedom for information and education. There should be the copies of the news papers of repute in the vernacular as well as in the national language. If there are illiterate or semi-literate inmates, then facility must be made to inform the news and other important events by reading the news papers during the time of breakfast or lunch. One of the inmates may be instructed with the duty and the authorities may see to it that he performs his duty in an acceptable way.

There are Centres where the news to be read by the inmates is censured. Sometimes the news is cut away or is blackened so that the inmates do not read it. This, to my view, is unnecessary and of bad taste. Therefore, it should be avoided. The cutting off or blackening of the news items appearing in the daily newspapers creates uncontrollable desire in some to know what is hidden. There are very many ways to know the news and daily happenings in these days. They can know it *via* television news telecast, radio news broadcast, channel talks, letters, visitors etc. so much so that a policy of let the inmates read everything which a free citizen outside the Centre reads. What is it? The news which comes in the dailies or on the T.V. screens etc., are read by little children to the oldest old alike. There is nothing wrong in knowing the news by the inmates whatever may be the nature of the news in the media or whatever may be the nature of crime one has committed.

There are journals and periodicals of repute. The inmates must read them for the development of their personality, for the inculcation of values, for entertainment, for education etc. Lectures must be arranged in the Centre and the author has several opportunities to address the inmates about values, community life, interpersonnel relations, rules of etiquette etc., and I could observe the earnestness and enthusiasm which they showed to listen to the lectures I have given to the inmates in a central prison in India. The situation will be same or similar in other countries too. Therefore, the revised text should have—

Rule 39 (a) "Inmates shall be kept informed regularly of the important items of news by reading of newspapers of repute in the vernacular as well as in the national language, journals, periodicals or special institutional publications, by hearing wireless transmissions, by lectures or by any similar means as authorized or controlled by the administration;

(b) For the benefit of the illiterate and semi-literate inmates, facility shall be made for the reading of the more important items of news by an educated inmate during the time of breakfast and lunch utilizing amplifiers and loud speakers;

(c) Blackening of the news items or cutting away of the news items from the daily papers/periodicals should be avoided unless otherwise it is found to be very essential to do so by the administration; and

(d) Those inmates who utilize the reading room for their enrichment of knowledge should be encouraged with incentives/remission marks."

Rule 40—That is, "Every institution shall have a library for the use of all categories of prisoners, adequately stocked with both recretional and instructional books and prisoners shall be encouraged to make full use of it"—is about the books and the library and the rule must be retained with the following changes in the revised text as—

Rule 40 (a) Every institution shall have a library for the use of all categories of inmates, adequately stocked with both recreational and instructional books, and the inmates shall be encouraged to make full use of it; and

(b) Those inmates who prove that they make use of the library and books to the development of their personality in an upright way in the right direction must be rewarded with remission marks."

FAITH AND RELIGION

Deism, theism, agnosticism, humanism, empiricism, rationalism, existentialism, epicureanism, hedonism, scepticism, etc., are in vogue. Precisely, therefore, a cross-section of the inmates in any Centre may be seen in every 'ism'. Everyone has his/her own faith, religion and philosophy and no doubt it must be honoured. An inmate has the freedom to uphold his/her faith and no one can or should interfere with it. The inmates represent a cross-section of the society and therefore, even among the theists, there may be people professing or practicing different faiths. People from tribes have their tribal gods and today some living people are adored and worshipped as the incarnation of god in human flesh. They establish their own worship centres and people gather in such centres. Some of them are detected as fake-gods and some such "fake gods" are arrested, charge-sheeted, prosecuted, tried and convicted. They too may become inmates in the Centres. Taking everything together, it is necessary to revise the existing Rule 41 (1, 2 & 3) which is –

Rule 41 (1) "If the institution contains a sufficient number of prisoners of the same religion, a qualified representative of that religion shall be appointed or approved. If the number of prisoners justifies it and conditions permit, the arrangement should be on a full-time basis.

(2) A qualified representative appointed or approved under paragraph (1) shall be allowed to hold regular services and to pay pastoral visits in private to prisoners of his religion at proper times.

(3) Access to a qualified representative of any religion shall not be refused to any prisoner. On the other hand, if any prisoner object to a visit of any religious representative, his attitude shall be fully respected."

The prison has a floating population and therefore, more often than not, it cannot be said that any institution will contain a sufficient number of prisoners of the same religion. There may be several denominations in one and the same religion. Every denomination has its own prayers and rituals. A religion may have many castes/sub-castes/divisions. There may be members of the tribes who may have their tribal gods. Appointment of a qualified representative of a particular religion/denomination/sect/caste/sub-caste/division, etc., will be undesirable and at times dangerous. Even in countries where such appointments do not take place, criticisms are heard that the representatives of certain religions come to the Centres to see the inmates with ulterior motives—i.e. conversion of religion. Hence, my revision will be—

Rule 41 (1) "A qualified representative of every religion may be approved by the administration and allowed to hold religious services subject to conditions imposed by the authority and accepted by the representative.

(2) Representatives of every religion may be approved to offer counselling to the inmates of their religion for a fixed length of time decided by the authority of the Centre.

(3) No representative of any religion shall be allowed to promote and propagate his faith to any other inmates belonging to other religion/sects/denomination/caste/sub-caste/division.

(4) Access to a qualified representative of any religion shall not be refused to an inmate belonging to his religion if it helps for the development of his personality in an upright way in the right direction.

(5) If an inmate objects to the visit of any religious representative to his private life, his attitude shall be fully respected.

(6) If an inmate wants to pray in silence or perform by himself some religious rituals without causing disturbance to other fellow inmates, his need shall be fully respected."

Religion, religious bigotary, religious fundamentalism, fanaticism or extremism etc., have caused many problems and havocs in society. Crimes are committed in the name of religion. Laws are violated for the religion. Religious differences create issues which may result in arson, murder or destruction of property. This is what is seen throughout the world and therefore, a Centre may not be an exemption to it. Therefore, facilities shall be provided to develop secularism among the inmates. They must stay together and the Centre shall make any and all efforts to see a harmonious human co-existence among the people who have different faiths, philosophy and religious beliefs. Hence, the revised text shall have—

Rule 41(7) "All attempts shall be made to develop secularism among the inmates. For this, religious festivals shall be organized by all belonging to different religions for harmonious co-existence within the Centre.

(8) Atheism, agnosticism, rationalism, humanism etc.,

which do not accept any religion shall be accepted as a reality and those who believe in such non-religious or anti-god philosophy shall be fully respected."

Rule 42 of the existing Standard Minimum Rules Reads: "So far as practicable, every prisoner shall be allowed to satisfy the needs of his religious life by attending the services provided in the institution and having in his possession the books of religious observance and instruction of his denomination."

The above rule may be revised as:

Rule 42 (1) "Every inmate shall be free to attend the services offered by his or any other religious groups.

(2) Every inmate shall be free to possess books of his or any religious observance and instruction of his denomination."

However, any special marks showing one's religious affinity, attachment etc., may be allowed by the authority if they do not disturb the community or community feelings. Excessiveness of anything is abnormal and unwanted. Therefore, all kinds of excessiveness in religious practices/rituals should be discouraged or avoided.

VALUABLES AND PROPERTY

A new entrant may have money, valuables, clothings and other effects when he comes to the Centre. There may be valuables—more valuable or costlier than money in some. They may be the wedding ring, Mangalya Sutra, medals of gods, articles of faith such as caskets of safety or those contain prayers or religious idols, relics of saints etc. To remove such valuables will make some depressed in life. Some may exhibit abnormality in behaviour or behavioural disorders. The existing rule is:

Rule 43 (1) "All money, valuables, clothing and other effects belonging to a prisoner which under the regulations of the institution he is not allowed to retain shall on his admission to the institution be placed in safe custody. An inventory thereof shall be signed by the prisoner. Steps shall be taken to keep them in good condition.

(2) On the release of the prisoner, all such articles and money shall be returned to him except in so far as he has been authorized to spend money or send any such property out of the institution, or it has been found necessary on hygienic grounds to destroy any article of clothing. The prisoner shall sign a receipt for the articles and money returned to him.

(3) Any money or effects received for a prisoner from outside shall be treated in the same way.

(4) If a prisoner brings in any drugs or medicine, the medical officer shall decide what use shall be made of them."

In my view, the inmate should be given the option either to deposit them in safe custody or return them to his near and dear, kith or kin or dependents. Why should a new entrant be compulsorily asked to deposit his valuables with the Centre's custody? Hence, the amended text shall be:

43(1) (a) "All money, valuables, clothing and other effects belonging to an entrant to a Centre, which under the regulations of the institutions, he is not allowed to retain shall on his admission to the Centre be placed, at his option, either in safe custody of the authorities or be entrusted to a person of his choice outside the Centre. In the former case, an inventory thereof shall be signed by the entrant. Steps shall be taken to keep them in good condition.

(b) Wedding ring, *Mangalya Sutra* in married women, any symbol of marriage in married people, articles of religious faith such as relics, symbols, caskets of safety or those containing prayers for self-protection etc., shall be items which one can at his option, retain to himself or entrust to the Centre/person outside the Centre whom he chooses.

(2) (a) On the release of the inmate, all such articles and

money, if they are in the safe custody of the Centre, shall be returned to him. On the death of the inmate, all such articles and money shall be returned to those who are the legal inheritants to his property. All lifers or long termers shall be asked to write a will in which the nominee who may receive his articles and valuables shall be specified. Alternatively, he shall nominate a person to receive the articles and valuables kept in safe custody of the Centre, if that is needed.

(b) On the release or death, the inmate or his nominee respectively shall receive only such articles and money except in so far as he has been authorized to spend money or send any such property out of the Centre, or it has been found necessary on hygienic grounds to destroy any article of clothing. The inmate or his nominee shall sign a receipt for the articles and money returned to him.

(3) Any money or effects received for an inmate from outside shall be treated in the same way.

(4) Any money received by him out of his labour in the Centre will be treated as money deposited in safe custody.

(5) Money deposited in safe custody shall be treated as money deposited with the Government and shall be given bank interest applicable in the country.

(6) If an inmate who has deposited money or valuables as per Rule 43 (1) (a) with the Centre may opt for entrusting the same to a person of his choice at any time during his stay in the Centre.

(7) If an entrant brings in any drugs or medicine, the medical officer shall decide what shall be made of them."

DEATH, ESCAPE, ILLNESS AND TRANSFER

An inmate in a Centre may die, may kill himself, may escape, may become seriously ill, may become mentally insane and we have any number of such cases down the centuries in many countries. The general attitude of the family, community or society, more often than not, may be to forget a person convicted to imprisonment. He is a burden for many and many a time people want to avoid him. Nevertheless, people who ought to know the whereabouts of an inmate incarcerated must know the death, illness, transfer etc. Hence, Rule 44 of the existing Rules reads:

Rule 44 (1) "Upon the death or serious illness of or serious injury to a prisoner or his removal to an institution for the treatment of mental affections, the director shall at once inform the spouse, if the prisoner is married, or the nearest relative and shall in any event inform any other person previously designated by the prisoner.

(2) A prisoner shall be informed at once of the death or serious illness of any near relative. In case of the critical illness of a near relative, the prisoner should be authorized, whenever circumstances allow, to go to his bedside either under escort or alone.

(3) Every prisoner shall have the right to inform at once his family of his imprisonment or his transfer to another institution."

No inmate in a Centre may be an island. He may have friends, relatives, kith and kin, dependants or those who may inherit his property if he dies in a Centre. Earlier, the necessity to ask every prisoner to write a will has been discussed. In any case, the natural death of an inmate, suicide or murder of a resident in a Centre ought to be informed to his near and dear/family. There may be cases of escape from the Centre. Some may be caught while others may not be. Sometimes, some escapees die or commit suicide. Some people leave the Centre under parole or under the ticket to leave system. They may not return after the period. In any case, the fact of such escape and not-returning of the inmates should be communicated to the kith and kin/family.

The inmates are under State's care and they are in prisons. In prisons, the medical facility may not be adequate and therefore, more often than not, many inmates affected/afflicted with serious illness or injury are taken to the civil hospital where the treatment may not be proper. "A prisoner after all" attitude and a "Government hospital approach" make the inmates unhappy and take everything from bad to worse. Therefore, in my view, the inmates may be allowed to have treatment in a specialist hospital at their expense, if that is possible. For, the right to get the best treatment is a human right not only of the civilians outside the prisons but also the residents in a Centre of incarceration. In my opinion, the Rule 44 must be amended or revised to read:

Rule 44(1) (a) "Upon the death, escape from the Centre's custody, non-return of the inmate after parole or ticket to leave or serous illness of or serious injury to an inmate, the director shall at once inform the spouse by the quickest means if the resident is married or the nearest relative and shall in any event inform any other person previously designated by the inmate.

(b) The director is bound to follow the same procedure said under Rule 44(1)(a) if an inmate is removed to an institution for the treatment of mental diseases or is removed to a civil hospital for the treatment of a serious physical illness or injury. The director shall allow the inmate to have specialist treatment in specialist hospitals or by specialist doctors if the expenses towards such treatment is met by the inmate or his family provided that the rules of custody in the Centre are fully honoured by the inmate/family and the hospital authorities as if his stay in that specialist hospital is an extension of his stay in the Centre.

(2) An inmate shall be informed softly at once of the death or serious illness of any near relative or severe mishap at his family or an unfortunate act of *vis major* at home. In case of the sudden death or critical illness of a near relative or severity of the mishap or the cruelty of the act of *vis major*, the inmate should be authorized whenever need and circumstances allow, to go to his home or wherever, at the expense of the Centre, either under escort or alone as the authorities deem fit and suitable.

(3) Every inmate shall have the right to inform at once his family or a near relative at his option and free of

cost, of his imprisonment or his transfer to another institution."

Why should an inmate be told about the death, illness etc., softly? The reason is that he is after all a human being and he too has soft feelings and emotions. The merciless and sudden information received may be too heavy for him to bear and therefore, the authorities ought to be kind and considerate when unpleasant matters are communicated. A severe mishap or an unfortunate act of *vis major* may be as painful as the sudden death or serious illness of a near relative. The whole edifice may be crumbled down when such incidents take place. He may have some solutions to solve the problem or escape from it. Let him participate in the sorrows of his family in such situations. It is not necessary that he must go home in all such circumstances. Everything depends upon the fair decision taken by the authorities in an objective and human way.

About Rule 44 (3), it may be said that the right of the inmate should be exercised at his option and that too free of cost. There are cases in which an inmate does not want anyone—the dear and near—to know anything about his incarceration, transfer, etc., and therefore, if that is the case, then his desire should be respected. Further, a transfer to another institution may be for the administrative convenience or efficiency of the department. Precisely, therefore, the expenses towards informing of one's imprisonment/transfer must be free of cost for the inmate who has only very little income (if he works) during the period of his incarceration. The transfer of an inmate often does not take place at his option. All depends upon the authorities to transfer or not to transfer an inmate to another institution or Centre. Though away from his family, he is or he should be a part of his family. Owing to his incarceration, he has a broken family and such a family has its negative sides on the development of his children. If he takes interest in his family, certainly, it will mitigate the seriousness of the situation and in order to facilitate such an atmosphere, the information about his transfer to another Centre may be of great use.

REMOVAL OF INMATES

Prisoners are 'human beings of curiosity' for many. People go to prisons to see the caged human beings and look at them as caged animals and birds. Some excursion parties visit the prisons almost daily and watch the inmates who often feel irritated at it. A handcuffed prisoner in public feels humiliated and often he covers his handcuffs with kerchiefs. Laws prohibiting public exhibition of prisoners in handcuffs are enacted in some countries. Rule 45 of the Standard Minimum Rules for the Treatment of Prisoners says:

> Rule 45 (1) "When the prisoners are being removed to or from an institution, they shall be exposed to public view as little as possible, and proper safeguards shall be adopted to protect them from insult, curiosity and publicity in any form."

Why should a prisoner be exposed? Certainly, it can help only to humiliate him. Instances are plenty to show that the prisoners were attacked by their enemies—were given opportunities for their escape from the custody. Sometimes, the prisoners are taken in vehicles which make the public know that the people seated inside are prisoners. The vehicle may have "Prisons" or "Prisons Department" or "Central Prison" or "District Jail" etc. written in bold letters and the general public look at such vehicles with curiosity—eyes widely open—with unpalatable comments and contemptuous looks. It is a horrible sight indeed! Hence, the revised text will be—

> Rule 45(1) "When the inmates are taken to or from a Centre, they shall not be exposed to/exposed as little as possible to the public view as inmates of a 'Centre of Personality Development' and proper safeguards shall be taken to protect them from insult, attack, curiosity, escape and publicity in any form."

Instances are not rare that the media men come after the prisoners with their camera in sensational cases and in such situations, it is the duty of the authorities to see that they are not exposed at all/exposed as little as possible. The media want to sensationalize many things and a prisoner is a news for them. Beware of it.

Rule 45 (2) That is, "The transport of prisoners in conveyances with inadequate ventilation or light or in any way which would subject them to unnecessary physical hardship, shall be prohibited"—has to be removed and substituted with—

"The transport of the inmates shall be in conveyances which are no way different from those used by the general public—which shall be adequate enough to ensure the safety of the inmate during the transport."

There is no need to make any changes in Rule 45(3) and therefore, the text will be—

Rule 45 (3) "The transport of the inmates shall be carried out at the expense of the administration." The rest of the Rule 45 (3) is deleted.

There are countries which take the inmates making use of the public transport system. This should, as far as possible, be avoided as it is difficult to ensure the safety and security. In some cases, the inmates have run away while in other cases, they have expressed their anger and hostility when they are exposed to the public view. Avoid such unpleasant situations.

INSTITUTIONAL PERSONNEL: RECRUITMENT AND SERVICE

A 'Centre of Personality Development' will have a variety of personnel—administrative, custodial and correctional as they are known today. A job in a prison is not a preferred one in many countries as many do not want to live and work amidst those who are convicted for committing crimes. Hence, candidates, as a rule, join the service if and only if they do not have other options. Most of those who opt for a job in prison are found to be not enviably qualified academically. Some may be graduates or post graduates, but their scoring in the examinations may be far away from being enviable. They are usually moderately qualified and join the service with an aim to leave the job if they get a better one. The job in the prison is a divine vocation and only those who have a religious desire, commitment and dedication will be successful in the service. The pay and perks are not presently attractive while the risk to life and safety is high. The social status in prison jobs is not very high. A job in police, forest, excise, customs, motor vehicle department etc. is rated to be always better than the same in prisons although all of them wear the same or similar uniform with minor differences. Yet, the Rule 46 of the Standard Minimum Rules for the Treatment of Prisoners reads:

Rule 46 (1) "The prison administration shall provide for the careful selection of every grade of the personnel since it is on their integrity, humanity, professional capacity and personal suitability for the work that the proper administration of the institution depends.

(2) The prison administration shall constantly seek to awaken and maintain in the minds both of the personnel and of the public the conviction that this work is a social service of great importance, and to this end all appropriate means of informing the public should be used.

(3) To secure the foregoing ends, personnel shall be appointed on a full-time basis as professional prison officers and have civil service status with security of tenure subject only to good conduct, efficiency and physical fitness. Salaries shall be adequate to attract and retain suitable men and women; employment benefits and conditions of service shall be favourable in view of the exacting nature of the work."

First of all, the selection or recruitment shall not be entrusted to the prison administration. For, they are not experts in the field. At the most, they can assist the Civil Service Recruitment Board or Public Service Commission. The prison jobs are generally not highly attractive owing to many reasons and therefore, there will not be a heavy rush from aspiring candidates in countries where unemployment is not a problem. Whatever that be, every candidate should be subjected to an intellectual test and those who come high in score in the written (above) test should be subjected to proper aptitude and personality tests. They should be specially designed and must be administered by experts in the specialized field. Integrity, humanness, devotion to work, commitment to correctional services, understanding fellow human beings especially the crime-doers, empathy, personal and physical suitability for the work, etc., must be assessed through the psychological tests. After all, the service in a prison is a man-oriented service and not material oriented. Precisely, therefore, everyone working with the inmates must have a human face.

Secondly, the work in a prison is not merely a social service or a charitable work. It is a paid work/service of great human importance. The output of the service ought to be the development of the personality of the inmates in an upright way in the right direction. It will or must ensure individual happiness and social welfare. People who appoint officials in prisons have expectations and correspondingly, the officials have obligations to the inmates and to the society. Therefore, the text must be revised accordingly.

Thirdly, of course, good conduct, efficiency and physical fitness are good and needed. Nevertheless, they are not all or everything. For example, efficiency is something different from effectiveness. What is the use of one becoming efficient without being effective? Good conduct is fine but what about the character? People with a bad character may show good behaviour. Character is something one has in himself while behaviour is something he exhibits. A person with a high dose of revenge in mind can utter sweet words if he has no character.

Presently, the salary of the prison officials in many countries is found to be far away from being satisfactory. No one will be pleased to take up a risky job for an inadequate pay and therefore, never offer peanuts which will attract only monkeys. A low paid employee will always be an expensive employee and in prison service, the output will be recidivism or relapsing into crime even after the incarceration. Hence, the revised text ought to be.

Rule 46 (1) "The Public Service Commission or the Civil Service Recruitment Board shall conduct a written test to measure the intellectual capability of the aspiring candidates to the service followed by psychological tests to assess the personality and aptitude of the candidates by suitably qualified experts in the field.

For the purpose of enlisting the members of the

custodial staff, a physical efficiency test of suitable standard shall be conducted.

On the basis of the tests conducted to measure the intellectual capability, to assess the aptitude to evaluate the personality traits like the humanness, integrity, understanding, empathy, devotion to work, service with a human face, etc., and steps to verify the physical fitness, etc., an interview board consisting of experts shall hold a face to face interview with the candidates to enlist the right personnel to the service.

(2) The administration shall constantly seek to awaken and maintain in the minds of the personnel, of the people and the inmates the conviction that the work in a 'Centre of Personality Development' is a human service of great social importance and to this end all appropriate means of informing and educating the public and the inmates should be used.

(3) To secure the foregoing ends, personnel shall be appointed on a full-time (permanent) basis and on contract basis as professional officials. Those who are appointed on full time basis shall have civil service status with security of tenure subject to good conduct and character, efficiency and effectiveness in a positive way and physical and mental fitness. Those who are on contract basis, if are appointed on full-time basis, shall have civil service status with security of tenure as and when they become full-time.

(4) Salary, perks, employment benefits and conditions of service shall be attractive to retain the best men and women in service."

It has been found acceptable to appoint personnel on contract basis. They may prefer to opt for the job on a permanent or full time basis only if they find that they are most suitable for the same.

INSTITUTIONAL PERSONNEL: EDUCATION AND TRAINING

Any investment on education and training is an investment on human resources. I have been a visiting member on the faculty of the State Institute of Correctional Administration (as the jail training centres are now called in India) and I have found that many new entrants to the service were from disciplines other than correction, criminology, sociology, victimology, social work, etc. so much so that many have little or no knowledge in man-oriented sciences. Some are qualified in science while others are in arts or commerce. They feel that 2 + 2 = 4 always and everywhere even when they deal with men and crime-doers. No doubt, 2 + 2 = 4 everywhere, but with crime-doers, it may be 3 or 5 depending upon several factors. A thorough understanding of human behaviour—especially of the crime-doer's behaviour is essential to do any job in a 'Centre of Personality Development'. What does Rule 47 say?

Rule 47 (1) "The personnel shall possess an adequate standard of education and intelligence.

(2) Before entering on duty, the personnel shall be given a course of training in their general and specified duties and be required to pass theoretical and practical tests.

(3) After entering on duty and during their career, the personnel shall maintain and improve their knowledge and professional capacity by attending courses of in-service training to be organized at suitable intervals."

The entire rule needs a thorough revision. What is the adequate standard of education and intelligence? In my view, 12 years of schooling can be considered as adequate standard of education and a pass in the examination of the 12th grade may be treated as adequate standard of education for the entry level jobs in the custodial staff. Moreover, their physical fitness like height, weight, measurements of chest etc. should be spelt out in clear terms in different countries. Hence, the revised text—

Rule 47(1) "The lowest entry level post shall be for personnel who possess an adequate standard of education—i.e., 12 years of schooling—and intelligence—i.e., a pass in the said examination—with body measurements to be physically fit to perform the work which is of an exacting and strenuous nature.

(2) Before entering on duty, the personnel in the custodial staff shall be given a course of training in their general and specific duties which shall include special lectures in criminology, correctional work, prison management, human behaviour, victimology, professional ethics and qualities of an official in the Centre of Personality Development.

(3) All personnel recruited to the custodial staff shall undergo special training in physical fitness which shall include weapon training, armed and unarmed combat, mob operation and physical training. All personnel in the custodial as well as correctional staff shall undergo a course on *yoga*, meditation, self-control and personality development.

(4) All undergoing the induction training shall be required to pass theoretical and practical tests.

(5) After entering on duty and during their career, the personnel shall maintain and improve their skill, knowledge, expertise and professional capacity by attending courses of in-service training—that is, orientation course, specialized courses, promotion courses, development courses, management courses etc., to be organized regularly at suitable intervals."

Orientation courses are intended to have the right orientation in the job. There should be special syllabus drawn for the purpose and the faculty should consist of the personnel from the prison administration as well as experts outside the department. They may include journalists, professors, politicians of integrity, social workers and public men. Specialized courses shall be on the management of special issues faced by the staff. For example, there may be terrorists, insurgents, economic offenders, extremists, offenders against women and so on. Necessarily, the staff need special knowledge, skill and expertise for such specialized services—all for the development of personality in an upright way in the right direction. The aim is to reduce recidivism and to ensure individual happiness and social welfare. Development courses are intended for the development of the personnel in many areas.

Promotion courses are very essential. As the officials go higher and higher in rank/position, their responsibilities too change a lot. They must know what to do and how to go about while they perform their duties at a senior level. Management is a highly developed science today and in every field, there exist management courses. Several universities are after such programmes and the principles of management are found to be very essential for the management of a Centre for Personality Development. The experts now say that the name 'prisons' is to be changed into Centres of Personality Development and the suggestion comes from the point of view of management.

Rule 48 reads: " All members or the personnel shall at all times so conduct themselves and perform their duties as to influence the prisoners for good by their example and to command their respect." This may be revised as—

Rule 48 "All members or the personnel shall be role models for the inmates in character and conduct so as to command their respect."

This may be a wishful thinking and will remain sometimes as unachievable in reality. For, allegations are plenty against the institutional personnel. They are accused of corruption and malpractices. They establish unholy relations with the inmates and sometimes, they are blamed to be more criminal(?) than the convicted criminals inside the Centre. Some of the personnel are really depressed and suffer from relative deprivation when compared to their fellow friends in police, forest, excise etc., departments. According to them, to live like a role model amidst the convicted crime-doers is indeed very difficult if not impossible. Still the rule can be retained as it gives meaning to one's devoted works in the Centre.

INSTITUTIONAL PERSONNEL: SPECIALISTS AND THE DIRECTOR

Development of the inmate's personality in an upright way in the right direction is the job of a specialist/team of specialists. The foundation of values, as said elsewhere, is laid and the personality infrastructure is constructed in an individual while he is an infant or a juvenile. In the Centre for Personality Development, one sees the inmates who are above 18 years of age and precisely, therefore, the services of specialists are a *conditio sine que non* for the development of personality further in an upright way in the right direction. A prison is a negativity having a positive aim. The convicts are not free, necessitated to work in spite of their disinterestness, forced to eat the food provided and are controlled everywhere in very many ways. In such a life of restrictions, controls, do's and don'ts, it is likely that they experience frustrations, tensions and mental conflicts. Even in religious nunneries and monasteries, the inmates are found to suffer from frustrations and mental conflicts and it is so in spite of their professed vow of chastity, poverty, and obedience. They have opted for a life of seclusion for spiritual achievements. There too, one may see spiritual counsellors and others to offer consolation at the moment of depression and tension. If it is so in a religious house, situation is no different in a Centre of Personality Development where the inmates stay out of compulsions. Hence, Rule 49 says:

Rule 49 (1) "So far as possible, the personnel shall include a sufficient number of specialists such as psychiatrists, criminologists, psychologists, social workers, teachers and trade instructors.

(2) The services of social workers, teachers and trade instructions shall be secured on a permanent basis without thereby excluding part-time or voluntary workers."

Why the phrase "so far as possible"?—no, there shall be sufficient number of specialists. In my opinion, presently in many countries, the custodial functions are given top priority more than correctional/personality development functions. There are Centres where no specialists are appointed. In custodial functions, the muscle power is more important than the mind power. The custodial staff, more often than not, may not be very much concerned with the development of the inmates' personality. They want to fulfil the orders of the court for incarceration. They may not be concerned at all about the correction, reformation, rehabilitation, resocialisation, personality development, reintegration, etc., of the inmates. Hence, researchers suggest that there should be specialists entirely devoting their time, initiative, energy and activities directed towards the development of personality of the inmates in an upright way in the right direction. According to my studies 1/3rd of the staff in a Centre should be specialists. Presently, in some countries there may not be any specialists or if at all they work, their number is far away from being satisfactory. I have seen that their number is less than 3 per cent in certain Centres. They may not be able to do anything constructively or substantially for the development of the personality of the inmates.

The specialists shall be from the fields of criminology, correctional work, psychology, psychotherapy, social welfare, psychiatry, education, trade and industry, counselling, sociology, art and culture, morality and ethics, management, law, all systems of medicine, nursing, child-care etc. They will be able to render their human services wherever necessary and whenever needed. They will be able to bring out enviable output in the inmates' reintegration to society. Hence, the revised text will be—

Rule 49 (1) "There shall be specialists not less than 33 per cent of the total staff in a Centre from various fields such as criminology, correctional work, psychology, social work, sociology, welfare, education, medicine, nursing, trade and industry etc. for the correction, reformation, rehabilitation, resocialisation, personality development and reintegration to the society and culture back.

(2) The services of the specialists shall be effectively and meaningfully secured and utilized on a permanent basis without thereby excluding part-time or voluntary specialists."

Part-time and voluntary specialists are required for the simple reason that trade instructors may have to be changed depending upon the job markets. In many Centres, traditional trades like carpentry, smithy, soap-making, mat-production, weaving, etc., may be seen. They may not have any job markets outside and precisely, therefore, some trained in a trade will be a waste outside. Today IT may be having good job market. Therefore, the inmates must be introduced to such new trades for which part-time, voluntary, contract specialists may be necessary.

What about the director of the Centre? Presently, the directors of a Centre in many countries are promotees from lower ranks. They may have entered service with academic background which may be enough for the lower level posts to which they were recruited. The director of the Centre should possess good academic qualifications and precisely, therefore, promotees with the required academic qualifications only shall be considered for the appointment of directors. Necessary facility should be provided by the administration to acquire the required academic qualifications while they are in service at a lower rank. The present Rule 50 is—

Rule 50 (1) "The director of an institution should be adequately qualified for his task by character, administrative ability, suitable training and experience.

(2) He shall devote his entire time to his official duties and shall not be appointed on a part-time basis.

(3) He shall reside on the premises of the institution or in its immediate vicinity.

(4) When two or three institutions are under the authority of one director, he shall visit each of them at frequent intervals. A responsible resident official shall be in charge of each of these institutions."

The whole Rule 50 needs an overhauling and a total revision. First of all Rule 50 (2) must be deleted as it is not necessary. The revised version will be—

Rule 50 (1) "The director of a Centre shall be appointed on full time basis. He shall be adequately qualified in social sciences for his job by academic education, character, knowledge, administrative effectiveness, proper training, reputation and experience.

(2) Every personnel shall be provided with adequate facilities and encouragement to acquire academic and on the job qualifications and excellence in the work and duties.

(3) The director and his staff shall reside on the premises of the Centre or in its immediate vicinity for which facilities shall be provided for family accommodation.

(4) When two or more Centres are under the authority of one director, he shall visit each one of them at frequent intervals regularly at irregular hours for performing his duties. A responsible, work-knowing and qualified subordinate/associate resident-official shall be in charge of each of these Centres."

The associate shall be under the functional control of the director. The area where the officials reside should have facilities for their children to study or engage in leisure-time activities—park, play courts, schools, travel facilities etc. For, the job in the Centre should be made more attractive for the best talents to join the service.

STAFF AND THEIR LANGUAGE

Any Centre is in a geographical area and accommodates usually the convicts from that area. The culture of the people, their language, their views and outlooks, values etc., affect their life in the Centre. The birds of the same feather—they are there in the Centre and amidst the inmates. There is interaction between the staff and the inmates. The interaction is *via* language, manners, mannerisms etc., and everything is a language in one sense. The verbal language and the non-verbal language—both are important. There is research evidence to show that the non-verbal language is more important than the verbal language. The nature of the transaction is decided by the nature of non-verbal language. 86 per cent of the transaction between the staff and the inmate is decided by the non-verbal signals emitted by the staff or by the inmates as the case may be. In my view, in some instances, even 100 per cent of the transaction will be decided by the non-verbal cues and therefore, the language means not only the spoken language but also the non-verbal language. The existing Rule is about the spoken language and reads:

Rule 51 (1) "The director, his deputy, and the majority of the other personnel of the institution shall be able to speak the language of the greatest number of prisoners, or a language understood by the largest number of them.

(2) Whenever necessary, the services of an interpreter shall be used."

Speaking language may be very nice, but the emitting (non-verbal) language may be bad. The tune of voice, the eye-contact, the body language, the propinquity etc., will decide the nature of the transaction. Every time, the staff communicate—the inmates communicate. Remember that many of the inmates are intuitive or perceptive which means that they are able to read and appreciate the non-verbal signals of the staff. The staff too must understand the non-verbal cues of the inmates. When people are happy, they smile—when they are sad, they frown. This is common among the people. In the Centre, many are sad and how do they behave? Experts on gestures say that the non-verbal language differs from culture to culture. The 'OK' gesture (The Ring), the Thumb-up Gesture, the V sign etc., have different meanings in different culture. Cultural misinterpretation of gestures may result in embarrassing situations and a person's cultural background should be taken into account before arriving at any conclusions about his or her body language or gestures. This being so the revised text will be—

Rule 51 (1) "All, if possible or as far as it is possible, employed in a Centre shall be able to communicate *via* verbal and non-verbal language to each other in a way understood by the greatest number of inmates housed there.

(2) The verbal and non-verbal language shall be for the development of the inmate's personality in an upright way in the right direction.

(3) Whenever, necessary, the services of an interpreter who knows the verbal and non-verbal language shall be used."

The director, deputy director or the staff under them in a Centre have status, power or prestige among the inmates. They are educated and, more often than not, more educated than many of the inmates. They have expectations as to how should each and every inmate must behave or communicate to them non-verbally. If the inmates do not behave the way these officials expect them to behave, it is likely that they interpret/misinterpret the behaviour of the inmates as undesirable. The officials ought to understand that the inmates behave not in the way they are told but in the way they understand. This is the reason why it is argued that every official must be a behavioural scientist who understands the inmates very well. Certainly, the officials, if they speak the same language and are from the same culture, will prove to be better than those who speak a different language and are from a different culture.

I am of the view that the present Rule 52 which reads: (1) "In institutions which are large enough to require the services of one or more full time medical officers, at least one of them shall reside on the premises of the institution or in its immediate vicinity, (2) In other institutions the medical officer shall visit daily and shall reside near enough to be able to attend without delay in case of urgency"—should be made applicable to all specialists like psychologists, psychiatrists, psychiatric social workers, welfare officers, criminologists and so on. If the development of the personality of the inmates in an upright way in the right direction is what is intended by incarceration, then the stay of all specialists in the premises or in its vicinity will be very fine. Hence, the revised text may be—

Rule 52 (1) "In Centres which utilize the services of the specialists for the development of the inmates' personality in an upright way in the right direction, all of them, as far as possible, shall reside on the premises of the Centre or in its immediate vicinity. The medical officer shall necessarily reside on the premises of the Centre or in its immediate vicinity.

(2) In Centres where specialists are not appointed, then the services of the specialists working in other Centres shall be made readily available. They shall visit the inmates daily to ensure their services at any time as they need them.

(3) In cases of emergency or immediate medical attention, arrangements shall be made with the civil hospital or any other private/specialist-hospital to attend the inmates as and when necessary and particularly when the medical officer of the Centre cannot offer his services as the situation demands."

MEN AND WOMEN IN THE SAME CENTRE

Sex is a very powerful energy and among the drives, sex occupies an important position. All men and women, doubtlessly, incarcerated suffer from sex starvation. Most of them suppress or repress their sex-urge and a few of them may sublimate it for the development of their personality in an upright way in the right direction or for some other nobler motives. In the society outside the Centre, the sex energy is manifested in a legitimate way or there may be the facilities to do so. Nevertheless, one may notice a lot of sex aberrations in the forms of masturbation (onanism, ipsation), incest, transvestitism, flagellation, homosexuality, (inversion and pervation) lesbianism, tribady, metatrophism, bisexuality, pederasty and sodomy, cunnilingus and fellaire, voyeurism (Scoptophilia), Exhibitiionism, frotteurs, infantilism, pedophilia, rape, fetishism, sathyriasis, nymphomania, sexual incendiarism, koprolangia and urolangia, bestiality and zoophila, necrophilia and thus goes a litany of sex disorder problems. The inmates in a Centre are not free from such sexual psychopathy so much so that the sex-life of the inmates is always a problem for the administration. Homosexuality and lesbianism are seen among the inmates and their frustrations/conflicts create a lot of adjustment problems. In my view, it is not desirable to have a Centre which accommodates male and female inmates in two apartments, however watertight they may be. The sex energy flies and the entire atmosphere will be contaminated by sex-smell. No, I do not recommend such a set-up in incarceration. Why to pour oil into a burning fire? Still, there may be special situations where men and women have to be housed in the same institution. Hence, Rule 53 reads:

Rule 53 (1) "In an institution for both men and women, the part of the institution set aside for women shall be under the authority of a responsible woman officer who shall have the custody of the keys of all that parts of the institution.

(2) No male member of the staff shall enter the part of the institution set aside for women without accompaning a woman officer.

(3) Women prisoners shall be attended and supervised

only by women officers. This does not, however, preclude male members of the staff, particularly doctors and teachers, from carrying out their professional duties in institutions or part of the institutions set aside for women."

Women inmates just like the male residents in a Centre are helpless and live under the mercy and consideration of the officials. Both of them will be susceptible to many temptations and the temptation a women may have may be sexual as well. Some of the women in the Centre may be convicted for sex work and precisely, therefore, they can be misused, abused or exploited by the male officials. Lesbianism is reported from the Centres where women are housed. Instances are reported that unscrupulous women officers connive with the sexual desires of their male associates. Whatever that be, a responsible woman officer who is in charge of the women's wing in a Centre should have sex values which are of unquestionable nature. Hence, the revised version shall be:

53 (1) "In an institution for both men and women, the part of the institution set aside for women shall be under the authority of a responsible woman officer having unblemished sex-values and she alone shall have the custody of the keys of all that parts of the institution.

(2) No male member of the staff shall enter the part of the institution set aside for women unless an entry is made in a register kept for the purpose and accompanied by two women officers of character and sexual integrity.

(3) Women inmates shall be attended and supervised only by women officers of proved sexual uprightness. This does not, however, preclude male members of the staff, particularly the specialists from carrying out their professional duties in a transparent way in Centres or parts of the Centres set aside for women.

(4) Guidelines laid under Rule 53 (1, 2 & 3) are strictly and meticulously applicable in the part of the institution set aside, *mutatis mutandis* for men and shall be strictly adhered to by substituting male for female and men for women in the above guidelines.

(5) As far as possible constructing the institutions

> exclusively meant for men geographically away from the institutions housing women shall be encouraged."

Why do I insist two women officials to accompany a male member of the staff? It is only for giving a trust for other female inmates. 1 + 1 (male and female) will create suspicion in some of the sexually starved women in the Centre. Let everything be transparent and beyond suspicion. Justice must be done-no-it should appear to others to be just. Transparency is very much desired and that is the reason why I insist transparency even when specialists perform their duties in a Centre. Let them be accountable for what they do.

A male in a female Centre or a female in a male Centre—both are attractions for the inmates. They have magnetic powers to attract the inmates who are sexually starved. There is no difference between man and woman in sexual matters and precisely, therefore, every precaution taken in a Centre for women shall be taken in a Centre for men as well.

OFFICIALS AND USE OF FORCE

Any prison is not a pleasant place to stay. They live under restrictions and controls which they do not like. They have anger, but cannot express it. They repress it and an energy created will be converted and not destroyed. Quarrels in prisons are reported; prison riots are seen; and escape from the jails do occur in many parts. People who go on a *ticket to leave system* do not return. The custodial staff in any Centre are responsible for the safe custody of the inmates. An escape of an inmate means definite suspension from service for the custodial staff. Allegations are sometimes heard that the inmates are tortured by the custodial staff or the inmates are tortured by other fellow inmates under the instigation of the staff in the Centre. Though the community is small in number, maintenance of discipline is indeed very difficult. If one goes through the punishment records (not official), he can see that many inmates are punished for quarrelling among themselves. Corporal punishments have been, officially speaking, done away with. Nevertheless, video-clippings are sometimes telecasted by the visual media and reports are published by the print media. What is more? The ex-inmates of many Centres speak loudly about the employment of corporal punishments in the prisons. Of course, Rule 54 says:

Rule 54(1) "Officers of the institutions shall not, in their relations with the prisoners, use force except in self-defence or in cases of attempted escape, or active or passive physical resistance to an order based on law or regulations. Officers who have recourse to force must use no more than is strictly necessary and must report the incident immediately to the director of the institution.

(2) Prison officers shall be given special training to enable them to restrain aggressive prisoners.

(3) Except in special circumstances, staff performing duties which bring them into direct contact with prisoners should not be armed. Furthermore, staff should in no circumstances be provided with arms unless they have been trained in their use."

Any prison is a heated oven as the inmates are chained in a way in many ways. Life in the prisons becomes meaningless for many of them—boring and monotonous—leading to nowhere! The anger can be expressed to self (and sometimes, reports of suicides appear in media), to the property belonging to the institution (major and minor punishments are awarded in such cases), to the fellow inmates (quarrels and even murders are reported), to the staff of the Centre. Some want to escape, a few do escape and all have always the thoughts of escape. Hence, the revised text shall be:

Rule 54 (1) "No official member in a Centre shall use physical force against an inmate/group of inmates except in self-defence or the defence of a fellow associate/fellow inmate or in cases of attempted escape or active or passive physical resistance to a reasonable order based on law or regulations.

(2) No official member in a Centre shall instigate or provoke, encourage or in any way cause a fellow inmate to use physical force against another inmate/group of inmates except in the circumstances enumerated under 54(1) above.

(3) Any official or at his need and request any fellow inmate who has recourse to force shall use it no more than is strictly necessary—a little more or a little less- and shall report the incident immediately to the authorities concerned."

Self-defence means not only the private defence of the official concerned but also of all who are around him. In case of need or necessity, an official can make use of the help of the fellow inmates. But in all such cases, use only the minimum force needed for the purpose.

When the authority to use physical force is exercised, it may be remembered that the authority extends even to the causing of death of the inmate. Hence, the amended text shall be—

Rule 54 (4) "When the authority to use physical force is exercised, the official or under his request any fellow inmate/ inmates may voluntarily cause the death of the inmate/inmates if his/their act which occasions the exercise of the authority be of any of the descriptions hereinafter enumerated, viz.—

First, Such an act as may reasonably cause the apprehension that death will be otherwise be the consequence of the act.

Secondly, such an act as may reasonably cause the apprehension that a serious injury will otherwise be the consequence of the act.

If the act be not of any of the descriptions stated above, the authority to use physical force does not extend to the voluntary causing of death to the inmate/inmates, but does extend to the voluntary causing to the inmate/ inmates of any harm other than death.

The authority to use the physical force commences as soon as a reasonable apprehension of danger to the body of the official/at his request, of the fellow inmate/inmate arises from an attempt or threat to commit the act though the act may not have been committed and it continues as long as such apprehension of danger to the body continues.

If in the exercise of the authority to employ

physical force against an inmate/inmates which reasonably causes the apprehension of death, the inmate/s be so situated that the official/at his request the fellow inmate/s cannot effectively exercise that authority without the risk of harm to an innocent person, his right of private defence extends the running of that risk."

Why do I say so?

The reasons are many and one of the reasons is that there have been situations when the official at his request, the fellow inmates have resorted to the killing of the residents in some Centres. In such situations, sometimes, innocent people too are killed. There, the officials/at their request, the fellow inmates do not have any option but to cause firing or to act in such a way that death or grievous hurt is caused. There, the authority must enjoy legal immunity for the act/s it does.

Presently, prisons in many countries give special training for the custodial staff in the use of weapons. At a time, terrorists and insurgents are housed in prisons, there is the immediate necessity to give training to the custodial staff in musketry as well. Hence, the revised text:

Rule 54 (5) "The custodial staff in a Centre shall be given special training in the use of weapons and musketry during their induction course and thereafter periodically as and when necessary. This shall be in addition to their physical training as well as training in unarmed combat and mob operation tactics.

(6) Except in situations which necessitate arms or ammunitions, the staff performing duties which bring them into direct contact with the inmates shall not be armed. No member of the staff shall, under any circumstances, use arms or ammunitions unless he is trained in their use."

The Centre of Personality Development is visited by many official authorities. They may include the Human Rights Commission, the Women's Commission, the Cabinet Sub-Committee, the members of the judiciary and so on. Nevertheless, the Centres must be inspected by qualified and experienced officials whose duty will be to ensure that the Centres are administered in accordance to the laws and regulations and with a view to see that the objectives of incarceration, fully or as far as possible, are materialized. Hence, the present Rule 55—i.e., "There shall be a regular inspection of penal institutions and services by qualified and experienced inspectors appointed by a competent authority. Their task should be in particular to ensure that these institutions are administered in accordance with existing laws and regulations and with a view to bringing about the objectives of penal and correctional tretment"—shall be revised—

Rule 55 "Over and above the inspections done by the official authorities, statutory or otherwise, there shall be regular inspections conducted by qualified and experienced officials appointed by a competent authority. Their task shall be to ensure that these Centres are administered in accordance with the existing laws and regulations and with a view to bring out about the objectives of incarceration, namely development of the personality of the inmates in an upright way in the right direction."

6

Rules Applicable to Special Categories

Part II of the existing Standard Minimum Rules for the Treatment of Prisoners-1957 is all about the rules applicable to special categories of inmates. Part II has 5 sections and they are—

1. **Section A:** Prisoners under sentence containing Rules 56 to 81—altogether 25 Rules. The guiding principle in the section contains 11 Rules followed by classification and individualization having 3 Rules. Privileges has only 1 Rule and work has 6 Rules, Education and Recreation has 2 Rules and Social Relations and After-care has 2 Rules.
2. **Section B:** Insane and mentally abnormal Prisoners has only 2 Rules
3. **Section C:** Prisoners Under Arrest or Awaiting Trial has 7 Rules
4. **Section D:** Civil Prisoners has only 1 Rule
5. **Section E:** Persons Arrested or Detained without charge has only 1 Rule.

To reiterate what has been stated elsewhere, the part II of the present Standard Minimum Rules for the Treatment of Prisoners, 1957 contains "rules applicable only to the special categories dealt with in each section. Nevertheless, the rules under section A, applicable to prisoners under sentence shall be equally applicable to categories of prisoners dealt with in sections B, C and D provided they do not conflict with the rules governing those categories and are for their benefit". Keeping this in mind, I may analyse the Rules 56 to 95 in the SMR for the Treatment of Prisoners, 1957.

Rule 56 under the **Guiding Principles** reads: "The guiding principles hereafter are intended to show the spirit in which penal institutions should be administrated and the purposes at which they should aim, in accordance with the declaration made under preliminary observation I of the present text."

This is not a Rule as it is only a statement. Hence, I wish to delete it from the text.

What about the Rule 57 of the existing text? It is about punishment and the philosophy behind it. This may be put under the Rule telling about punishment, i.e. Rules 27 to 34 (both inclusive) and the rule may be put under the Rule 32 of the present text. Hence, Rule 57 in the existing text is deleted. Again Rules 58 and 59 of the existing text are deleted as the objectives or purposes and justifications of a sentence of imprisonment are well spelt out throughout the text. About the remedial, educational, moral, spiritual and other forces and forms of assistance are dealt with extensively in the Rules and therefore, Rule 59 has no scope in the revised text.

PRISON LIFE AND LIFE IN LIBERTY

Rule 60 of the Standard Minimum Rules-1957 is reproduced as under.

Rule 60 (1) "The regime of the institution should seek to minimize any differences between prison life and life at liberty which tend to lessen the responsibility of the prisoners or the respect due to their dignity as human beings.

(2) Before the completion of the sentence, it is desirable that the necessary steps be taken to ensure for the prisoner a gradual return to life in society. This aim may be achieved, depending on the case by a pre-release regime organized in the same institution or in another appropriate institution, or by release on trial under some kind of supervision which must be entrusted to the police but should be combined with effective social aid."

Though researchers and prison authorities (authorities of the Centre) accept the fact that the development of the intimates' personality in an upright way in the right direction is the prime aim of imprisonment, this conceptual or theoretical acceptance does not often reflect in the practical life. In practice, the life in the prison is punitive or made punitive by various attitudes and approaches of the institutional staff who have an upper hand over the intimates. As such, the prison justice in theory, more often than not, is not seen in prison justice in practice. Hence, there is a lot of difference between the life in prison and the life in a free society. It may be accepted in fairness that the difference between the life in prison and the same in society should be or ought to be that the former life is a life in confinement while the latter is that it is a life in freedom. Hence, the revised Rule should be—

Rule 60 (1) "Every step shall be initiated and the meaningfully implemented in the Centre so that there should be, as far as possible, only minimum difference between the life in the Centre and the same outside which tend to lessen the responsibility of the inmates or the respect due to their dignity as human beings."

The very purpose of imprisonment is or should be the return of the inmate with a personality formed in an upright way in the right direction. Hence, the revised Rule 60 (2) will be—

Rule 60 (2) "From the moment of an inmate's entry in to the Centre and throughout his life in the Centre, especially before the completion of the sentence, necessary steps and strategies be taken to ensure for the inmate's return to life in a free society as a person developed in his personality in an upright way in the right direction. In order to achieve this, the Centre shall—

(a) Organize periodical courses and particularly a pre-release course to make the inmate understand the philosophy behind.
(b) Allow the inmate to stay in a half way home established under the Centre's administrative authority or the authority of an NGO approved by the Centre.
(c) Grant parole under the supervision of Parole Officers."

Researches show that parole granted at the appropriate time to the inmates is always better than their continued stay in confinement.

COMMUNITY AGENCIES AND THE CENTRE

There are any number of community agencies interested in the inmates. Some of them are religiously committed or otherwise devoted. In my opinion, they must be promoted and their association ensured. Rule 61 of the existing Standard Minimum Rules, 1957 says—

Rule 61: "The treatment of prisoners should emphasize not their exclusion from the community but their continuing part in it. Community agencies should, therefore, be enlisted wherever possible to assist the staff of the institution in the task of social rehabilitation of the prisoners. There should be in connection with every institution social workers charged with the duty of maintaining and improving all desirable relations of a prisoner with his family and with valuable social agencies. Steps should be taken to safeguard, to the maximum extent compatible with the law and the sentence, the right relating to civil interests, social security rights and other social benefits of prisoners."

Most of the inmates inside a Centre may have his one leg in the free society and the other in the institution of confinement. I have seen it not only in films and TV serials but also in real life in front of the Centres. The queue of the family members, kith and kin, friends, near and dear ones of the incarcerated in or around a Centre in India (Similarly in other countries too) is incredible. It shows that an inmate may not be alone in a Centre. He lives amidst many near and dear ones even when he is isolated to live in confinement. I am of the view that every inmate should have sufficient facility to interact with his dear and near ones if his contacts are not injurious to himself, to the institution, to the family, to the community, to the society or to the nation. Hence, social service agencies and NGOs may be welcomed and encouraged to interact with the authorities of the Centre as well as with the inmates, if possible. In my view, Rule 61 should be revised as under:

Rule 61 (a) "Every inmate shall be encouraged to have loving and caring relations with his family, kith and kin, friends and decent members of the public provided his relationship is for the mutual benefits of the inmate and the contact-party outside as well as not harmful to the Centre and its functionings.

(b) The Centre shall maintain a list of community agencies, social workers, NGOs etc. so that their services can be effectively made use of for the development of the personality of the inmates in an upright way in the right direction and for the correction, rehabilitation, reformation, resocialisation and reintegration of the inmates to the society back.

(c) All steps and strategies shall be initiated and implemented to the maximum extent, compatible with the law and the sentence, the rights relating to civil interest, social security rights and other social benefits of the inmates."

Rule 62, that is, "The medical services of the institution shall seek to detect and shall treat any physical or mental illness or defects which may hamper a prisoner's rehabilitation. All necessary medical, surgical and psychiatric services shall be provided to that end"—has been extensively dealt with in the revised text elsewhere. Hence, I wish to delete Rule 62 from the revised text.

INDIVIDUALIZATION, SECURITY AND SIZE OF THE CENTRES

About classification and individualization, there exists a separate section in the present Standard Minimum Rules, 1957. Over and above, Rule 63 of the text says:

Rule 63(1) "The fulfilment of these principles requires individualization of treatment and for this purpose, a flexible system of classifying prisoners in groups; it is therefore, desirable that such groups should be distributed in separate institution suitable for the treatment of each group."

There are long termers and short termers. The treatment that is offered to short termers must be short and long termers ought to be long. The courts punishing a culprit may not be concerned with long-term or short-term treatments of the inmates. My observations show that some of the short termers need long term treatment. What to do and how to go about? I have seen jail birds who come to prisons, stay there and go out with no treatments whatever. I have also seen lifers who need no more treatment. What to do with them? The courts are not concerned with such aspects. Prisons are presently overcrowded. A prison which can accommodate only 1000 inmates may be forced to accommodate 1500 or 1600 or 1800 people. What type of individualization and classification may be possible in such situations? The courts convict and send culprits to prisons and the prisons have to accommodate them. Some of the prisons—most of them or all of them—are understaffed. There may be only a few correctional staff and what to do then? Rule 63 (1) may be revised—

Rule 63 (1) "For developing the personality of an inmate in an upright way in the right direction, individualization of the inmates (for the purpose of fulfilling the objectives) shall be inevitable, classification of the inmates will be necessary, accommodation in separate *cameratae* suitable for achieving the aims will be needed. It shall be the duty of the Centre to implement the programmes in a meaningful way for correction, reformation, resocialization, rehabilitation and reintegration of the inmate to society back."

What does the Rule 63 (2) in the existing Standard Minimum Rules, 1957 say? The Rule 63(2) reads:

Rule 63(2) "These institutions need not provide the same degree of security for every group. It is desirable to provide varying degrees of security according to the need of different groups. Open institutions by the very fact that they provide no physical security against escape but rely on the self-discipline of the inmates, provide the conditions most favourable to rehabilitation for carefully selected prisoners."

Today in various parts of the world, one observes "Maximum Security Institutions, Medium Security Institutions and Minimum Security Institutions". Maximum Security Institutions are for housing the terrorists, insurgents, fanatics, fundamentalists, extremists and so on and the purpose is to keep them under tight confinement with maximum physical security so that their escape from the prisons becomes impossible. Medium Security Institutions have security– physical and otherwise—in a lesser way. The inmates seldom escape the prison custody. One sees transparency in such a set up and a trust on man's good behaviour. The Minimum Security Institutions are open prisons which provide no physical security against escape. Such open institutions work on the mutual trust of the Centres' authority and the inmates who claim to have achieved self-discipline and near-total personality development. Hence, Rule 63 (2) may be revised to:

Rule 63 (2) "The inmates, after examining them by a team consisting of a medical doctor, psychologist, psychiatrist, psychiatric social worker, welfare officer, trade instructor and so on shall be classified and accommodated in a Centre taking in to account the security needs and the inmate's need for personality development. The Centres may be "Maximum, Medium, or Minimum Security" institutions in which the last (open institutions) one which relies on the self-discipline and development of the inmate's personality is found to be most favourable to the correction, reformation, resocialisation, rehabilitation and reintegration of the inmate to society back."

The Maximum Security and the Medium Security (the former are closed while the latter are transparent) institutions in some countries are very large institutions which accommodate large number of convicts. There are prisons, I am told, which accommodate 10000 or more people. Incredible! But real!

Rule 63 (3) reads: "It is desirable that the number of prisoners in closed institutions should not be so large that the individualization of treatment is hindered. It is considered that the population of such institutions should not exceed five hundred. In open institutions the population should be as small as possible."

Prisons are classified in some countries into 5 categories, i.e.

Category I which accommodates 1000 inmates.
Category II accommodates inmates between 500-1000
Category III accommodates inmates between 300-500
Category IV accommodates inmates between 100-300
Category V accommodates inmates below 100

I do not know the criteria or scale for such a classification. I am not in favour of it and the revised Rule 63 (3), according to me, will be—

Rule 63(3) "A Centre in whatever category it belongs shall be a fit institution for the development of the inmate's personality in an upright way in the right direction. For it, it shall be neither very large nor very small. Five hundred inmates in an institution is ideal for a Centre of Personality Development."

Rule 63 (4) is an extension of Rule 63 (3) and it reads:

Rule 63(4) "On the other hand, it is undesirable to maintain prisons which are so small that proper facilities cannot be provided".

In my view, it is not only undesirable but also or rather is purposeless to have small Centres to effect personality changes in inmates. Hence, the amended or revised text will be—

Rule 63 (4) "It is purposeless to maintain small institutions which cannot provide proper facilities to the inmates for their personality development."

SOCIETY AND REINTEGRATION TO SOCIETY

Centres of Personality Development are very much a part of the society like hospitals, educational institutions, religious temples, churches, mosques, etc. The society has a responsibility to maintain such institutions and to provide facilities for the people to develop their personality in an upright way in the right direction. The jails and the inmates in the Centres are no exception to this principle. Rule 64 of the Standard Minimum Rules, 1957 tells—

> "The duty of society does not end with a prisoner's release. There should, therefore, be governmental or private agencies capable of lending the released prisoner efficient after-care directed towards the lessening of prejudice against him and towards his social rehabilitation."

The revised text shall be–

Rule 64 (1) "Every assistance shall be ensured to NGOs and other governmental agencies to provide meaningful and effective after-care services to released inmates for their reintegration to a life in a free society and to live there in dignity.

(2) Every step shall be initiated and implemented for educating the society about its role in the rehabilitation and reintegration of a released inmate to society back."

The education here means formal, informal and non-formal. Schools and the institutions of learning, religious platforms, media including the visual, cultural, print etc. must be made use of to transform the people to accept a released inmate as a person in dignity. For this, every prejudice formed against the ex-inmates of the Centres of Personality Development ought to be eradicated.

Rule 65 of the existing Standard Minimum Rules-1957 says:

> "The treatment of persons sentenced to imprisonment or a similar measure shall have as its purpose, so far as the length of the sentence permits, to establish in them the will to lead law abiding and self supporting lives after their release and to fit them to do so. The treatment shall be such as will encourage their self-respect and develop their sense of responsibility."

I am not in favour of retaining the Rule 65. Once, the development of personality in an upright way in the right direction is accepted as the main objective of imprisonment, there is no meaning in saying a 'derivative of such an aim'. "A will lead a law abiding and self-supporting life after the release and to fit one to do so" is just a logical consequence of the Personality Development. Proper Development of the inmates' personality will ensure—

(1) values in life,
(2) development of a social, ethical and legal conscience,
(3) life in dignity,
(4) sharing of responsibilities and performing of duties, and
(5) self-respect and what not? Hence, the Rule 65 of the present text is deleted in the revised text as it is no more necessary or needed.

METHODS AND STRATEGIES FOR DEVELOPMENT OF PERSONALITY

Superego Formators—Value Creation Agencies, Conscience Makers and so on are seen in any texts on Personality Development. They work from the early infancy of a new born child. Home, religion, school, community, media, family members, neighbourhood of a child etc. individually and jointly work for the development of child's personality. In the case of an inmate in a Centre of Personality Development, there is the need for "Personality Formators" and precisely, therefore, Rule 66 of the present Standard Minimum Rules-1957 reads:

Rule 66 (1) "To these ends, all appropriate means shall be used, including religious care in the countries where this is possible, education, vocational guidance and training, social casework, employment counselling, physical development and strengthening of moral character in accordance with the individual needs of each prisoner, taking into account of his social and criminal history, his physical and mental capacities and aptitudes, his personal temperament, the length of his sentence, and his prospectus after release."

Rule 66 (2) says further: "For every prisoner with a sentence of suitable length, the director shall receive, as soon as possible after his admission, full reports on all the matters referred to in the foregoing paragraph. Such reports shall always include a report by a medical officer, wherever possible qualified in psychiatry, on the physical and mental condition of the prisoner."

Rule 66 (3) adds again: "The reports and other documents shall be placed in an individual file. This file shall be kept up-to-date and classified in such a way that it can be consulted by the responsible personnel whenever the need arises."

While I appreciate very much the contents of the Rule 66(1), I have the following amendments to make. By the time a convict comes to the Centre, he will be 18 years of age or more. By the time he comes to the Centre, the foundation of his personality is already laid up as the basic values are formed by the time a child reaches around 14 years of age. This is what the psychologists say and precisely, therefore, a total personality change is not possible. At the same time, behavioural modification is quite possible. There may take place some changes in the value system as well. This is the reason why it is emphatically stated that the purpose of imprisonment is and ought to be the development of the inmate's personality in an upright way in the right direction. Hence, the following changes may be necessary in Rule 66 (1) of the existing text.

Rule 66(1) "For the development of the inmate's personality in an upright way in the right direction, all appropriate means, methods and strategies shall be used including religious instructions and care in countries where this is possible and if it is not possible, then moral instructions and care should invariably be given. Academic education, vocational training and guidance, individual centred clinical method and group relations method of treatment, social case work, employment counselling, intellectual development by reading, education, library use, listening to lectures and exposure to media, physical development and strengthening of moral character, effective use of leisure time activities, works in industries or otherwise in accordance with the individual needs of each inmate taking account of his family, school, social and crime history, his physical and psychological capacities and aptitudes, his personal temperament, the length of his sentence and his prospectus after release. To these end, appropriate tools should be developed and experts ought to be appointed.

(2) For every inmate with a sentence of suitable length, the director shall receive, as soon as possible after his admission full reports on all the matters referred to in the foregoing paragraph. Such report shall always include an assessment or evaluation report by a medical officer, psychologist, psychiatrist, psychiatric social worker, welfare officer, the trade instructor and the teacher on the physical, mental, intellectual and emotional conditions of the inmate.

(3) The reports and other relevant documents shall be placed in individual and in computer files. It shall be kept up-to-date and classified in such a way that it can be consulted by the concerned and responsible personnel whenever the need arises."

CLASSIFICATION AND INDIVIDUALIZATION

The *camerata* system of accommodation, discussed elsewhere in this book, may be the best way of accommodating the inmates after their classification. In some countries, the inmates are classified on the basis of age, sex, mental health, nature of offence, frequency of the commission of crimes etc. The Standard Minimum Rules, 1957 are intended for adult prisons and of course, provisions are there for the male and female convicts. Under Rule 67 it is written: "The purpose of classification shall be:

(a) To separate from others those prisoners who, by reason of their criminal records or bad characters are likely to exercise a bad influence.

(b) To divide the prisoners into classes in order to facilitate their treatment with a view to their social rehabilitation."

Classification of prisoners—it is easier said than done. In certain countries, the inmates are classified as habituals and casuals. But how? The casual inmates are further subdivided into Star and General Classes. But how? The habitual inmates are further subdivided into professional and non-professional. But how? How are they described or defined?

(1) A *casual prisoner* is one who is a first offender and who lapses into crime not because he has a criminal mentality but on account of his surroundings, physical disability and mental deficiency, etc. Are there any scientific criteria to decide all those factors like physical surroundings, mental deficiency, etc.? Will there be sufficient time to apply the scale on short-term prisoners? Will there be enough space for accommodating the inmates who commit various categories of crimes? Questions are many, but answers are nil.

(2) A 'Star' category inmate is a casual prisoner whose previous character is good, whose antecedents are not criminal and whose crimes do not indicate grave cruelty, gross moral turpitude or depravity of mind. Again how to decide all those parameters within a short time by the prison administration—and particularly in the cases of short-term inmates? Does the administration have sufficient field staff to do the strenuous tasks? The classification of inmates is "nice to hear" but difficult (very difficult) to implement in practical situations.

(3) '*Casual prisoners*' who are not put under the Star Category are enlisted under the 'general sub-category'.

(4) Who are the *non-professional habitual* prisoners? They are those who lapse into crimes owing to their surroundings or some physical or mental defects and who are not first offenders.

(5) Those who are not put under the '*Non-professional habitual*' category are enlisted in the category of '*other habitual criminals*'. For example, those who are men with an object, sound in mind and mostly sound in body, often highly skilled, who deliberately and with their eyes open prefer a life of crime and know the tricks and manoeures necessary for that life.

Classification of Crimes on the Basis of Frequency of Committing Crimes

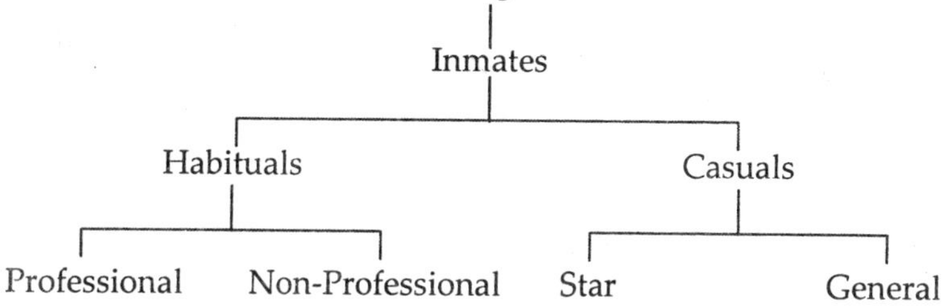

I have discussed the above classification process with some prison officials in India and most of them said that the classification could be done in an *adhoc* manner or in an arbitrary way. Who has the time to do it? Who has the skill to do it? Hence, the classification is seen more on paper and not in reality.

Of course, the Standard Minimum Rules-1957 say about *classification and individualization* under Rule 67. How many countries do it scientifically? How many countries have the necessary personnel and skill to do it scientifically? In my view, the very purpose of *classification and individualization* given under Rule 67 must be changed to read:

Rule 67: 'The purpose of classification shall be—

(a) to develop the personality of the inmate in an upright way in the right direction; and
(b) To correct, reform, resocialize, rehabilitate and reintegrate the inmate back to society."

In order to decide the ways in which an inmate must develop his personality, the prison administration ought to develop many tests and specialists must work on development of such tests, their administration, evaluation and implementation. It calls for investment and such investment ought to be an investment on human resources. On the basis of the classification made by the experts, the inmates may be housed separately and the *camerata* model suggested by me elsewhere can be effectively and meaningfully made use of. Therefore, I suggest a revision of the existing Rule 68 which reads:

"So far as possible separate institutions shall be used for the treatment of the different classes of prisoners"—may be revised to:

Rule 68: "Separate *cameratae* of the Centre shall be used for accommodating different categories of inmates after classification for the development of their personality in an upright way in the right direction."

At present, the problem is that the sentencing judge does have little or no information academically and otherwise about the various methods and strategies employed by the Centre for the development of the personality of the inmates after careful classification. The judge adjudicates every case in a manner, as per law, without giving little or least importance for the personality development of the inmates or their classification. This is one of the reasons for the failure of initiating and implementing effective methods/strategies for the development of the inmates' personality in an upright way. Hence, the authorities of the Centre face severe problems for a meaningful classification. Yet, Rule 69 of the Standard Minimum Rules, 1957 says:

Rule 69: "As soon as possible after admission and after a study of the personality of each prisoner with a sentence of suitable length, a programme of treatment shall be prepared for him in the light of the knowledge obtained after his individual needs, his capacities and dispositions."

I propose that the same Rule 69 may be retained in the revised text with the following changes, that is—

Rule 69: "As soon as possible— that is, in any case within 72 hours—after admission and after a thorough study of the personality, aptitude, attitude, values, etc. of each inmate with a sentence of suitable and sufficient length, a detailed programme for the development of an inmate's personality in an upright way in the right direction shall be prepared for him by a team of

> experts consisting of a psychologist, psychiatric social worker, welfare officer, trade instructor, medical officer and so on in the light of the data, information and knowledge gathered or obtained about his individual needs, his capacities and dispositions."

In other words, every strategy is individual based or tailor cut for each inmate.

PRIVILEGES

What are the privileges of an inmate in a Centre? Many, especially the short termers are not informed of them. If at all they are told about them, it is of no use to the short termers as the period of their stay in the Centre will be almost nearing completion then. In my view, education, recreation, social relations and many such facilities are in every sense privileges to an inmate at present. The privileges are enjoyed sometimes by the inmates on the mercy of the prison staff. In a Centre, there may be very *irksome* jobs and some inmates may be forced to do them for no valid reasons at all. An assignment to a work may be treated as a privilege and in some countries there exists convict official system. The convict official system is a privilege as the inmates enjoy a lot of benefits. Thus the privileges may be formal or informal. What have been said above are put under informal privileges. Even in the Centres, there are powerful and influential inmates who demand privileges from the prison staff. I am told that in some democratic countries the inmates having political affiliation with the ruling Government demand many informal privileges from the Centre. They may include good food, better accommodation, pleasant works in the work-shop etc. If they are denied of such privileges, then the officials in the Centre have to suffer many evil consequences. The rich and the affluent inmate who has political affiliation to the ruling Government, or to a powerful politician gets the services of other fellow inmates for preparation of special food for him, for washing of his clothes etc. Why think in a rigid way? The powerful and influential inmate may get special ticket to leave. In one case, I have noticed that an inmate has stayed more days outside the Centre than inside on the strength of the special orders issued by the Government in power. It is not an isolated case. Many inmates enjoy such privileges in an informal way and there is justification for many things—legal or illegal.

Researches show that even the privileges can be purchased and corruption rules even the granting of privileges in some countries. The Standard Minimum Rules-1957 tells about formal privileges and Rule 70 is about it. It reads:

Rule 70: "Systems of privileges appropriate for the different classes of prisoners and the different methods of treatment shall be established at every institution, in order to encourage good conduct, develop a sense of responsibility and secure the interest and co-operation of the prisoners in their treatment." Fine. The questions are—

(1) Who knows the systems of privileges appropriate for the different classes of prisoners?
(2) Who tells the new entrants about the system of privileges?
(3) What are the different methods of treatment?

In some countries, many of the inmates are illiterate or semi-literate. They do not know to read or write. For example, REMISSION is a privilege and there are many ways to earn remission marks. Who knows about them? Or, who tells the inmates about them? Many officials who work in a Centre may be unaware of the remission-rules and what good may be expected from such ignorant officials in uniform? Hence, the revised text will be—

Rule 70 (1) "The system of privileges appropriate for different classes of inmates and the different methods of treatment shall be established at every institution. They shall be told to every inmate at the time of admission.

(2) The systems of privileges and the different methods of treatment shall be exhibited in a conspicuous way in the Centre so that the inmates may know about them.

(3) No informal privileges shall be granted to any inmate under any circumstances. If a privilege is granted on special reasons, the grounds should be specified and it is an exception and not a general rule.

(4) The sole purpose of the system of privileges and different methods of treatment shall be to encourage good conduct, develop a sense of responsibility, secure

the interest and willing co-operation of the inmates in their personality development in an upright way in the right direction, have a feeling of living in dignity both inside the Centre and afterwards in a free society on release.

(5) An illiterate/semi-literate inmate or an inmate who does not know the language of the inmates in a Centre should be informed of the privileges orally by the authorities of the Centre themselves or by using an interpreter or a translator."

In some of the Centres, the inmates form informal groups on the basis of their political affiliation or otherwise and establish unholy nexus with officials who have similar interests. They exploit the relationship and enjoy many privileges informally. This should be discouraged or eliminated.

WORK IN THE CENTRE: A SHORT HISTORY AND NATURE

"Imprisonment of either description" in any Penal Code means "either simple imprisonment or rigorous imprisonment". Rigorous imprisonment means that the inmate should work and simple imprisonment means that he needs not work. "Live without works"—whose idea it is to allow a person convicted for having committed an offence to live without working is not clear, but it has been there for centuries. The makers of such a law never knew the human psychology that man would prefer to work than to remain idle. Look at the Pennsylvania Prison system (introduced in 1790) in America. Prisoners were segregated and lived in isolated cells without any work. Evidence in hand showed that a good number of inmates died prematurely owing to cruelly unbearable monotony and idle living without any work. In order to avoid it they introduced labour and work. The inmates were allowed to work in isolated cells and never in congregate shops. How unfortunate was it that the prison planners did not know the A, B, C of inmates' psychology and behavioural dynamics. What happened at Auburn Prison System (1818-19) in U.S.A.? There, the inmates were allowed to work in shops—but in absolute silence. To begin with, the inmates were not allowed to work and experience taught them that the solitary life resulted in many becoming mental patients and some of them committed suicide.

In 1823, a new system was adopted and it was known as Auburn System. The system permitted congregate work in shops during day time. Nevertheless, they had to maintain absolute silence. Those corrigible inmates were made to work in shops in silence during day time. Those who broke the rule were flogged. The prison authorities understood that work in shops was essential for the physical and mental fitness of the inmates. In short, the inmates worked under extreme fear. No doubt, the system was inhuman and never resulted in the reformation of the inmates.

Elmira Movement in U. S. A. finally admitted that the prisons should never be dump houses for the incarcerated, but should be places of industry to train inmates for skilled work. Such an approach had many advantages including rehabilitation, engagement during day time in prisons, physical and mental fitness, better return to society, etc. All these realities were understood meaningfully only in the beginning of the twentieth century. By 1930, the prisoners were graded according to their individual needs and chances of rehabilitation.

What happened in England? By virtue of an Act in 1778, the inmates of the English prisons were put to work during day. They were detained in solitary cells during night. In 1894, Gladstone Committee recommended the abolition of unproductive work as well as work in groups in prisons. The Prison Act in England was passed in 1898. Sir Arthur Waller, the Chairman of Prison Commission for England and Wales suggested to the International Penal and Penitentiary Congress in 1925 to draw up a set of general rules for the treatment of prisoners. In 1929, the international Penal and Penitentiary Commission took up the work, but failed in their attempts owing to the differences in geographical, physical and political conditions in different countries. In 1949, the United Nations came forward and thus came out the Standard Minimum Rules for the Treatment of Prisoners in 1957.

Rule 71 of the existing Standard Minimum Rules, 1957 reads:

(1) "Prison labour must not be of an afflictive nature.

(2) All prisoners under sentence shall be required to work, subject to their physical and mental fitness as determined by the medical officer.

(3) Sufficient work of a useful nature shall be provided to keep prisoners actively employed for a normal day.

(4) So far as possible, the work provided shall be such as will maintain or increase the prisoner's ability to earn an honest living after release.
(5) Vocational training in useful trades shall be provided for prisoners able to profit thereby and especially for young prisoners.
(6) Within the limits compatible with proper vocational selection and with the requirements of institutional administration and discipline, the prisoners shall be able to choose the type of work they wish to perform."

Everyone today accepts the physical and psychological need for labour in prisons, nevertheless, the provisions of the law in some countries still lay down "imprisonment of either description" and the courts unfortunately consider the work in prisons as an additional punishment for the convicts. Many prisons in many parts of the world have works of no utility and the prisoners work in prisons as an additional punishment for them. Works for work's sake is of no use for the prisoners. Since, many of the works in prisons are of an afflictive nature even today, it must be presumed that the Rule 71(1) has no effect on the nature of the work given to prisoners in many countries. One of the major reasons for it has been that the Rule 71(1) was not positive on its structure and content. ".....must not be of an afflictive nature" ought to be redrafted to read as: "....ought to be such that correction, reformation, rehabilitation, reintegration to society back must be ensured".

Rule 71(2) says "required to work" and it is not a 'nice to hear' expression. "Shall work" is a better way to communicate the idea to the inmates. The desire to work shall come from within the inmates and the expression "shall work" creates such an attitude and approach and, therefore, the proposed revision can be:

> "All inmates shall work subject to their physical and psychological fitness determined by a team consisting of the medical officer, a psychologist, a psychiatric social worker, trade instructor and the welfare officer".

If the convicted inmates under sentence need work for their well-being in the institution, the same is equally applicable for all types of inmates. This is the reason why "All Prisoners under sentence" was amended to read: "All inmates".

Rule 71(3) speaks of "sufficient work, a useful work" without any clarity and certainly with vagueness. What is the meaning of "sufficient work?" and how to decide the "sufficiency of work?" Again of a "useful nature" brings confusion to the administration as well as to the inmates. "useful to whom?" Works which may be useful to the administration/institution may be useless-even harmful- to the inmates. As far as the 'Best Interest of the Inmate' is the sole objective of prison labour, the 'useful nature' means "useful to the inmate"—that is, useful for the correction, reformation, resocialization, rehabilitation, reintegration to the society back. In other words the work should be for the development of the inmates' personality in an upright way in the right direction. Accordingly, the revised Rule can be—

Rule 71(3) "Work for the development of the inmate's personality in an upright way in the right direction giving emphasis to the best interest of the inmates shall be provided."

Certainly, such works will keep the inmates actively employed and, therefore, the said provision is removed. No body understands the meaning of 'a normal working day' as there is or there cannot be an abnormal working day.

In some countries the works provided in the prisons have no purpose. For example, what is the meaning in teaching the inmates "mat-making, phenol preparation, washing shop production, etc."? They are taught as a "time pass or hobby" for the housewives in some countries. Multinational companies are in perpetual competition to sell their products and they spend a lot of money for advertisement. In such a market situation everyone knows that studying to make "soup, detergents, phenol" etc. will help to the least to make an honest living after the release of the inmate from the Centre. Rule 71(4) says: "So far as possible, the work provided shall be such as will maintain or increase the prisoners' ability to earn an honest living after release. The Rule is to be amended making the following changes.

(1) "So far as possible" should be erased. There is no question

of such a charity included in the amended Rule. The inmates have a human right to live after their release. Enjoyment of the human rights should not come from 'charity'.

(2) 'Honest living' should be submitted by living in dignity. Hence, the amended Rule will be Rule 71(4) "The work shall be such that the inmates should be able to live in dignity after their release."

Rule 71(5) may be amended to read: 71(5) "Vocational training in income generating trades shall be the prerogative of the inmates able to profit thereby and necessarily for young persons."

At present, the Rule 71(5) in the existing Standard Minimum Rules is—71(5): "Vocational training in useful trades shall be provided for prisoners able to profit thereby and especially for young prisoners". Some trades in some countries are attached to castes/sub-castes, etc. Precisely, therefore, the inmates belonging to other castes/sub-castes do not want to enter into a trade which they do not do traditionally for many generations. For example, the carpentry, smithy, etc., belong to such categories in India. This is the reason a trade—that is, income generating—not attached to religion, caste, sub-caste, traditions etc. is suggested in the amended Rule 71(5).

What does the Rule 71(6) say? It is as under:

Rule 71(6) "Within the limits compatible with proper vocational selection and with the requirements of institutional administration and discipline, the prisoners shall be able to choose the type of work they wish to perform."

In my considered view, the option to choose the works/trade shall be given entirely to the inmates. The administration should not have a say in such matters as the inmates alone know better how they can live a life in dignity after their release and the employment potentials/market facilities, etc. Therefore, I propose that the amended Rule shall be—

Rule 71(6) "Every inmate has a right to opt for a trade/work on admission to a Centre as well as a right for a change in the trade/work available in the Centre as he decides."

Putting everything together, the new Rule will be—

Rule 71(1) "Labour in the Centre shall be for the development of the inmates' personality in an upright way in the right direction.

(2) All inmates under sentence shall work, subject to their physical and psychological fitness determined by a team consisting of the medical officer, a psychologist, a psychiatric social worker, trade instructor and the welfare officer. All inmates who are not under sentence shall be free to opt for a work if they so desire.

(3) The work shall be for the development of the inmates' personality in an upright way in the right direction giving emphasis to the best interest of the inmates—best for the correction, reformation, resocialization, rehabilitation and reintegration to the society back after release.

(4) The work shall be such that the inmates should be able to live in dignity after their release.

(5) Vocational training in income generating trades shall be the prerogative of the inmates able to profit thereby and necessarily for young prisoners.

(6) Every inmate has a right to opt for a trade/work on admission to a Centre as well as a right for a change in the trade/work available in the Centre as he decides."

PRISON LABOUR: OBJECTIVES, WORK AND REST

What are the objectives of prison labour? The objectives of prison labour are the same as one may see of labour in the society outside. There cannot be two types of objectives for one and the same. People work for their livelihood—for living in dignity. The XIIIth International Penal and Penitentiary Congress (Hague, 1950) thought that "work" in prisons was the best alternative to channelise the prisoners' potential for useful or meaningful purpose. Remember always that the prisoners are not a special species. They are human beings just like anybody outside the prison. The only difference is that a convict is a detected and punished offender whereas the one outside is not. If work outside the prison can channelise (it does channelise) a man's potential for useful and meaningful purpose, the same will do the same thing with those who are incarcerated. Work helps all for their physical and mental fitness. The prisoner is not an exception to this rule. Work infuses self-confidence among the people and same is with an inmate in the Centre. As I said earlier the "Best Interest of the Inmate" should be the main objective of prison labour. Presently, the Rule is—

Rule 72(1) "The organization and methods of works in the institutions shall resemble as closely as possible those similar work outside institutions, so as to prepare prisoners for the conditions of normal occupational life.

(2) The interests of the prisoners and of their vocational training, however, must not be subordinated to the purpose of making a financial profit from an industry in the institution."

Every industry has a work structure, organization, management style, infrastructure, work environment, discipline, interpersonnel communication etc. and a prison industry should also have everything which similar industries outside the prison are having. Hence, the amended Rule will be—

Rule 72 (1) "The organization, methods of work, work environment, management style, discipline, interpersonnel communication etc. in the Centre shall be, as far as possible, the same as seen in similar institutions outside the Centre, the purpose being to prepare the inmates for the conditions of normal occupational life in dignity.

(2) Every inmate is entitled to get a certificate of experience/employment on his release from the Centre with all details related to the trade, designation, duration, performance, character and conduct, etc.

(3) The interest of the inmates and of their work and vocational training must never be subordinated to the purpose of making a financial profit or any other pecuniary advantage from an industry in the Centre."

Recently a trend is found to be developing in some prisons that the work and the vocational training of the inmates are made use of to make financial profit to the Centre. They do business and appear to enter into areas from where they can make more and more financial profit. In such situations the *best interest of the inmates* is sacrificed. In some countries prisoners are asked to work free of wages or to accept a wage which is no wage at all. It is almost like receiving of arms by the inmates for the hard labour extracted from them under controlled and deterrent conditions. This attitude is violative of the legal rights of the workmen to get wages as well as a violation of the ethical principles accepted in every society. The inmates are deputed to do some works earmarked by the Public Works Departments of the Government. Though the scheme is found to be somewhat good, the wages received by the department are not fairly given to them, rather are taken by the department for no justifiable reasons.

Rule 73 of the existing Standard Minimum Rules read:

Rule 73(1) "Preferably institutional industries and farms should be operated directly by the administration and not by private contractors.

(2) Where prisoners are employed in work not controlled by administration, they shall always be under the supervision of the institution's personnel. Unless the work is for other departments of the Government, the full normal wages for such works shall be paid to the administration by the prisoners to whom the labour is supplied, account being taken of the output of the prisoners."

Where the operation of institutional industries and farms directly by private contractors may be accepted as a desirable option, I fail to understand why can't such operations be entrusted to NGOs having necessary suitability and eligibility? Some of the NGOs are committed to give training to ex-inmates of the Centres and they can usefully be entrusted with this noble task. While the operations of the institutional industries and farms be operated by the administration directly, the experience hitherto shows that the performance is far away from being satisfactory, Why? Some of the personal entrusted with the tasks suffer from lack desirable personality traits and needed psychological suitability to do the job. They perform the works under the strict disciplinary controls—without understanding the objectives of prison labour—with the sole intention of custodial control. *The best interest of the inmates* often does not come to the picture or often the "best interest of the institution" alone is taken into account. Hence, my suggested amendment is:

Rule 73 (1) "Preferably, institutional industries and farms should be operated directly by the administration only with the help of specialists in institutional training with an objective of the 'best interests' of the inmates.

(2) The institutional industries and farms may be operated directly by NGOs committed in activities connected to inmates' welfare and after-care services under the control of the administration. The administration may impose reasonable and necessary conditions for the eligibility and suitability for such NGOs. In any case, the best interests of the inmates shall be the ultimate aim in such decisions.

(3) Institutional industries and farms shall never be operated by private contractors for their benefit.

(4) The operation of the institutional industries and farms and their interest shall not be subordinated to the purpose of making a financial profit or any other pecuniary benefits from an industry or farm in the Centre."

The existing Rule 73(2) is to be deleted from the amended text as it is no more found necessary, Why? Any such employment will defeat the purpose of prison labour and will be motivated by interests which may not be strictly "the best interest" of the inmates.

What does the Rule 74 (Standard Minimum Rules-1957) say about the protection of the safety and health of the inmates. It reads:

Rule 74 (1) "The precautions laid down to protect the safety and health of the free workmen shall be equally observed in institutions.

(2) Provisions shall be made to indemnify prisoners against industrial injury, including occupational

disease on terms not less favourable than those extended by law to free workmen."

Every country has its own labour laws which are made on certain principles as accepted at the national and/or international level. The inmate of a Centre is just like any other labourer and precisely, therefore, all provisions of the labour laws, not only of the protection, safety and health, etc., but also on other aspects must also be made applicable to the inmates with necessary changes naturally seen during incarceration. This is not a charity but an inevitable necessity or better their human rights. Hence, the revised Rule shall be—

Rule 74 (1) "The provisions of the labour laws in force in the country shall be made applicable to the inmates, *mutatis mutandis* in all Centres of Personality Development.

(2) Provisions of laws laid down in any statutes/ administrative orders to protect the safety and health of free workmen shall be equally observed in Centres of Personality Development.

(3) Provisions shall be made and enacted to indemnity the inmates against any industrial or otherwise injury, including occupational disease and loss of life expectancy on the same terms applicable by laws to free workmen."

A worker is a workman, no matter he is in prison or otherwise. His fundamental rights are not denied to him just because of the fetters imposed on his freedom to movement in accordance to law.

According to the Rule 75(1&2), [Standard Minimum Rules-1957], the working hours and rest, etc. have been fixed. Accordingly,

Rule 75 (1) "The maximum daily and weekly working hours of the prisoners shall be fixed by law or by administrative regulation taking into account local rules or customs in regard to the employment of free workmen.

(2) The hours so fixed shall leave one rest day a week and sufficient time for education and other activities required as part of the treatment and rehabilitation of the prisoners."

What about the leave, emergency or casual leave, provident fund and other benefits which a free workman enjoys in the society? The inmates' earnings have a purpose. In my view, an inmate must have enough money (after a life sentence) or as much money as possible (after a period of incarceration) to start a meaningful life outside the prison. Presently, it is difficult or even impossible for ex-convicts to raise money from financial institutions to start a business or other enterprises. As a result, some of them—if they are pick pockets, thieves, burglars and so on—return to their commission of crimes. Moreover, there should be the services of the After-care Organizations to settle the released inmates in society. Presently, some suggestions exist in some countries and they call for discussions and debates. For example, some Prison Reform Committees or even judges of the Higher Courts recommend that the earning of the inmates should be utilized in the following ways— that is, (1) A portion of the earnings of the inmates should be given to him for his personal needs; (2) Another portion should be for the institution for the maintenance of the inmate, (3) Another portion should be given for victimlogical compensation or needs. I am just laughing at their suggestions. I think that some of them are in the fool's paradise as they think that the inmates make a lot of income by their work in the institution. Their wages are nominal and until recently, in some countries, they were not given any wages at all. The work was extracted from them forcefully and strong objections to such prison-controlled situations created a lot of murmur everywhere and protests in some countries which ultimately forced the authorities to take merciful decisions which in my opinion, are not realistic. The inmates get very little wages even in the background of mercy, sympathy, consideration and what not. The saddest part or culmination of such unrealistic wage structure is that all of the inmates leave the Centres after incarceration with an empty pocket. Sometimes, the prison authorities are morally forced to give them minimum money for their travel and other necessities until they reach home. What can such inmates do with an empty pocket to start a life in dignity? The suggested amendment is—

Rule 75 (1) "The maximum daily and weekly working hours of the inmates shall be fixed by law or by administrative regulations, taking into account the local rules or customs in regard to the employment of free workmen.

(2) "The hours so fixed shall leave one rest day a week and all holidays declared by the Government for institutions outside and sufficient time for education, physical exercises, spiritual needs (optional to the inmates) and other activities as are required as part of the personality development, correction, reformation, resocialization, rehabilitation and reintegration to the society of the inmates.

(3) Every inmate shall be entitled to have provident fund, gratuity and other benefits which employees in similar works are eligible to receive outside the Centre."

What does the existing Rule 76 say? The Rule 76 reads:

Rule 76 (1) "There shall be a system of equitable remuneration of the work of prisoners.

(2) Under the system, prisoners shall be allowed to spend at least a part of their earnings on approved articles for their own use and to send a part of their earnings to their family.

(3) The system should also provide that a part of the earnings should be set aside by the administration so as to constitute a savings fund to be handed over to the prisoner on his release."

When one reads Rule 76 (1, 2 & 3), he is simply taken up. He gets an impression that an inmate gets a lot of money for his work in the Centre. Presently, he does not get any wages worth mentioning or appreciating. The wages may be minimum wages, fair wages, equitable wages etc. In Rule 76(1) 'equitable remuneration' has been suggested. It is fine and no change is suggested except those seen under Rule 76 (1, 2 & 3) as follows:

Rule 76 (1) "There shall be a system of equitable remuneration of the work of the inmates.

(2) Under the system, the inmates shall be allowed to spend at least a part of their earnings on approved articles for their own use and to send a part of their earnings to their family.

(3) The system should also provide that a part of the earnings should be set aside by the administration so as to constitute a saving fund to be handed over to the inmates on his release. If the fund is very meagre, provisions shall be made to provide him a minimum fund for his living in dignity outside the Centre."

EDUCATION AND TRAINING

Rule 77 (1&2) seems to be very interesting and it reads:

Rule 77(1) "Provision shall be made for the further education of all prisoners capable of profiting thereby, including religious instruction in the countries where this is possible. The education of the illiterates and young prisoners shall be compulsory and special attention shall be paid to it by the administration.

(2) So far as practicable, the education of prisoners shall be integrated with the educational system of the country so that after their release, they may continue their education without difficulty."

The prisoners are of many kinds and backgrounds. There are illiterates, semi-literates, moderatly educated and so on. The prisoners are long termers and short termers. The prisoners come to the jails not in groups. Individuals come to jails and they belong to different age groups with different educational backgrounds. Prisoners are many and they have different attitudes and approaches to academic education. The questions are—

(1) What to do with short-termers? What kind of education can be designed for them? Where can the teachers be found out?
(2) What type of education should be designed for the illiterate, semi-illiterate or moderately educated? What to do for different inmates who talk different languages?
(3) What type of education should be given to better the educated inmates? Where do we educate them? Where can we find out facilities for their further education? What type of education be given to people qualified in Arts?—

in Science? In Commerce? In Social Sciences?—in Engineering?—in Fine Arts?—in Music, etc. Where can the teachers be found out?

(4) What to do with the inmates who show positive reluctance or hostility to education? What to do with those inmates incarcerated with a condition to do hard labour? Where or how do they find time for education?

(5) Is it not better to introduce some training in SKILL DEVELOPMENT instead of academic education to those who cannot benefit by academic education? If so, what sort of skill training may be thought of or introduced.

Generally, it is seen that many highly educated people do not normally come to prisons as incarcerated. The affluent and the influential people too rarely come to prisons as incarcerated. Hence, what to do with the poor, poorer, very poor, poorest inmates in matters of education? There may be inmates from the unprivileged community, tribal society, forests, etc. How to educate them with those who are from the privileged community? Hence, problems are many or perhaps questions are more than solutions. Remember always that any kind of forceful education or compulsory education to fairly elderly people does not work. Sometimes, such approaches become counter-productive resulting in negative reactions. Hence, my recommended amendments are—

Rule 77 (1) "Provisions shall be made and implemented for the further education of the inmates willing to study further.

(2) Provisions shall be made and implemented for obtaining a recognized certificate, diploma or degree for the education they undertake.

(3) Provisions shall be made and implemented for hiring out teachers to provide instructions for those who prosecute their education further. NGOs willing to offer assistance may be purposefully utilized for the purpose.

(4) Books, fees for the course and examination, study and writing materials shall be provided free of cost by the administration. On completion of the course or on obtaining a pass in the examination, special remission marks should be given to the successful inmates.

(5) Inmates who show good character and conduct may be sent to academic institution outside the Centre if they show satisfactory performance or success in education and subsequent examinations. All expenses towards such courses of study shall be borne by the Government.

(6) Inmates who are short-termers shall attend training in skill development and facilities shall be provided so that they make a living after their release.

(7) The education or training for skill development shall be compulsory and the short-termers are free to opt for any available in the Centre.

(8) So far as practicable, the education or training for skill development shall be integrated with the educational system of the country so that after their release they may continue their education or skilled work without difficulty. If needed, the inmates' stay in the Centre shall be extended till the completion of the course, if so desired by the individual inmate.

(9) Besides the academic education or training for skill development, provision shall be made and implemented for giving instructions in religious teachings in countries where this is possible at the option of the inmates concerned or in moral teachings in a compulsory and secular way.

(10) Where there are inmates from many religions accommodated in a Centre, instructions in religious teachings of each and every religion may be imparted by representatives of each religion approved by the authorities of the Centre.

(11) Provision shall be made and implemented for imparting literary and cultural education to inmates capable of profiting thereby by approved teachers or the NGOs."

RECREATION AND CULTURAL ACTIVITIES

Rule 78 of the existing Standard Minimum Rules for the Treatment of Prisoners – 1957 is about recreation and cultural activities. The Rule speaks about recreation in a general way or does not say anything in a specific manner. As it is now, the Rule 78 is:

"Recreational and cultural activities shall be provided in all institutions for the benefit of the mental and physical health of prisoners."

Yes, recreation is very essential for mental relaxation and the inmates should be encouraged to smile and laugh. Outside the prison, there exists "Laughter-Clubs" for people to laugh and to release their tension. There are older people too who need to have mental relaxation. Hence, there should be any number of indoor games in prisons. Therefore, the amended version of the Rule will be—

Rule 78 (1) "There shall be facilities for recreation in every Centre and it shall be different and many consisting of as many indoor games as possible for the inmates to congregate together and release their tension.

(2) Inmates shall be encouraged to participate in cultural activities of all kinds and every Centre shall make arrangements for conducting competitions in cultural activities either in individual capacity or on group basis. Prizes and remission marks shall be awarded to the winning individuals and groups.

(3) There shall be provisions for literary activities and competitions in every Centre. Creative writings and fine arts, drawings, paint works etc. shall be encouraged.

(4) Inmates shall be allowed to participate in tournaments conducted among the inmates of other Centres in the country. There shall be inter-centre competitions in indoor or/and outdoor games, literary or/and cultural activities. The winners shall be given prizes and remission marks.

(5) In consultation with the sports council, friendly matches shall be organized within the Centres for the inmates to compete with players outside the Centre. Prizes shall be instituted for the winning team in addition to the remission marks if they are the inmates.

(6) Periodically, film shows, dramas, mimicry, dance, songs, concerts or other performing arts shall be arranged in the Centre's auditorium for the inmates to enjoy and to relax their tensions. Provision shall be

> made for the inmates to listen to radio and see television programmes. Lectures of eminent personalities on topics of interests for the inmates shall be arranged. Radio and television programmes by the inmates shall be broadcasted/telecasted for the general public to accept the talents and capabilities of the incarcerated."

People call prisons "Hells" and the inmates too, at times, feel so. Why? Presently, no one seems to give any importance to the literary, cultural and recreational aspects of the inmates' life inside the Centre. Even animals need recreation and entertainment. They respond to music and tunes. If so, humans do need them. Why do we deny such human necessities for personality development for the inmates just because they are detected, convicted and incarcerated? This is cruel and needs to be changed.

SOCIAL RELATIONS AND CONTACTS WITH OUTSIDE WORLD

About social relations, Rule 79 and Rule 80 of the present Standard Minimum Rules-1957 say—

Rule 79: "Special attention shall be paid to the maintenance and improvement of such relation between a prisoner and his family as are desirable in the best interest of both."

Rule 80: "From the beginning of a prisoner's sentence, consideration shall be given to his future after release and he shall be encouraged and assisted to maintain or establish such relations with persons or agencies outside the institution as may promote the best interests of his family and his own social rehabilitation."

In my considered view, the expression 'special attention' given in Rule 79 does not have any special meaning. It should be made clear and specific. Every inmate is a member in a family—a son/daughter, a father/mother, a brother/sister as the case may be. There may be kith and kin, dear and near ones and, therefore, the expression FAMILY should be taken in its widest meaning. It may be remembered that the very incarceration is and should be for rehabilitation and reintegration of the inmates to society back. Many inmates may not require any correction or reformation as they have been living in their family, community and society without involving themselves in committing any crimes until they are sent to the Centre for personality development.

What is meant by the maintenance and improvement of SUCH RELATIONS........ ARE DESIRABLE? In my view, they are and should be a mutual relationship of care, concern, consideration, mutual acceptance, recognition, love, help etc. Home means a place where a lot of pleasant human emotions which establish bonds between/among the members are seen. Family is the basic unit of any society wherein homely emotions are seen—a place pregnant with desirable human emotions. Therefore, the amended Rule will be—

Rule 79 (1) "Very special and specific strategies shall be designed and implemented for the maintenance and positive improvement of homely relations between the inmate and his family as are desirable in the best interests of both and the society at large.

(2) Such strategies will include visits, correspondence and communication to and from the inmates with his family.

(3) Family is taken in its widest meaning possible and includes parents, spouse, children, kith and kin, dear and near and so on with whom and for whom the inmates desire to have human relations and exchange of homely emotions."

Rule 80 of the present Standard Minimum Rules for the Treatment of Prisoners – 1957 ought to be redrafted, in my view, in the following way:

Rule 80: "From the beginning of an inmate's entry to a Centre, special care, attention and consideration shall be given to his life in society after his release. He shall be encouraged and assisted to maintain and establish desirable human relations with all persons and agencies outside the Centre for promoting the best interest of

> his family and his own rehabilitation and reintegration to the community/society back. After-care agencies and concerned citizens may be incorporated to offer assistance to fulfil the above objectives."

This is easier said than done. For, the administration in general may not get sufficient time to spare for promoting the above noble objectives. Therefore, AFTER-CARE agencies and concerned citizens may do everything possible for promoting the best interest of the inmate's family and his rehabilitation/reintegration to the community/society back.

AFTER-CARE SERVICES

Rule 81 of the existing Standard Minimum Rules for the Treatment of Prisoners – 1957 is about After-Care Services and Agencies. It reads:

Rule 81 (1) "Services and agencies, governmental or otherwise, which assist released prisoners to re-establish themselves in society shall ensure, so far as is possible and necessary, that released prisoners be provided with appropriate documents and identification papers, have suitable homes and work to go to, are suitably and adequately clothed having regard to the climate and season, and have sufficient means to reach their destination and maintain themselves in the period immediately following their release.

(2) The approved representatives of such agencies shall have all necessary access to the institution and to prisoners and shall be taken into consideration as to the future of a prisoner from the beginning of his sentence.

(3) It is desirable that the activities of such agencies shall be centralized or co-ordinated as far as possible in order to secure the best use of their efforts."

I am of the view that the existing Rule 81 above has been drafted without giving any thoughts to the rehabilitation and reintegration of the inmate after his release from the Centre. The end portion of the Rule 81 (1) reads: ".... and have sufficient means to reach their destination and maintain themselves in the period immediately following their release". Rehabilitation and reintegration do not mean and stop during the period immediately following the release of the inmates. They must mean and continue till their death. It is ridiculous to say that the Services and Agencies should see to it that the inmates have sufficient means to reach their destination. They were working and they have been receiving little wages for the work they were doing. At last, when they are released a situation arises and they do not have sufficient means to reach their destination and it shows and implies how meaningless has been the wage-structure in the Centres? Do the inmates released from the Centre need "re-establishment"? Some of them are fully established and they do not require any re-establishment. The rich and the affluent, the influential and the well-to-do, the social higher-ups and the well-established do not normally require any re-establishment. What they need may be "to reintegrate" themselves in a legally acceptable way in dignity. Therefore, the entire Rule 81 may be redrafted as:

Rule 81 (1) "Services and agencies, governmental or otherwise, which assist released inmates to reintegrate themselves in the family, community and society, shall ensure, so far as possible and necessary, that released inmates be provided with

- (a) appropriate documents and identification papers,
- (b) have suitable home and works to go to with equitable wages,
- (c) are suitably and adequately clothed having regard to the climate and season,
- (d) have ways and means to have their medicines, treatment and medical care,
- (e) have fund and facilities to make an earning to live in dignity in the family, community and society under the care and concern of the agencies or services until such time they do not need their continued care, concern and support."

The Services and Agencies in some countries are seen to be agencies of suspicious integrity. They have been blamed for their nefarious activities to raise funds from various sources in the name or pretext of extending After-care services to released inmates from the Centres of Personality Development. These "FAKES and FRAUDS" ought to be guarded against. Therefore, the proposed amendments will be—

Rule 81(2) "The approved representatives of such agencies having proved integrity shall have necessary access to the Centre and to the inmates for taking up their correctional, reformative, rehabilitative mission for reintegrating them back to their family, community and society during the period of incarceration from its beginning and shall be taken into consideration as to the life of the inmates after their release.

(3) It is inevitable that the activities of such agencies are audited and shall be centralized or co-ordinated as far as possible in order to secure the best use of their efforts recognizing the principle that the reintegration of an inmate to his family, community and society is a shared responsibility of the agencies and services with all interested in his reintegration to his family, community and society back."

It is to be accepted that the desirability is not what is required—rather is the inevitability that is most warranted. The efforts should be a shared responsibility.

INSANE AND MENTALLY ABNORMAL INMATES

The insane and the mentally abnormal inmates are a special category dealt with in the present Standard Minimum Rules for the Treatment of Prisoners-1957. It reads:

Rule 82(1) "Persons who are found to be insane shall not be detained in prisons and arrangement shall be made to remove them to mental institutions as soon as possible.

(2) Prisoners who suffer from other mental diseases or abnormalities shall be observed and treated in specialized institutions under medical management.

(3) During their stay in a prison, such prisoners shall be placed under the special supervision of a medical officer.

(4) The medical or psychiatric service of the penal institutions shall provide for psychiatric treatment of all other prisoners who are in need of such treatment."

Insane people are insane people who do not know why they are in a Centre for Personality Development. Insane people are no more prisoners and therefore, existing Rule 82(1)—that is, "Persons who are found to be insane shall not be detained in prisons and arrangements shall be made to remove them to mental hospitals as soon as possible"—shall be deleted. In some countries, there are prisoners' ward in the mental hospitals and therefore, it is proposed that the Rule 82(1) may be rewritten as—

Rule 82(1) "Any incarcerated diagnosed to be insane shall be admitted to the Mental Health Hospital forthwith for treatment."

Rule 82(2) may be redrafted as:

Rule 82(2) "Inmates who are diagnosed to suffer from mental disorders other than insanity proper shall be admitted to Mental Health Centre for specialized treatment."

Rule 82(3) "There shall be an 'Inmates' Ward' attached to all Mental Health Centres under the Government. The Medical, Psychiatric, Psychiatric Social Work Services in the Mental Health Centres shall render all their services and assistance to every inmate who needs such assistance and services in all Centres of Personality Development."

Rule 83 of the existing Standard Minimum Rules for the Treatment of Prisoners-1957 is retained as it is to read: "It is desirable that steps should be taken, by arrangement with appropriate agencies, to ensure, if necessary, the continuation of psychiatric treatment after release and the provision of social psychiatric after-care". Instead of "it is desirable" I may propose "It is necessary"—for desirability is one thing and necessity is quite another thing. Let it be a necessity and let the Rule 83 begin with: "It is necessary......". O.K., Fine.

In my view, the old and the infirm inmates should be treated as a special category as they are found to be a group who need no further development in their personality. If we accept the sociological classification of "*The old, The old old, The older old, The oldest old*" in the present context, the oldest old (those who are 80 years of age or above) do not need any incarceration at all whatever may be the type of offences they have committed. Nevertheless, offences like waging war against one's own country, terrorism, insurgency etc. are very heinous offences and precisely, therefore, they must be counted seriously. Excepting such crimes of treason or affecting the security of the nation, all sentenced to undergo incarceration if they belong to the *Oldest Old* category, need to be dealt with leniently just like juveniles or women under certain categories. They are people suffering from many weaknesses, handicapedness and debilities. Hence, I propose probation of good conduct to such *oldest old* incarcerated.

What about those who are in the category of the Older Old? (i.e., between 75-80 years of age). They are those found to be suffering from many physical ailments. They need special and specialized treatment from specialists and specialized institutions, sometimes, outside the Government administration and management. In my view, subject to scrutiny, examination and evaluation, they may be granted *probation of good* conduct or treatment in special institutions and treatment by specialists in Government hospitals. What about those who are in the category of *old old*?

Of course, many Governments all over the world are concerned about the old (those who are 60 years of age and above up to 65 years) and they make special policies for their welfare. I propose that the existing provisions of law will be applicable to them. Therefore, as an annexure to Rule 83, I propose:

Rule 83A(1) Laws shall be specially enacted for the release of offenders above the age of 80 years under probation of good conduct except in those cases which are coming under the category of offences against the State.

(2) Inmates in the age-group of 75-80 years of age shall

be allowed to have specialists' treatment for their diseases either in a specialist institution or in Government hospitals or in the Centre for which the expenditure incurred shall be borne entirely by the inmates. In case, they are people of good character and conduct, they may be granted pre-mature release under parole conditions for treatment and reintegration to the family, community and society back.

(3) Inmates in the age-group of 70-75 years shall be allowed to have specialists' treatment at their expenses and depending upon each case, specialities and needs, they may be granted pre-mature release for treatment outside.

(4) Inmates who are in the age-group of 60-70 shall be granted privileges given to the inmates under Rule 83A(3) except that they will not be considered for pre-mature release in relaxation of the existing rules governing the eligibility and suitability for the granting of parole in every country.

7
Custodial Facilities

The International Penal and Penitentiary Commission (IPPC), as said earlier—they have the credit for bringing out the Standard Minimum Rules for the Treatment of Prisoners. *Penal and Penitentiary* have pain attached to them. Penitentiary means a place for imprisonment or punishment and penal means pertaining to punishment. Punishment means subjecting a person to pain—physical, mental, or both. All those words are used for a convict and not at all for a suspect in a crime, a detainee in a crime or an accused in a crime. If imprisonment means confinement and consequent sufferings (pain) attached to such a penal confinement, then there is no meaning in subjecting a suspect, an arrested, a detainee, an accused and so on to such a penal treatment. For imprisonment as a penalty has–

(1) Social stigma attached to it.
(2) Physical sufferings and mental pain consequent to imprisonment as a penalty.
(3) Neglect of the imprisoned by his dear and near ones in some cases and a feeling of isolation and segregation as a consequence.
(4) Treatment of a "Prisoner After All"—an attitude of contempt, avoidance and fear.
(5) Once a convicted prisoner, then always a convicted prisoner—approach by the administration and people alike.

Amidst these and similar realities, there are people who think that the convicted prisoners are not the *last, least and lost* people in society. Such a humanitarian concern for the imprisoned goes back to 250 years or more. Forget about the lost past and the history of humanitarian concern to the imprisoned. In 1926, July 1, the IPPC (International Penal and Penitentiary Commission) in their meeting held in Berne (seep. Cornil, international Standards for the treatment of offenders, International Review of Criminal Policy, No. 26 (United Nations Publication Sales No E-70.IV.I) accepted the proposal to consider the granting of minimal rights for all deprived of their liberty by a judicial decision. All deprived of their liberty include untried detainees, civil prisoners and persons arrested or detained without charge and so on. They cannot be or ought not to be treated on par with the convicted prisoners. They are on a different plane altogether. But, it seems that the U.N. Standard Minimum Rules for the Treatment of Prisoners-1957 took everyone on the same ground and made Rules for each one of them. Thus an untried detainee, an arrestee in police custody, a remanded in judicial custody, a civilian detained in prisons under any non-criminal process and so on were treated as imprisoned and the UN Standard Minimum Rules for the Treatment of Prisoners-1957 has sections C, D, E (under part-II giving Rules applicable to special categories for the purpose.) This is not correct as I find that people kept in a custodial facility under the police or under the judiciary (under a judicial order) cannot be or ought not be treated as persons detained under jail custody or in a prison manned and managed by the Prisons Department (The Department of Correction as it is known in some countries today).

Persons detained temporarily in police (for a few days) or in judicial custody (for days/weeks generally) do not require any long-term treatment or programmes designed for developing their personality in an upright way in the right direction. Untried prisoners may be a wrong way of addressing suspects under custody of the police or in judicial custody. People who are confined owing to several reasons are not prisoners although some may figuratively call them so. In law there is no one called an Untried Prisoner and precisely, therefore, the Rules 84 to 93 (both inclusive) have no scope in a Standard Minimum Rules for the Treatment of Prisoners-1957. What is the meaning of "Unconvicted" when a person is just confined in a custodial facility manned and managed by the police or judiciary? In any case, they are not prisoners in any sense what so ever.

The custodial facility of the police or judiciary does not have anything to do with the prisons and therefore, the questions of separation of the prisoners in jails and detainees in the custodial facility does not arise. What is meant by work by 'Untried Prisoners?' Why should they work? What works can be given to them for a few days they stay? Persons who are remanded to judicial custody may remain in the custodial facility, sometimes for a long period if they do not go on bail. Even in such cases, one is to be treated as innocent. Penal stay, penal treatment, penal food etc. do not have any meaning in his case. Correctional strategies do not have anything to do with him. Everything taken into account, I am of the firm view that the entire section C in part II of the existing Standard Minimum Rules for the Treatment of Prisoners-1957 must be deleted forthwith as they do not have any space or scope in the revised version of the *Rules or Guidelines or Directives*, whatever. Though a revision of the existing Rules under section C of the part II is not required, I do it just to make everything in order knowing fully well that my exercise may be futile in the revised version.

Imprisonment for debt or by an order of a court under any other non-criminal process—again ununderstandable as imprisonment has meaning only as a punishment for an offence committed. I do not find any place or space for the inclusion of section D in part II of the existing Standard Minimum Rules for the Treatment of Prisoners-1957 in the Revised Edition. Hence, I am inclined to omit the same.

What is meant by persons arrested or detained without charge? Are they the people kept under *Preventive Detention*? Or are they arrested by Mistake of Fact? Why do the police arrest people if they do not have any probable cause for their arrest? Why does the justice system detain people without any charge? If they are detained informally or illegally, then it is a violation of human rights and they need to get victimological compensation. If they are detained under preventive detention sections of law for preventive detention, then special rules must be framed for them. Such Rules do not have any relevance or scope in the revised version of the Standard Minimum Rules for the Treatment of Prisoners-1957. Hence, I am inclined to omit them or I want to delete Section E in the revised text.

PRISONERS UNDER ARREST OR AWAITING TRIAL (REVISED: DETAINEES UNDER ARREST OR AWAITING TRIAL)

How can a detained person be a prisoner? It is a historical fact that from time antiquity, people were caught and kept in confinement by the strangers. Whether or not one was convicted to be imprisoned was not a concern for those who confined him. 'Organised Police' is of recent origin and they did not have a 'prison'; yet they called their custodial facility to be a "Lock-up" which meant a prison. They have treated the confined worse than prisoners and they left the police stations with a life-long stigma.

"Prisoners under Arrest"—this is an expression which I do not understand. Why should a person undergo "prisonship" so long as the crime against him is not proved? Prisonership has many sufferings, pains, hardships and stigma. Why should a detainee—if he is innocent—suffer them? Just go through Rule 84(1) in Part II (i.e., Rules Applicable to Special Categories) of the Standard Minimum Rules for the Treatment of Prisoners, 1957, that is,

Rule 84(1) "Persons arrested or imprisoned by reason of a criminal charge against them, who are detained either in police custody or in prison custody (jail) but have not yet then tried and sentenced, will be referred to as "untried prisoners", hereinafter in these rules". If one refers a dictionary to find out the meaning of a 'PRISON', he may read that a prison is a building for the confinement of persons accused or convicted of crimes. Hence, there is no justification for calling an arrested to be a prisoner. His status is different. Merely because a married person lives like a bachelor (without family life, away from the family—i.e., enforced bachelorhood) it does not mean that he can be called a "married bachelor". Likewise, a person who is arrested or detained by reason of a suspicion of having committed an offence in a prison, it does not mean that he can be called an "untired prisoner." He is just a detainee—nothing more, nothing less. Judicial custody and police custody—these are often heard and widely used in legal circles. I have been always against the use of expression "JUDICIAL CUSTODY" for "PRISON CUSTODY UNDER A JUDICIAL ORDER". A detention under a judicial order can be a detention under judicial order and not "judicial custody" so long as the detained is not kept in an institution manned and managed by judicial officers. A detention in an institution managed by the executive or prison officers of the Government will be an executive custody and not a judicial custody. Suppose, "*sandalwood paste*" is put in a bottle and a label "*gold paste*" is put on the bottle. Just because there is a label of 'gold paste', it does not mean that the "sandalwood paste" becomes 'gold paste'. Similarly, just because a detention under *executive custody* is called *judicial custody*, it does not become judicial custody. Precisely, therefore, the detainees in police custody or judicial custody cannot be or should not be called "PRISONERS". There are countries where the detainees under a judicial order are detained in institutions manned and managed by the judiciary. They do not maintain prisons or jails and therefore, they get the status of "untried detainees". The entire Rule 84(1) must be amended to read as:

Rule 84(1) Persons arrested or detained by reason of a suspicion of having committed an offence and who are kept either in the custodial facility of the police or in the custodial centres manned and managed by the judiciary, will be called untried detainees hereinafter in these rules. Countries where they are called "untried prisoners", they shall make necessary changes in law and the criminal justice system to adopt to this rule." Accordingly, the heading of Part II will be rewritten as "Detainees under Arrest or Awaiting Trials."

The existing Rule 84(2) is: "Unconvicted prisoners are presumed to be innocent and shall be treated as such." This rule appears to be funny and is against the basic principles of human psychology. Of course, detinues or untried detainees can be presumed to be innocent and I do not know how can one treat a person to be a prisoner on the basis of such a presumption? Presumption is only a presumption and a reality is a reality. Hence, presumption is one thing and reality is quite another thing. This can be illustrated further:

1. Presume that A is the wife of B and treat A as B's wife.
2. Presume that A is laughing when actually he is crying. Treat him as laughing.

Here, the untried under arrest is a person arrested with a probable cause. He is merely a suspect and precisely, therefore, he can be treated only as a suspect in reality and not as innocent. A suspect is a suspect and an innocent is an innocent. Suspicion however strong it is cannot be a substitute for guilt or innocence. Hence, the entire Rule 84(2) must be revised to read:

Rule 84 (2) "Unconvicted detainees are suspects in crime and shall be treated as such". Remember always that, "nothing comes out from nothingness". Hence, only a presumption comes out from a presumption. "Treatment in reality" cannot come out from a presumption.

What does Rule 84(3) say?

Rule 84(3): "Without prejudice to legal rules for the protection of individual liberty or prescribing the procedure to be observed in respect of untried prisoners, these prisoners shall benefit by a special regime which is described in the following rules in its essential requirements only."

The word "prisoners" shall be substituted by "Detainees".

Rule 85 (1) "Untried prisoners shall be kept separate from convicted prisoners."

I am of the firm view that untried detainees are entirely different from convicted inmates and, therefore, they must not be mixed or allowed to mingle. They are different in many or almost in all aspects legally and otherwise. Therefore, I want to strike off the entire Rule 85(1) from the amended text. Police custodial facility, judicial custody and prison custody—All are different and, therefore, separation of them in different buildings does not arise. Police custodial facility is manned and managed by police officials while the judicial custodial facility is manned and managed by the judiciary. They cannot be one and the same.

Rule 85 (2) "Young untried prisoners shall be kept separate from adults and shall in principle be detained in separate institutions."

What is the meaning of "in principle". If the rules are intended for the well-being of humanity, they should be enforced in reality and not in principle only. Hence, the amendment is—

Rule 85 (2) "Young untried detainees shall be kept separate from adults and shall be detained in reality in separate institutions manned and managed by the police or judiciary as the case may be."

Who are young detainees? What is their age? Everyone below 18 years of age is a juvenile. Who is an adult detainee? There are countries were 'Youth' or 'Adult' means people below the age of 35. Does the Rule 85(2) mean those who are below the age of 35 to be "young"? Anyway, it must be clarified.

Rule 86, that is, "Untried prisoners shall sleep singly in separate rooms, with the reservation of different local custom in respect of the climate." This is not practically possible or in reality feasible to provide single room accommodation for every untried detainee in a police custodial facility. In a police custodial facility, they can be accommodated in dormitories located centrally for a fixed number of police stations. Most of the untried detainees in police custodial facility will be tensed and their stress should be minimised by such a stay in a group in dormitories having medical assistance. Instances are not rare that detainees in police custodial facility have committed suicide. Again, instances are plenty to show that those detained in police custody are tortured or tortured to death. It may be remembered that the detention in police custody is for a short period and precisely, therefore, a dormitory type of accommodation under medical supervision, pharmacy assistance and surveillance by police officials will be the best. Therefore, the revised Rule 86 will be—

Rule 86 "Untried detainees shall sleep in dormitories equipped with medical and pharmacy facilities under the surveillance of police. In the case of judicial custody, the detainees shall sleep in dormitories if that is possible; if not they shall be detained in single rooms."

The existing Rule 87 is fine as an untried detainee is only a suspect in a crime. It reads: "Within the limits compatible with the good order of the institution, untried prisoners may, if they so desire, have their food procured at their own expense from the outside, either through the administration or through their family or friends. Otherwise, "the administration shall provide their food." Here many questions are raised and they are—

(1) Who can or will ensure the safety and security of the detainee in case the food is poisonous? The so-called friends or so-named family members can be coerced to give food mixed with deadly poison.
(2) The rich detainee will have rich food and the poor will have the food from the institution. This sort of a double treatment will create problems and the administration will find it extremely difficult to manage peace and order in custodial facility.
(3) All untried detainees are under the State's care and protection. The State has a responsibility to maintain them in dignity with food and other facilities. Is it just and fair to ask the family or friends to provide food for those detained under State's care and protection?

My considered view is to make the State responsible for providing food to the untried detainees and therefore, the amended Rule 87 will be—

Rule 87 "The untried detainees will be provided with food at State expense and it shall be qualitatively and quantitatively healthy and good."

According to the present "Rule 88(1) "an untried prisoner shall be allowed to wear his own clothing if it is clean and suitable." Many detainees come to police custody or judicial custody without adequate number of dress or clothing. Many a time, it may not be clean and suitable too. Why to think in this way? They may not bring any item to maintain a good appearance compatible with their self-respect. I have seen many detainees from police custody appearing before the courts without shaving. In my view, they must be allowed to have all equipments/materials for shaving and as far as the women are concerned everything to attend to their special needs of nature.

Hence, the Rule 88(1) "An untried detainee shall be allowed to wear his own clothing if it is clean and suitable. He shall be allowed to procure clean and suitable clothing at his expense, if that is necessary. The clothing shall be clean and kept in proper condition. Underclothings shall be changed and washed as often as necessary for the maintenance of hygiene. Both men and women shall maintain a good appearance compatible with their self-respect. Facilities shall be provided for the proper care of hair and beard for men who shall be enabled to shave it regularly if that is desired. For women, facilities shall be provided for the proper care of their hair and for attending the special needs of nature."

How long will a detainee be there in police custody? It may be for a few hours, days or weeks. There will not be any prolonged stay in the police custodial facility. It depends upon whether or not he gets bail from the courts. If one does not get bail or is not prepared to go on bail, he will have to remain there until his case is disposed of by the courts. In any case, untried detainees who have spent more than 5 years are many in some countries. Therefore, in my view, the rules will have to be framed taking into account of these hard realities.

Rule 88(2) reads: "If he wears prison dress, it shall be different from that supplied to convicted prisoners." The above rule is to be revised to read:

Rule 88(2): "No detainee shall be provided with dress by the State if he is in police custodial facility or in judicial custody till he is granted bail in the ordinary course of legal procedure. If a detainee remains in judicial custody without obtaining bail for a longer period beyond three months, he shall be provided with clothing at the State expense. Such clothing shall be dignified respecting the dignity of man."

The existing Rule 89 reads: "An untried prisoner shall always be offered opportunity to work, but shall not be required to work. If he chooses to work, he shall be paid for it" needs an amendment. Why? In police custody, there is no time to apply the above rule and in judicial custody which lasts for a few days, weeks or months too does not need the application of the above rule. The above rule can be thought of in the case of untried detainees who spend prolonged time in the judicial custodial facility and in my view, any stay beyond three months may be treated as "prolonged stay". Hence, the revised Rule 89 will be—

Rule 89 "An untried detainee in judicial custody for a prolonged time lasting more than 3 months shall always be offered opportunity to work, but shall not be forced or required to work. If he chooses to work, he shall be paid for it. Those who stay in judicial custody for a prolonged time shall be detained in a facility separate from those who stay for a short period. Centres for prolonged stay must be equipped with facilities to work."

What is stated in the existing Rule 90? It is written. "An untried prisoner shall be allowed to procure at his own expense or at the expense of a third party such books, newspapers, writing materials and other means of occupation as are compatible with the interest of the administration of justice and the security and good order of the institution." The idea is good, nevertheless, there must be some modifications. In police custodial facility where dormitory accommodation, dining halls, facilities for small scale indoor recreation/games, reading rooms and library etc. are not provided, newspapers and a few periodical publications must be procured at the State's expense. The rest of the portion in the original Rule 90 is to be deleted as I find them unnecessary. If needed, radio and T.V. can be provided. The same provision may be followed in institutions where detainees under judicial custody are accommodated for a short period. In such centres, procuring of books at the expense of the detainee or at the expense of a third party may be allowed. The books must be of good quality—morally and otherwise. Procuring of newspapers/periodicals at the expense of the detainee or at the expense of the third party too may be permitted over and above the same purchased at the State's expense. But, with regard to the centres for judicial custody for a long period the entire Rule 90 may be accepted and implemented. Hence, the revised Rule 90 will be—

Rule 90 "Every police custodial facility shall be provided with non-partisan newspapers, periodicals, radio and television at the expense of the State. In addition to what is stated above, a detainee in every Centre for judicial custody for short-stay shall be allowed to procure at his own expense or at the expense of a third party books and periodicals of good quality—morally and otherwise. A detainee in judicial custody for a long stay shall be allowed to procure at his own expense or at the expense of a third party such books, newspapers, periodicals of good quality, morally and otherwise, writing materials and other means of occupation as are compatible with the interests of the administration of justice and the security and good order of the institution."

"An untried prisoner shall be allowed to be visited and treated by his own doctor or dentist if there is reasonable ground for his application and he is able to pay any expenses incurred." This is what is stated in the present Rule 91 and I find it extremely difficult for practical implementation for the simple reason that there will be a feeling of discrimination getting developed among the detainees. Hence, a revision is suggested and that is:

Rule 91 "An untried detainee shall be allowed to be visited and treated by the institutional doctor or dentist. However, if there is reasonable ground for getting him treated by a doctor of his choice, his application must be considered by the institutional doctor/dentist and thereafter, he shall be allowed to be visited and treated by his own doctor or dentist provided there is reasonable and genuine grounds for allowing his application. If allowed, the entire expenses incurred shall be paid by the detainee himself."

Coming to the existing Rule 92, it is stated: "An untried prisoner shall be allowed to inform immediately his family of his detention and shall be given all reasonable facilities for communicating with his family and friends, and for receiving visits from them, subject only to restrictions and supervision as are necessary in the interests of the administration of justice and of the security and good order of the institution." As usual, the word 'prisoner' should be substituted by 'detainee' and the provision to inform his family should be extended not only at the time of admission but also at every time he is transferred from one Centre to another. This takes place in Centres where the detainee is kept for longer periods. Hence, the revised Rule 92 will be—

Rule 92: "An untried detainee shall be allowed to inform immediately his family of his detention on admission to an institution as well as on his transfer from one Centre to another and shall be given all reasonable facilities for communicating with his family and friends and for receiving visits from them, subject only to restrictions and supervision as are necessary in the interests of the administration of justice and of the security and good order of the institution."

The present Rule 93 is—

"For the purpose of his defence, an untried prisoner shall be allowed to apply for free legal aid where such aid is available and to receive visits from his legal adviser with a view to his defence and to prepare and hand to him confidential instructions. For these purposes, he shall if he so desires be supplied with writing material. Interviews between the prisoner and his legal adviser may be within sight but not within the hearing of a police or institutional staff."

Though this is a good rule for acceptance and implementation, it needs amendment in the following ways: "Where such legal aid is available"—the entire portion may be deleted, because the free legal aid is a right of the untried detainee if he so desires. It is not a charity shown by the administration. Free legal aid must be available in all countries as it is a basic and fundamental human right. It has been reported that certain authorities permit interviews between the legal adviser and the detainee. Nevertheless, they do not provide any facility to write.

Hence, the revised Rule 93 will be—

Rule 93: "For the purpose of his defence, an untried detainee shall be allowed to apply for free legal aid which must be provided forthwith and to receive visits from his legal adviser with a view to his defence and to prepare and hand to him confidential and other instructions. For these purposes, he shall if he so desires be supplied with writing material and physical facilities. Interviews between the detainee and his legal adviser shall be within the sight but not within the hearing of a police or other institutional official or others."

Sections D and E are omitted as they are no more needed in the revised text.

8

Guidelines for the Management of a Centre of Personality Development

United Nations have decided to revise, amend and bring out a new Standard Minimum Rules for the Treatment of Prisoners for the years to come. The work has been entrusted to experts to proceed further and the issue is discussed in international conferences. I am of the view that the revision now brought out by me will be a timely contribution for the experts to deliberate and discuss. I had close connections with the prison system and prison administration in India. I conducted a study on those life convicts who spent 8 years or more in a jail. I had occasions to interact with prison officials—both custodial and correctional. I had been a member on the Faculty of the State Institute of Correctional Administration and a member of the Prison Advisory Board and the Sentence Review Committee. I could feel the pulse of the petitioners, their thinking, attitude to prison life, miseries and pleasures of confinement, role of the prison staff in correction and thus I have a wealth of experience and information to draft the revised version for international debate and discussion.

Prison architecture is not a developed branch in engineering and the life in prisons is not a fascinating subject for many to study. A few universities have special courses of study in prison management and correctional work. The job opportunity is not bright and, therefore, only a few in academics or in administration have special interest and religious commitment to improve the prevailing situations in the prisons. "Let the prisoner suffer"—for he committed a crime. This is the general attitude and approach of the bureaucrats and politicians in general. Some politicians consider their life in a prison during their career as politicians is a feather in their cap and invariably they put it in their bio-data and take pride of their prison life. Their troubles, sufferings, hardships, pains and tribulations in the prison make them glorified among the followers and, therefore, they take little or no interest to improve the conditions in the prisons. Although the U.N. Standard Minimum Rules for the Treatment of Prisoners came into existence as early as in 1957, they were indifferently implemented in some countries. There has been no determined will or committed interest for the ruling political parties in many countries to enforce the UN Rules and implement them in letter and spirit. The 1957 Rules have become obsolete or have outlived their utility although many countries have reluctantly implemented a few, some or none of them. What a pity indeed!

Whether or not the 1957 Rules have been implemented by the member countries of the United Nations is not the question now. It is time that the old or antiquated 1957 Rules must be amended, revised or substituted by another well thought out guidelines. I take up the pleasant task proudly and thus present this revision for international consideration. This is only a draft and the United Nations have to consider it from many angles before it being accepted. I do not claim that this is a perfect revision, nevertheless I have the honour to request the United Nations to consider and evaluate this draft too when they finally approve or adopt a revised text. As stated earlier, my book titled *The UN Universal Declaration of Human Rights and Criminal Justice: The Total Revision* published by the Concept Publishing Company (Pvt.) Ltd., New Delhi has been well received by the international community. Likewise, it is my hope that this revision too will receive an international acceptance and approval.

Draft

Preamble

To consolidate and revise the Standard Minimum Rules for the Treatment of Prisoners adopted on August 30, 1957 by the First United Nations Congress on the Prevention of Crime and the Treatment of Offenders and approved by Economic and Social Council on 31 July, 1957;

To provide proper care, protection, education and training to all inmates incarcerated for the development of their personality in an upright way in the right direction *via* correction, reformation, resocialization, rehabilitation and reintegration back to society.

To make all to ensure a human rights friendly attitude and approach in their interaction with the inmates—in the best interest of the inmates and for their ultimate personality development in an upright way in the right direction through various means and methods resorted to in the Centre of Personality Development—

Whereas, the Universal Declaration of Human Rights has, in several of its Articles, imposes on the Member States of the United Nations a primary responsibility of ensuring that all the needs of the incarcerated are met and their basic human rights are fully protected;

And whereas the General Assembly of the United Nations has requested the Commission on Crime Prevention and Criminal Justice to establish an open-ended Inter-governmental Expert group on the revision of the existing United Nations Standard Minimum Rules for the Treatment of Prisoners on 21 December, 2010;

And whereas the UN instruments focusing on the Treatment of Prisoners and the same relevant for the Treatment of Prisoners have prescribed a set of Standards to be adhered to by State Parties in securing the best interests of the inmate incarcerated to a Centre of Personality Development;

And whereas it is expedient to revise the existing Standard Minimum Rules relating to the treatment of prisoners, be it adopted by the Member States of the United Nations as their guidelines or directives in the management and running of the Centres of Personality Development henceforth.

REGISTER, IDENTITY AND AUTHORITY

Rule 7—"In every place where persons are housed for the development of personality in an upright way in the right direction by an order of conviction by a competent court of law, there shall be kept a Bound Registration Book with numbered pages in which shall be entered in respect of everyone received—

(1) Information concerning his identify which will further be recorded electronically containing his fingerprints, palm-

prints, signature, photographs, Iris ID and Lip-print ID and Portrait Parle.

(2) (a) Judicial reasons for his commitment and the authority, therefore, which will further be recorded in detail electronically containing a brief summary of the offence as narrated by the convict along with a brief summary of any situational or environmental factors which contributed to the offence.

(b) Special information collected from the convict about his family, attitude, approach and expectation in his life in the Centre for Personality Development, economic/occupational and social background, values towards family, observance of law, police, courts, Centre authorities, duties, works etc., in the Centre and any other information essential for his personality development in an upright way in the right direction.

(3) The day and hour of his admission and release which will further be recorded electronically with details about his life during the pre-incarceration period, during investigation, during trial and the way he managed to live a law abiding life till the date of his admission. His attitude, approach and values towards domestic life, religious life, moral life, social life, leisure-time activities, profession, occupation etc., must be recorded by experts.

(4) Every convict on his admission must be given a copy of the Register so recorded along with a copy of the Centre's Rules which he must observe while he is inside the Centre free of cost and in a language understandable to him.

(5) Every convict on his entry to a Centre has a right to attend a pre-entry course to learn the rules of the Centre along with the conduct norms, rules for the staff-inmate interaction, etiquette in community living and such other matters found necessary for the best interest of the inmate and the institution.

SEPARATION OF CATEGORIES

Rule 8

(a) The different categories of residents in a Centre of

Personality Development shall be housed in separate Institutions or parts of the Institution ***(Cameratae)*** taking into account of their (1) sex, (2) age, (3) crime record, (4) marital status, (5) professional or occupational status, (6) economic background, (7) length of stay, (8) necessities of treatment after diagnosis or any other special ground as may be found necessary.

(b) Men and women shall be housed in separate institutions which are located in different places geographically.

SLEEPING ACCOMMODATIONS

Rule 9

(1) "Sleeping accommodation shall be provided in cubicles in *Cameratae* for 16-20 inmates to enable them to develop community life.

(2) Sleeping accommodation in individual rooms shall be allowed only in rarest of rare cases, or in special circumstances if possible.

(3) Sleeping accommodation in individual cubicles having safety walls with bars and security doors in *cameratae* shall be allowed in all cases where Rule 9(2) is not applied"

Rule 10 is retained as—

"All accommodations provided for the use of the inmates and in particular all sleeping accommodation shall meet all requirements of health, due regard being paid to climatic conditions and particularly to cubic content of air, minimum floor space, lighting, heating and ventilation."

Rule 11

(a) "In all places where the inmates are required to work, there shall be *sufficient* natural light for them to read and work. If it is not possible, the artificial lights provided should be pleasant enough for their eyes to read or work.

(b) There shall be free flow of fresh air whether or not there is artificial ventilation."

SANITARY AND BATHING INSTALLATIONS

Rule 12

"There should be sufficient number of latrines and bathrooms not only in the *camerata* where the inmates stay, but also outside to enable the residents to comply with the needs of nature when necessary and to use them keeping their privacy and human decency attached to such use."

Rule 13

"Every inmate shall be compulsorily required to have a bath or shower, at a temperature suitable to the climate as frequently as necessary for the general hygiene according to season and geographical region decided by the medical doctor attached to the institution:

Provided that the inmates who work as per the judgments of the courts ought to have the bath or shower at least once a day:

Provided further that taking a bath or shower in public or in the visibility of other inmates is degrading and should be avoided at any cost."

Rule 14

"All parts of an institution regularly used by prisoners shall be properly maintained and kept scrupulously clean at all times."

PERSONAL HYGIENE

Rule 15

"Inmates shall keep their person clean in a psychologically conducive atmosphere and to this end, they shall be provided with sufficient time, water and with such other toilet articles along with disinfectants without too much rationing and free of cost as are necessary for maintaining health and cleanliness."

Rule 16

(a) "In order that the inmates may maintain a good appearance compatible with their self respect, facilities shall be provided for the proper care of hair, beard and their private parts. Men shall be enabled to shave regularly and old men shall be provided with assistance/assistants to shave regularly, if needed. Women shall be provided with necessary sanitary articles free of cost for attending their special needs of nature every month. Old men and women should be given every assistance and assistants to keep their body clean taking into account of their physical disabilities to perform the functions related to hygiene.

(b) Every inmate shall be required to wear clean uniform which is neat and tidy. They must change their uniform everyday after the cleaning of their body by bath or otherwise or as and when the change of shabby uniform is necessary.

(c) Every Centre should have facilities for washing clothes by the use of washing machines and the facility should be provided with sufficient washing materials to keep the inmates' uniform and other personal belongings clean, neat and tidy."

CLOTHING, UNIFORM AND SLEEP

Rule 17

(1) "Every inmate shall be provided with an outfit of clothing prescribed by a medical team of experts and such an outfit shall ensure the well-being of the inmate in every aspect.

(2) (a) Underclothing shall be changed and washed as often as necessary and in any case once in everyday.

(b) The underclothing for the inmates in general and for the women or the aged and infirm in particular shall be prescribed by a medical team of experts and everyone shall be educated and introduced to the use of underclothing in daily life.

(3) Whenever, an inmate goes outside the Centre for an authorized purpose, he shall be allowed to wear a clothing

which does not reveal his identity as an inmate of a Centre."

Rule 18

"Every new inmate has a right to get new uniforms issued and they shall be tailor-cut and not mass-produced."

Rule 19

"Every inmate has a right to get a coat issued along with a separate bed, pillow or bedding which shall be clean when issued and throughout his stay in the Centre, kept in good order and changed often to ensure the cleanliness."

FOOD AND WATER

Rule 20

(1) "Every inmate shall be provided with enough food of nutritional value well prepared qualitatively at the usual hours and shall be served in a dining hall having tables and seats to eat it in dignity. The food shall be of wholesome quality adequate for health and strength.

(2) Drinking water shall be made available to all inmates who may drink it lavishly whenever he needs it."

EXERCISE AND SPORTS

Rule 21

(1) "Every inmate who is not employed—i.e., those who are incarcerated with simple imprisonment—shall be persuaded and encouraged to engage in a work of his interest available in the Centre. If he is unwilling to do a work, he shall have one hour of suitable exercise—indoor or outdoor—daily as decided by the medical officer in consultation with the instructor of physical training.

(2) Inmates who are aged and unable to work in spite of a sentence of rigorous imprisonment shall have one hour

(more or less) of suitable exercise—indoor or outdoor—daily as decided by the medical officer in consultation with the instructor of physical training. If no exercise is advised, he shall do *yoga* daily as decided and controlled by an instructor of yogic culture.

(3) Women inmates undergoing simple imprisonment, if not employed at her option, pregnant women, aged women, sick or unhealthy women shall have physical exercise or *Yoga* as the case may be utilizing the indoor or outdoor facility, daily as decided by the medical officer in consultation with a lady instructor of physical training/Yogic culture.

(4) Physical exercise or *Yoga* shall be done only under the supervision of a qualified instructor who shall be a man for the male inmates and a woman for the female inmates separately.

(5) Any inmate who does not belong to any of the categories stated above wants to do physical exercise/*Yoga* along with those mentioned above, facilities shall be provided for the fulfilment of his/her decision.

(6) Every Centre shall have indoor and outdoor facility to do the physical exercise, to receive physical training and to do *Yoga*. To this end, space, installations and equipments shall be provided. The inmates shall be given special physical exercise dress/*yoga* dress free of cost for the purpose. After the physical exercise/*Yoga*, they must have a bath and washing of the dress for which facilities shall be provided and washing materials given free of cost.

(7) Facilities for indoor and outdoor games shall be provided in every Centre and every inmate may be encouraged to make use of the facility. Every inmate shall be provided with sports dress free of cost. Outdoor games shall be played by the inmates under the guidance and supervision of an instructor of physical education and training. The instructor shall be male for male inmates and female for female inmates.

(8) Facilities for playing indoor games shall be provided. Every Centre should have a recreation hall and the kinds of indoor games shall be decided by the instructor of physical training in consultation with the director of the Centre.

MEDICAL OFFICERS AND TREATMENT

Rule 22

(1) "At every Institution there shall be available the services of at least one qualified medical officer from at least two systems of medicine. As many diseases are psychosomatic in origin, the qualified medical officers thus appointed should have good knowledge of Psychiatry.

The medical services should be organized in close relationship with the services rendered by a qualified Psychiatrist, Clinical Psychologist and a Psychiatric Social Worker who are on the medical team of the Centre.

The medical services should be organized further in close relationship to the general health administration of the community or nation. They shall include the services of all systems of medicine for the proper diagnosis and treatment of physical, mental or psychosomatic diseases.

(2) Sick persons who require specialist treatment shall be transferred to specialized institutions or to civil hospitals. Where hospital facilities are provided in an institution, their equipment, furnishings and pharmaceutical supplies shall be proper for the medical care and treatment of sick persons, and there shall be a nursing staff of suitably trained officers.

(3) The specialist institutions or civil hospitals to which a sick inmate is transferred does not have facilities to accommodate the inmate with safety and security, then the services of the specialist medical officers available in such institution/hospital is to be made available to the hospital attached to the Centre.

(4) The services of specialist hospitals owned and operated by private individuals or organizations shall be made available, if needed, to the sick inmate who is in the hospital attached to the Centre. If the services of such doctors cannot be made available to the hospital attached to the Centre, then the sick inmate may be transferred to such private institution on condition that—

(a) The expenditure necessary for such treatment shall be borne by the inmate.

(b) The private institution or the ward/room where the inmate is accommodated shall be declared as an extension of the hospital attached to the Centre.

(c) The institution/ward/room shall have all the necessary requirements to have the safety and security of the inmate accommodated there. The rules and conduct norms applicable to the Centre will be strictly made applicable to such extension of the Centre.

(5) Where hospital facilities are provided in an institution, there shall be a staff of suitably trained persons who shall be male in men's institutions and female in women's institutions. The nursing staff in the Centre's institution should be adequate to provide proper nursing care to the inpatients if facilities for treating the inmates as inpatients is provided.

(6) The Services of a qualified dental officer shall be available to every prisoner."

MEDICAL SERVICES IN WOMEN'S INSTITUTIONS

Rule 23

(1) (a) "At every women's institution or part of the institution where female convicts are housed, there shall be the services of at least one lady medical officer who should be solely responsible for making arrangements for specialist treatment, if that is needed for women-inmates in accordance with the guidelines given under Rule 22.

(b) The sentence of conviction to imprisonment may be stayed in the case of pregnant women until her delivery. If that is not possible, the pregnant women shall be accommodated in a facility available in Government hospitals until her delivery for pre-natal care and treatment. After the delivery of a baby, she shall be admitted in a women's institution where all facilities to provide post-natal care and treatment are available.

(2) (a) Where babies who are breast-fed are in the institution with their mothers, provision shall be made for

accommodating the mothers and babies in a *camerata* physically separated from other *cameratae;*

(b) Where nursing infants are allowed to remain in the institution with their mother, provision shall be made for a nursery separated physically from the institution by a wall in a different compound staffed by qualified persons, where the infants shall spend their time when their mothers are away for work or similar activities; and

(c) Where infants stay with their mothers in the institution, provision shall be made for the infants to meet and mingle with their father as often as found necessary and in any case at least once in a month."

MEDICAL OFFICERS AND EXAMINATION OF THE NEW ENTRANTS

Rule 24

(1) "The medical officer shall examine every new entrant as soon as possible after his/her admission with a view particularly to the discovery of any physical illness, infectious or contagious diseases, diseases which need prolonged treatment or treatment by specialists or in specialist institutions. The medical officer shall see that all necessary measures are taken for the segregation/ isolation of inmates suffering from any infectious or contagious or communicable diseases.

(2) The Psychiatrist, Psychiatric Social Worker, Clinical Psychologist, the workshop chief, the chief of the teaching staff, the welfare officer shall examine every inmate immediately after his/her admission and jointly take a decision for the total development of his/her personality in a upright way in the right direction."

Rule 25

(1) "A health-care and welfare team consisting of the medical officer, psychiatrist, clinical psychologist, psychiatric social worker and the welfare officer shall

have the care of the physical and psychological health of the inmates.

(2) Any member of the health-care and welfare team or all of them shall be free to see, talk and understand all sick persons—that is, physical, psychologically disturbed or psychosomatic–all who complain of illness and any inmate to their—individually or jointly—attention is specially directed. The director of the Centre will be the co-ordinator of the advice and activities of the medical team.

(3) Any member of the health-care and welfare team is free to report to the director whenever he considers that an inmate's physical, psychological (or both) health has been or will be injuriously affected by continued imprisonment or any condition of imprisonment. The director, on receipt of such an information, shall act positively keeping in mind the development of the personality of the inmate in an upright way in the right direction.

(4) Any inmate who is diagnosed to be affected by insanity proper shall be transferred to the Government hospital for such patients for free treatment or to any specialist hospitals for treating them at their expense. The director of the Centre shall be free to make arrangements to have the services of the specialists in specialist hospitals to the Government hospitals, if that is needed—all with the sole purpose of developing the personality of the inmates in an upright way in the right direction."

HEALTH CARE AND WELFARE TEAM AND THEIR ADVICE

Rule 26

(1) "Any member of the health-care and welfare team shall regularly inspect, get the feed-back from the inmates and advise the director upon:

(a) The quality, quantity, preparation and service of the food;

(b) The hygiene and cleanliness of the toilet, bathing and washing facilities provided in the institution;

(c) The personal hygiene of the inmates and the

cleanliness of the inmates' clothings, undergarments, beds and bedding;

(d) The hygiene and cleanliness of the institution, waste management, hygiene in the workshops, hospital, schools, *cameratae,* recreation hall, canteen etc.

(e) The sanitation, heating, lighting, ventilation, air-flow of every building in the Centre;

(f) The purity, purification and quality of the drinking water, food-materials given, vegetables and anything purchased from outside or produced inside the Centre;

(g) Suitability, dignity and neatness of the inmates' uniform and the uniform (dress) of the officials employed in the service of the institution; and

(h) Observance of the rules concerning physical education and sports, work in the Centre, leisure-time activities in cases where there is no technical personnel in charge of these activities.

(2) The director shall take into consideration the reports and advice that any member of the health-care and welfare team presents before him in accordance to 25(3) and 26 and in case he concurs with the recommendations made, shall take immediate steps to rectify the defects or to give effect to those recommendations *mutatis mutandis*; if they are not within his competence or if he does not concur with them, he shall immediately submit his own report justifying his position and the advice of the member of the health-care and welfare team to his higher authority."

DISCIPLINE AND PUNISHMENT

Rule 27

(1) "Discipline and order shall be maintained with firmness both among the staff and among the inmates. No unholy nexus between the staff and the inmates shall be allowed and any violation of the rule owing to the unholy nexus between the staff and the inmates shall be treated as an offence under the criminal laws.

(2) No corporal punishment shall be inflicted on inmates in

disciplinary cases. Any torture in any capacity from the staff to an inmate or by an inmate at the instigation of any member/s of the staff shall be treated as an offence against the criminal laws.

(3) No inmate shall be punished without holding an inquiry in the matter keeping all principles of natural justice.

(4) Forfeiture of the remission marks, withholding of the privilege enjoyed by the inmate, refusal to grand *ticket to leave* for the inmates may be included as punishments in diciplinary cases."

DISCIPLINE AND PERSONALITY DEVELOPMENT

Rule 28

(1) "No prisoner shall be employed in the service of the institution, in any disciplinary capacity.

(2) This rule shall not, however, impede the proper functioning of the systems based on self-Government, under which specified social, educational or sports activities or responsibilities are entrusted under supervision, to inmates who are formed into groups for the purposes of personality development in an upright way in the right direction."

DISCIPLINARY OFFENCE, PUNISHMENT AND AUTHORITY

Rule 29

"There shall be written laws, rules or regulations—

(a) Defining a violation—commission or omission—to be a disciplinary misconduct;

(b) Prescribing the procedure for the conduct of the inquiry and the evidence to be taken;

(c) Clearly specifying the type, intensity, nature and duration of the punishment which may be inflicted;

(d) Specifying the authority competent to impose such punishment;

(e) Stating the procedure for making appeals and the authority to decide on the appeal and pronounce a judgment; and

(f) All steps must be initiated and executed with an objective of developing the personality of the inmate in an upright way in the right direction."

CONDUCT OF DISCIPLINARY CASES

Rule 30

(1) "No inmate under a disciplinary inquiry shall be punished unless he has been issued with charges which must be specific and precise and should convey to the delinquent in the clearest possible terms the act of misconduct under law or regulation levelled against him.

(2) No inmate under a disciplinary inquiry shall be punished unless he is given a reasonable opportunity to defend his case.

(3) Every incarcerated under disciplinary inquiry has a right to—

   (a) adduce all relevant and material evidence on which he relies his defence;

   (b) have the evidence of the witness/es against him taken in his presence and to cross-examine such witness/es;

   (c) See all relevant documents to which he is entitled to have accessibility;

(4) All the acts done and decisions taken must be done in good faith;

(5) No incarcerated under inquiry shall be punished twice for the same offence and no one shall be punished without giving him an opportunity to make representations as to why the proposed punishment should not be inflicted on him and get his representation to make a through examination of the case under inquiry; and

(6) No incarcerated under inquiry shall be punished unless the delinquent is allowed to be represented by a fellow associate or by himself or by an official employee of the Centre on whom he has trust. Under no circumstances, a lawyer shall be allowed to represent the incarcerated under inquiry in disciplinary matters. Where necessary, the incarcerated under inquiry shall be allowed to make his defence through an interpreter."

PUNISHMENTS IN DISCIPLINARY INQUIRIES

Rule 31

(1) Where a disciplinary authority is satisfied on the conduct of a disciplinary inquiry that an incarcerated has committed a misconduct or violated a conduct norm/Centre's rule/regulation etc., the disciplinary authority may if it thinks so fit,

(a) allow the incarcerated delinquent to abide by the norms/rules/regulations after an advice or admonition with or without attending special counselling session arranged by the authorities for developing his personality and values in an upright way;

(b) direct the incarcerated delinquent to participate in group counselling and similar activities for a period of time regularly arranged by authorities for similar inmates;

(c) order the incarcerated delinquent to perform some community services inside the prison as chosen by him from a list prepared by the authorities for a period of time;

(d) order the incarcerated delinquent to pay a fine if he works in the prison;

(e) direct the incarcerated inmate to be under the special care, watch and surveillance of a specified officer of the Centre for a period of time provided that the officer so entrusted takes the responsibility for his good behaviour for a period of time as fixed by the disciplinary authority;

(f) direct the incarcerated delinquent to do some extra work in addition to the normal hours of work, if he works or to do some extra work for fixed hours, if he does not work;

(g) order for the forfeiture of the remission marks earned by him during his stay;

(h) order for delaying the consideration for pre-mature release (Parole) for a specified period of time as decided by the authority;

(i) order for refusing the grant of "ticket to leave" or home visit for a period of time as decided by the authority;

(j) order for the withholding of the privileges enjoyed by the inmate for a period of time; and

(k) order for a change of labour for a stated period to some irksome or severe form.

(2) Corporal punishments, punishments by placing in a dark cell, separate or solitary confinement for a prolonged period exceeding 14 days, reduction of diet and all cruel, inhuman, sub-human or degrading punishments for disciplinary offences shall be completely prohibited."

MEDICAL OFFICERS AND PUNISHMENTS

Rule 32

(1) "The disciplinary authority shall obtain an investigation—medical, social, clinical—psychological, psychiatric, welfare, educational, professional/occupational/work—report on the inmate through anyone or more of the professional staff in the Centre and shall take into consideration the findings of such report before passing the order.

(2) No incarcerated inmate who violates the norms, rules or regulations shall be punished to close confinement unless it is certified by the health-care and welfare team that he is fit to sustain it and is not detrimental to the development of the personality of the inmate. In cases, the professionals in the health-care and welfare team are not in a position to file a consensus report jointly, the disciplinary authority may take a decision evaluating the majority opinion. If that too is not possible, the disciplinary authority shall take a decision in good will or faith for the best interest of the incarcerated inmate.

(3) The same principle shall apply to any other punishment that may be prejudicial to the physical or psychological health of the inmate. In any case, the order shall be passed in goodwill, in fairness, equity and good conscience for the best interest of the inmate—for the development of his personality in an upright way in the right direction.

(4) Any or all members of the health care and welfare team shall allow the inmates undergoing punishments to visit

him/them as and when necessary for obtaining advice. The medical officer along with the psychiatrist shall visit daily inmates undergoing close confinement or such other punishment that may be prejudicial to the physical or psychological health of the inmate and shall advise the director if he considers the termination or alteration of the punishment necessary on grounds of physical or psychological health.

(5) The director of the Centre may if he is satisfied that having regard to the nature of the misconduct or violation of the rule and the circumstances of the case and the good behaviour shown by the inmate after the order of punishment has been passed, it is expedient to do, for reasons to be recorded, reduce the intensity of the punishment, change the type or nature of the punishment to a lesser one or to cancel the order of punishment of the disciplinary authority in goodwill for the best interest of the inmate and for developing his personality in an upright way in the right direction.

(6) Imprisonment and other measures which result in cutting of an offender from the outside world are afflictive by the very fact of taking from the person the right of self-determination by depriving him of his liberty. Therefore, the system shall not, except as incidental or justifiable segregation or the maintainance of discipline, aggravate the suffering inherent in such a situation."

INSTRUMENTS OF RESTRAINT

Rule 33

"Instruments of restrains, such as handcuffs, chains, irons and strait jacket shall never be applied as a punishment.

(1) Instruments of restrains shall not be used as a precaution against escape during a transfer as the transport must be done in a protected vehicle with the help of adequate number of trained personnel (with arms, if necessary) or as the transport may be avoided by video-presentation, a 3-tier system of justice administration or the authority

situated in the vicinity of the Centre or any other ways by virtue of which the escape of the inmate can be prevented.

(2) Instruments of restrains shall not be used on medical grounds without obtaining the direction from the health-care and welfare team or a medical board which shall give such directions only for the best interest of the inmate without jeopardizing the objective of incarceration which is the development of the inmates' personally in an upright way in the right direction."

Rule 34

"The patterns and manner of instruments of restraint, if needed, shall be decided by the health-care and welfare team/medical board. Such instruments shall be approved by the Central administration of the Centres of Personality Development and such instruments shall not be applied for any longer time that is strictly necessary for the development of the inmates' personality in an upright way in the right direction."

INFORMATION TO AND COMPLAINTS BY PRISONERS

Rule 35

(1) "Every new entrant admitted to a Centre shall be provided with written information about—
   - (a) time-table of the Centre;
   - (b) disciplinary rules;
   - (c) misconduct and violations of rules including punishments;
   - (d) purpose of incarceration for personality development and the need for co-operation;
   - (e) rules relating to labour, education, leisure-time activities, religious performances, workshop, neatness, hygiene, cleanliness, behaviour in the dining hall and *camerata*, interpersonal relations, interaction with the Centre's staff etc.;
   - (f) rights, duties, responsibilities and obligations of the inmates;
   - (g) rules of remission, privileges, canteen and correspondence with family and outside world;

(h) authorized methods of seeking information and making complaints;

(i) authorized methods to get counselling, moral training, use of library and reading rooms, etiquette, manners and good behaviour; and

(j) facilities in the Centre and the behavioural principles, values and traits for the development of personality in an upright way in the right direction.

(2) If an inmate is illiterate, semi-literate or moderately educated, the aforesaid information shall be conveyed to him orally through an orientation course lasting at least two days. Those who attend the orientation course on admission shall be asked to attend a refresher course at least once in an year.

(3) Boards containing the information shall be displayed in a conspicuous manner in the Centre. Audio-visual gadgets may be used for the purpose."

REQUESTS AND COMPLAINTS

Rule 36

(1) "Every inmate, orally or in writing, shall have the opportunity each week day of making requests or complaints to the director of the Centre or the officer authorized to represent him. A box with a lock and key to receive the requests/complaints should be kept in every institution and its key should be kept in the personal custody of the director. Requests and complaints made in an anonymous way shall be accepted for making inquiries to find out remedial solutions, if that is needed. No action, disciplinary or otherwise, shall be initiated against an inmate making requests and/or complaints. No request or complaint shall be made to be a cause of persecution for the inmates individually or for the institution generally.

(2) (a) It shall be possible for the inmates to make requests and complaints to the Head of the Department during his inspection. The inmates shall have the opportunity to talk to the Head of the Department *in camera* without anyone of the staff being present.

(b) The Head of the Department shall convene a general meeting of the inmates during his inspection to receive requests and complaints so that solutions to the common problems of the inmates can be solved instantly or otherwise.

(c) The Guideline 36 (2) (a) is applicable to all authorities like the Human Rights Commission, Sub-committees of the Legislature, Minister of the State empowered' to inspect and hold discussions with the inmates and the staff. All such authorities empowered shall make attempts to solve the problems and settle the issues and complaints which have a common interest in consultation with or without the Head of the Department.

(3) Every inmate shall have the freedom to make a request or complaint, without censorship as to substance but in proper form, to the Head of the Department, the judicial authority and other proper authorities like the Minister in charge of the Centres of Personality Development, Human Rights Commissions, Sub-committee of the Legislature empowered to inspect the Centre through means and methods ensuring to protect the secrecy and even anonymity.

(4) Unless it is evidently frivolous or groundless, every request or complaint—anonymous or otherwise—shall be promply dealt with by an Inquiry Board/Committee with its investigating team and replied to the inmates if their identity is revealed or otherwise informed to the inmates in a common way, if it is anonymous, by methods and means adopted in each Centre for the information of the inmates in general within 30 days or earlier after the request or complaint has been received."

CONTACT WITH THE OUTSIDE WORLD

Rule 37

(a) "Inmates shall be allowed under necessary camera surveillance (CCTV) to communicate with their family and reputable friends enlisted by them, at the time of admission, at regular intervals, both by correspondence and by receiving visits;

(b) The authorities of the Centre shall verify the character, antecedents and reputation of the family members and friends enlisted by them immediately after the admission. Persons other than those enlisted by them as members of their family or friends come to visit them, the authority may refuse permission if they fail to or refuse to prove their identity and reputation; and

(c) The correspondence of the inmates to outside the Centre shall be screened for the purpose of security and welfare of the society in general and institution in particular. The correspondence may be *via* letters or land line telephones (Under Camera Surveillance) and under no circumstances shall be through internet or other electronic means of communication. No mobile phones will be permitted to communicate between an inmate and the people outside."

Rule 38

(1) "Inmates who are foreign nationals shall be allowed reasonable facilities to communicate with the diplomatic and consular representatives of the State to which they belong.

(2) Prisoners who are nationals of States without diplomatic or consular representation in the country and refugees or Stateless persons shall be allowed similar facilities to communicate with the diplomatic representative of the State which takes charge of their interests or any national or international authority whose task it is to protect such persons:

Provided that (a) the communication allowed under 38 (1 & 2) shall be with the consent of the Centre's authorities for a fixed time decided by the authorities;

(b) The communication shall be under camera surveillance and the video of the communication shall be kept under the custody of authorities; and

(c) The expenditure shall be met by the inmate who communicates with the diplomatic/consular/others in all cases stated under 38 (1 & 2)."

LIBRARY AND READING ROOM

Rule 39

(a) "Inmates shall be kept informed regularly of the important items of news by reading of news papers of repute in the vernacular as well as in the national language, journals, periodicals or special institutional publications, by hearing wireless transmissions, by lectures or by any similar means as authorized or controlled by the administration;

(b) For the benefit of the illiterate and semi-literate inmates, facility shall be made for the reading of the more important items of news by an educated inmate during the time of breakfast and lunch utilizing amplifiers and loud speakers;

(c) Blackening of the news items or cutting away of the news items from the daily papers/periodicals should be avoided unless otherwise it is found to be very essential to do so by the administration; and

(d) Those inmates who utilize the reading room for their enrichment of knowledge should be encouraged with incentives/remission marks."

Rule 40

(a) "Every institution shall have a library for the use of all categories of prisoners, adequately stocked with both recretional and instructional books and prisoners shall be encouraged to make full use of it;

(b) Those inmates who prove that they make use of the library and books to the development of their personality in an upright way in the right direction must be rewarded with remission marks."

FAITH AND RELIGION

Rule 41

(1) "A qualified representative of every religion may be approved by the administration and allowed to hold

religious services subject to conditions imposed by the authority and accepted by the representative.

(2) Representatives of every religion may be approved to offer counselling to the inmates of their religion for a fixed length of time decided by the authority of the Centre.

(3) No representative of any religion shall be allowed to promote and propagate his faith to any other inmates belonging to other religion/sects/denomination/caste/sub-caste/division.

(4) Access to a qualified representative of any religion shall not be refused to an inmate belonging to his religion if it helps for the development of his personality in an upright way in the right direction.

(5) If an inmate objects to the visit of any religious representative to his private life, his attitude shall be fully respected.

(6) If an inmate wants to pray in silence or perform by himself some religious rituals without causing disturbance to other fellow inmates, his need shall be fully respected.

(7) All attempts shall be made to develop secularism among the inmates. For this, religious festivals shall be organized by all belonging to different religions for harmonious co-existence within the Centre.

(8) Atheism, agnosticism, rationalism, humanism etc., which do not accept any religion shall be accepted as a reality and those who believe in such non-religious or anti-god philosophy shall be fully respected."

Rule 42

(1) "Every inmate shall be free to attend the services offered by his or any other religious groups.

(2) Every inmate shall be free to possess books of his or any religious observance and instruction of his denomination."

VALUABLES AND PROPERTY

Rule 43

(1) (a) "All money, valuables, clothing and other effects

belonging to an entrant to a Centre, which under the regulations of the institutions, he is not allowed to retain shall on his admission to the Centre be placed, at his option, either in safe custody of the authorities or be entrusted to a person of his choice outside the Centre. In the former case, an inventory thereof shall be signed by the entrant. Steps shall be taken to keep them in good condition.

(b) Wedding ring, *Mangalya Sutra* in married women, any symbol of marriage in married people, articles of religious faith such as relics, symbols, caskets of safety or those containing prayers for self-protection etc., shall be items which one can at his potion, retain to himself or entrust to the Centre/person outside the Centre whom he chooses.

(2) (a) On the release of the inmate, all such articles and money, if they are in the safe custody of the Centre, shall be returned to him. On the death of the inmate, all such articles and money shall be returned to those who are the legal inheritants to his property. All lifers or long termers shall be asked to write a will in which the nominee who may receive his articles and valuables shall be specified. Alternatively, he shall nominate a person to receive the articles and valuables kept in safe custody of the Centre, if that is needed.

(b) On the release or death, the inmate or his nominee respectively shall receive only such articles and money except in so far as he has been authorized to spend money or send any such property out of the Centre, or it has been found necessary on hygienic grounds to destroy any article of clothing. The inmate or his nominee shall sign a receipt for the articles and money returned to him.

(3) Any money or effects received for an inmate from outside shall be treated in the same way.

(4) Any money received by him out of his labour in the Centre will be treated as money deposited in safe custody.

(5) Money deposited in safe custody shall be treated as money deposited with the Government and shall be given bank interest applicable in the country.

(6) If an inmate who has deposited money or valuables as per 43(1)(a) with the Centre may opt for entrusting the same to a person of his choice at any time during his stay in the Centre.

(7) If an entrant brings in any drugs or medicine, the medical officer shall decide what shall be made of them."

DEATH, ESCAPE, ILLNESS AND TRANSFER

Rule 44

(1) (a) "Upon the death, escape from the Centre's custody, non-return of the inmate after parole or ticket to leave or serous illness of or serious injury to an inmate, the director shall at once inform the spouse by the quickest means if the resident is married or the nearest relative and shall in any event inform any other person previously designated by the inmate.

(b) The director is bound to follow the same procedure said under 44(1)(a) if an inmate is removed to an institution for the treatment of mental diseases or is removed to a civil hospital for the treatment of a serious physical illness or injury. The director shall allow the inmate to have specialist treatment in specialist hospitals or by specialist doctors if the expenses towards such treatment is met by the inmate or his family provided that the rules of custody in the Centre are fully honoured by the inmate/family and the hospital authorities as if his stay in that specialist hospital is an extension of his stay in the Centre.

(2) An inmate shall be informed softly at once of the death or serious illness of any near relative or severe mishap at his family or an unfortunate act of *vis major* at home. In case of the sudden death or critical illness of a near relative or severity of the mishap or the cruelty of the act of *vis major*, the inmate should be authorized whenever need and circumstances allow, to go to his home or wherever, at the expense of the Centre, either under escort or alone as the authorities deem fit and suitable.

(3) Every inmate shall have the right to inform at once his

family or a near relative at his option and free of cost of his imprisonment or his transfer to another institution."

REMOVAL OF INMATES

Rule 45

(1) "When the inmates are taken to or from a Centre, they shall not be exposed to/exposed as little as possible to the public view as inmates of a Centre of Personality Development and proper safeguards shall be taken to protect them from insult, attack, curiosity, escape and publicity in any form.

(2) The transport of the inmates shall be in conveyances which are no way different from those used by the general public—which shall be adequate enough to ensure the safety of the inmate during the transport.

(3) The transport of the inmates shall be carried out at the expense of the administration."

INSTITUTIONAL PERSONNEL: RECRUITMENT AND SERVICE

Rule 46

(1) "The Public Service Commission or the Civil Service Recruitment Board shall conduct a written test to measure the intellectual capability of the aspiring candidates to the service followed by psychological tests to assess the personality and aptitude of the candidates by suitably qualified experts in the field.

For the purpose of enlisting the members of the custodial staff, a physical efficiency test of suitable standard shall be conducted.

On the basis of the tests conducted to measure the intellectual capability, to assess the aptitude to evaluate the personality traits like the humanness, integrity, understanding, empathy, devotion to work, service with a human face etc., and steps to verify the physical fitness etc., an interview board consisting of experts shall hold a face to face interview with the candidates to enlist the right personnel to the service.

(2) The administration shall constantly seek to awaken and maintain in the minds of the personnel, of the people and the inmates the conviction that the work in a Centre of Personality Development is a human service of great social importance and to this end all appropriate means of informing and educating the public and the inmates should be used.

(3) To secure the foregoing ends, personnel shall be appointed on a full-time (permanent) basis and on contract basis as professional officials. Those who are appointed on full time basis shall have civil service status with security of tenure subject to good conduct and character, efficiency and effectiveness in a positive way and physical and mental fitness. Those who are on contract basis, if are appointed on full-time basis, shall have civil service status with security of tenure as and when they become full-time.

(4) Salary, perks, employment benefits and conditions of service shall be attractive to retain the best men and women in service."

INSTITUTIONAL PERSONNEL: EDUCATION AND TRAINING

Rule 47

(1) "The lowest entry level post shall be for personnel who possess an adequate standard of education—that is, 12 years of schooling—and intelligence—that is, a pass in the said examination—with body measurements to be physically fit to perform the work which is of an exacting and strenuous nature.

(2) Before entering on duty, the personnel in the custodial staff shall be given a course of training in their general and specific duties which shall include special lectures in criminology, correctional work, prison management, human behaviour, victimology, professional ethics and qualities of an official in the Centre of Personality Development.

(3) All personnel recruited to the custodial staff shall undergo special training in physical fitness which shall include weapon training, armed and unarmed combat, mob operation and physical training. All personnel in the custodial as well as correctional staff shall undergo a course on *yoga*, meditation, self-control and personality development.

(4) All undergoing the induction training shall be required to pass theoretical and practical tests.

(5) After entering on duty and during their career, the personnel shall maintain and improve their skill, knowledge, expertise and professional capacity by attending courses of in-service training—i.e., orientation course, specialized courses, promotion courses, development courses, management courses etc., to be organized regularly at suitable intervals."

Rule 48

"All members or the personnel shall be role models for the inmates in character and conduct so as to command their respect."

INSTITUTIONAL PERSONNEL: SPECIALISTS AND THE DIRECTOR

Rule 49

(1) "There shall be specialists not less than 33 per cent of the total staff in a Centre from various fields such as criminology, correctional work, psychology, social work, sociology, welfare, education, medicine, nursing, trade and industry, etc. for the correction, reformation, rehabilitation, resocialization, personality development and reintegration to the society and culture back.

(2) The services of the specialists shall be effectively and meaningfully secured and utilized on a permanent basis without thereby excluding part-time or voluntary specialists."

Rule 50

(1) "The director of a Centre shall be appointed on full time basis. He shall be adequately qualified in social sciences for his job by academic education, character, knowledge, administrative effectiveness, proper training, reputation and experience.
(2) Every personnel shall be provided with adequate facilities and encouragement to acquire academic and on the job qualifications and excellence in the work and duties.
(3) The director and his staff shall reside on the premises of the Centre or in its immediate vicinity for which facilities shall be provided for family accommodation.
(4) When two or more Centres are under the authority of one director, he shall visit each one of them at frequent intervals regularly at irregular hours for performing his duties. A responsible, work-knowing and qualified subordinate/associate resident-official shall be in charge of each of these Centres."

STAFF AND THEIR LANGUAGE

Rule 51

(1) "All, if possible or as far as it is possible, employed in a Centre shall be able to communicate *via* verbal and non-verbal language to each other in a way understood by the greatest number of inmates housed there.
(2) The verbal and non-verbal language shall be for the development of the inmates' personality in an upright way in the right direction.
(3) Whenever necessary, the services of an interpreter who knows the verbal and non-verbal language shall be used."

Rule 52

(1) "In Centres which utilize the services of the specialists for the development of the inmates' personality in an upright way in the right direction, all of them, as far as possible, shall reside on the premises of the Centre or in its

immediate vicinity. The medical officer shall necessarily reside on the premises of the Centre or in its immediate vicinity.

(2) In Centres where specialists are not appointed, then the services of the specialists working in other Centres shall be made readily available. They shall visit the inmates daily to ensure their services at any time as they need them.

(3) In cases of emergency or immediate medical attention, arrangements shall be made with the civil hospital or any other private/specialist—hospital to attend the inmates as and when necessary and particularly when the medical officer of the Centre cannot offer his services as the situation demands."

MEN AND WOMEN IN THE SAME CENTRE

Rule 53

(1) "In an institution for both men and women, the part of the institution set aside for women shall be under the authority of a responsible woman officer having unblemished sex-values and she alone shall have the custody of the keys of all that parts of the institution.

(2) No male member of the staff shall enter the part of the institution set aside for women unless an entry is made in a register kept for the purpose and accompanied by two women officers of character and sexual integrity.

(3) Women inmates shall be attended and supervised only by women officers of proved sexual uprightness. This does not, however, preclude male members of the staff, particularly the specialists from carrying out their professional duties in a transparent way in Centres or parts of the Centres set aside for women.

(4) Guidelines laid under 53 (1, 2 & 3) are strictly and meticulously applicable in the part of the institution set aside, *mutatis mutandis* for men and shall be strictly adhered to by substituting male for female and men for women in the above guidelines.

(5) As far as possible constructing the institutions exclusively

meant for men geographically away from the institutions housing women shall be encouraged."

OFFICIALS AND USE OF FORCE

Rule 54

(1) "No official member in a Centre shall use physical force against an inmate/group of inmates except in self-defence or the defence of a fellow associate/fellow inmate or in cases of attempted escape or active or passive physical resistance to a reasonable order based on law or regulations.

(2) No official member in a Centre shall instigate or provoke, encourage or in any way cause a fellow inmate to use physical force against another inmate/group of inmates except in the circumstances enumerated under 54(1) above.

(3) Any official or at his need and request any fellow inmate who has recourse to force shall use it no more than is strictly necessary—a little more or a little less—and shall report the incident immediately to the authorities concerned.

(4) When the authority to use physical force is exercised, the official or under his request any fellow inmate/inmates may voluntarily cause the death of the inmate/s if his/their act which occasions the exercise of the authority be of any of the descriptions hereinafter enumerated, such as:

First, such an act as may reasonably cause the apprehension that death will be otherwise be the consequence of the act.

Secondly, such an act as may reasonably cause the apprehension that a serious injury will otherwise be the consequence of the act.

If the act be not of any of the descriptions stated above, the authority to use physical force does not extend to the voluntary causing of death to the inmate/s, but does extend to the voluntary causing to the inmate/s of any harm other than death.

The authority to use the physical force commences as soon as a reasonable apprehension of danger to the body of the official/at his request, of the fellow inmate/s arises from an attempt or threat to commit the act though the act may not have been committed and it continues as long as such apprehension of danger to the body continues.

If in the exercise of the authority to employ physical force against an inmate/inmates which reasonably causes the apprehension of death, the inmate/s be so situated that the official/at his request the fellow inmate/s cannot effectively exercise that authority without the risk of harm to an innocent person, his right of private defence extends the running of that risk.

(5) The custodial staff in a Centre shall be given special training in the use of weapons and musketry during their induction course and thereafter periodically as and when necessary. This shall be in addition to their physical training as well as training in unarmed combat and mob operation tactics.

(6) Except in situations which necessitate arms or ammunitions, the staff performing duties which bring them into direct contact with the inmates shall not be armed. No member of the staff shall, under any circumstances, use arms or ammunitions unless he is trained in their use."

Rule 55

"Over and above the inspections done by the official authorities—statutory or otherwise, there shall be regular inspections conducted by qualified and experienced officials appointed by a competent authority. Their task shall be to ensure that these Centres are administered in accordance with the existing laws and regulations and with a view to bring out about the objectives of incarceration, namely development of the personality of the inmates in an upright way in the right direction."

Note: [Rules 56, 57, 58, 59 in Part II of the existing Standard Minimum Rules-1955 are omitted]

PRISON LIFE AND LIFE IN LIBERTY

Rule 60

(1) "Every step shall be initiated and the meaningfully

implemented in the Centre so that there should be, as far as possible, only minimum difference between the life in the Centre and the same outside which tend to lessen the responsibility of the inmates or the respect due to their dignity as human beings.

(2) From the moment of an inmate's entry into the Centre and throughout his life in the Centre, especially before the completion of the sentence, necessary steps and strategies be taken to ensure for the inmate's return to life in a free society as a person developed in his personality in an upright way in the right direction. In order to achieve this, the Centre shall—

(a) Organize periodical courses and particularly a pre-release course to make the inmate understand the philosophy behind.

(b) Allow the inmate to stay in a half way home established under the Centre's administrative authority or the authority of an NGO approved by the Centre.

(c) Grant parole under the supervision of Paroie Officers."

COMMUNITY AGENCIES AND THE CENTRE

Rule 61

(1) (a) "Every inmate shall be encouraged to have loving and caring relations with his family, kith and kin, friends and decent members of the public provided his relationship is for the mutual benefits of the inmate and the contact-party outside as well as not harmful to the Centre and its functionings.

(b) The Centre shall maintain a list of community agencies, social workers, NGOs etc. so that their services can be effectively made use of for the development of the personality of the inmates in an upright way in the right direction and for the correction, rehabilitation, reformation, resocialisation and reintegration of the inmates to the society back.

(c) All steps and strategies shall be initiated and implemented to the maximum extent, compatible with the law and the sentence, the rights relating to civil interest, social security rights and other social benefits of the inmates."

Rule 62 ***is deleted***

INDIVIDUALIZATION, SECURITY AND SIZE OF THE CENTRES

Rule 63

(1) "For developing the personality of an inmate in an upright way in the right direction, individualization of the inmates (for the purpose of fulfilling the objectives) may be inevitable, classification of the inmates will be necessary, accommodation in separate *cameratae* suitable for achieving the aims will be needed. It shall be the duty of the Centre to implement the programmes in a meaningful way for correction, reformation, resocialisation, rehabilitation and reintegration of the inmate to society back.

(2) The inmates, after examining them by a team consisting of a medical doctor, psychologist, psychiatrist, psychiatric social worker, welfare officer, trade instructor and so on shall be classified and accommodated in a Centre taking into account the security needs and the inmate's need for personality development. The Centres may be "Maximum, Medium, or Minimum Security" institutions in which the last (open institutions) one which relies on the self-discipline and development of the inmate's personality is found to be most favourable to the correction, reformation, resocialization, rehabilitation and reintegration of the inmate to society back.

(3) A Centre in whatever category it belongs shall be a fit institution for the development of the inmate's personality in an upright way in the right direction. For it, it shall be neither very large nor very small. Five hundred inmates in an institution is ideal for a Centre of Personality Development.

(4) It is purposeless to maintain small institutions which

cannot provide proper facilities to the inmates for their personality development."

SOCIETY AND REINTEGRATION TO SOCIETY

Rule 64

(1) "Every assistance shall be ensured to NGOs and other governmental agencies to provide meaningful and effective after-care services to released inmates for their reintegration to a life in a free society and to live there in dignity.

(2) Every step shall be initiated and implemented for educating the society about its role in the rehabilitation and reintegration of a released inmate to society back."

Rule 65 ***is deleted***

METHODS AND STRATEGIES FOR DEVELOPMENT OF PERSONALITY

Rule 66

(1) "For the development of the inmate's personality in an upright way in the right direction, all appropriate means, methods and strategies shall be used including religious instructions and care in countries where this is possible and if it is not possible, then moral instructions and care should invariably be given. Academic education, vocational training and guidance, individual centred clinical method and group relations method of treatment, social case work, employment counselling, intellectual development by reading, education, library use, listening to lectures and exposure to media, physical development and strengthening of moral character, effective use of leisure time activities, works in industries or otherwise in accordance with the individual needs of each inmate taking account of his family, school, social and crime history, his physical and psychological capacities and aptitudes, his personal temperament, the length of his sentence and his prospectus after release. To these end,

appropriate tools should be developed and experts ought to be appointed.

(2) For every inmate with a sentence of suitable length, the director shall receive, as soon as possible after his admission full reports on all the matters referred to in the foregoing paragraph. Such report shall always include an assessment or evaluation report by a medical officer, psychologist, psychiatrist, psychiatric social worker, welfare officer, the trade instructor and the teacher on the physical, mental, intellectual and emotional conditions of the inmate.

(3) The reports and other relevant documents shall be placed in individual and in computer files. It shall be kept up to date and classified in such a way that it can be consulted by the concerned and responsible personnel wherever the need arises."

CLASSIFICATION AND INDIVIDUALIZATION

Rule 67

'The purpose of classification shall be—

(a) To develop the personality of the inmate in an upright to way in the right direction.
(b) To correct, reform, resocialize, rehabilitate and reintegrate the inmate back to society."

Rule 68

"Separate *cameratae* of the Centre shall be used for accommodating different categories of inmates after classification for the development of their personality in an upright way in the right direction."

Rule 69

"As soon as possible—i.e., in any case within 72 hours—after admission and after a thorough study of the personality, aptitude, attitude, values etc. of each inmate with a sentence of suitable and sufficient length, a detailed programme for the development of an inmate's personality in an upright way in the right direction shall be prepared for him by a team of experts consisting of a psychologist, psychiatric social worker, welfare officer, trade instructor, medical officer and so on in the light of the data, information and knowledge gathered or obtained about his individual needs, his capacities and dispositions."

PRIVILEGES

Rule 70

(1) "The system of privileges appropriate for different classes of inmates and the different methods of treatment shall be established at every institution. They shall be told to every inmate at the time of admission.
(2) The systems of privileges and the different methods of treatment shall be exhibited in a conspicuous way in the Centre so that the inmates may know about them.
(3) No informal privileges shall be granted to any inmate under any circumstances. If a privilege is granted on special reasons, the grounds should be specified and it is an exception and not a general rule.
(4) The sole purpose of the system of privileges and different methods of treatment shall be to encourage good conduct, develop a sense of responsibility, secure the interest and willing co-operation of the inmates in their personality development in an upright way in the right direction, have a feeling of living in dignity both inside the Centre and afterwards in a free society on release.
(5) An illiterate/semi-literate inmate or an inmate who does not know the language of the inmates in a Centre should be informed of the privileges orally by the authorities of the Centre themselves or by using an interpreter or a translator."

WORK IN THE CENTRE

Rule 71

(1) "Labour in the Centre shall be for the development of the

inmates' personality in an upright way in the right direction.

(2) All inmates under sentence shall work, subject to their physical and psychological fitness determined by a team consisting of the medical officer, a psychologist, a psychiatric social worker, trade instructor and the welfare officer. All inmates who are not under sentence shall be free to opt for a work if they so desire.

(3) The work shall be for the development of the inmates' personality in an upright way in the right direction giving emphasis to the best interest of the inmates—best for the correction, reformation, resocialization, rehabilitation and reintegration to the society back after release.

(4) The work shall be such that the inmates should be able to live in the dignity after their release.

(5) Vocational training in income generating trades shall be the prerogative of the inmates able to profit thereby and necessarily for young prisoners.

(6) Every inmate has a right to opt for a trade/work on admission to a Centre as well as a right for a change in the trade/work available in the Centre as he decides."

PRISON LABOUR: OBJECTIVES, WORK AND REST

Rule 72

(1) "The organization, methods of work, work environment, management style, discipline, interpersonnel communication, etc. in the Centre shall be, as far as possible, the same as seen in similar institutions outside the Centre, the purpose being to prepare the inmates for the conditions of normal occupational life in dignity.

(2) Every inmate is entitled to get a certificate of experience/employment on his release from the Centre with all details related to the trade, designation, duration, performance, character and conduct, etc.

(3) The interest of the inmates and of their work and vocational training must never be subordinated to the purpose of making a financial profit or any other pecuniary advantage from an industry in the Centre."

Rule 73

(1) "Preferably, institutional industries and farms should be operated directly by the administration only with the help of specialists in institutional training with an objective of the 'best interests' of the inmates.

(2) The institutional industries and farms may be operated directly by NGOs committed in activities connected to inmates' welfare and after-care services under the control of the administration. The administration may impose reasonable and necessary conditions for the eligibility and suitability for such NGOs. In any case, the best interests of the inmates shall be the ultimate aim in such decisions.

(3) Institutional industries and farms shall never be operated by private contractors for their benefit.

(4) The operation of the institutional industries and farms and their interest shall not be subordinated to the purpose of making a financial profit or any other pecuniary benefits from an industry or farm in the Centre."

Rule 74

(1) "The provisions of the labour laws in force in the country shall be made applicable to the inmates, *mutatis mutandis* in all Centres of Personality Development.

(2) Provisions of laws laid down in any statutes/administrative orders to protect the safety and health of free workmen shall be equally observed in Centres of Personality Development.

(3) Provisions shall be made and enacted to indemnity the inmates against any industrial or otherwise injury, including occupational disease and loss of life expectancy on the same terms applicable by laws to free workmen."

Rule 75

(1) "The maximum daily and weekly working hours of the inmates shall be fixed by law or by administrative regulations, taking into account the local rules or customs in regard to the employment of free workmen.

(2) The hours so fixed shall leave one rest day a week and all

holidays declared by the Government for institutions outside and sufficient time for education, physical exercises, spiritual needs (optional to the inmates) and other activities as are required as part of the personality development, correction, reformation, resocialization, rehabilitation and reintegration to the society of the inmates.

(3) Every inmate shall be entitled to have provident fund, gratuity and other benefits which employees in similar works are eligible to receive outside the Centre."

Rule 76

(1) "There shall be a system of equitable remuneration of the work of the inmates.

(2) Under the system, the inmates shall be allowed to spend at least a part of their earnings on approved articles for their own use and to send a part of their earnings to their family.

(3) The system should also provide that a part of the earnings should be set aside by the administration so as to constitute a saving fund to be handed over to the inmates on his release. If the fund is very meagre, provisions shall be made to provide him a minimum fund for his living in dignity outside the Centre."

EDUCATION AND TRAINING

Rule 77

(1) "Provisions shall be made and implemented for the further education of the inmates willing to study further.

(2) Provisions shall be made and implemented for obtaining a recognized certificate, diploma or degree for the education they undertake.

(3) Provisions shall be made and implemented for hiring out teachers to provide instructions for those who prosecute their education further. NGOs willing to offer assistance may be purposefully utilized for the purpose.

(4) Books, fees for the course and examination, study and writing materials shall be provided free of cost by the administration. On completion of the course or on

obtaining a pass in the examination, special remission marks should be given to the successful inmates.

(5) Inmates who show good character and conduct may be sent to academic institution outside the Centre if they show satisfactory performance or success in education and subsequent examinations. All expenses towards such courses of study shall be borne by the Government.

(6) Inmates who are short-termers shall attend training in skill development and facilities shall be provided so that they make a living after their release.

(7) The education or training for skill development shall be compulsory and the short-termers are free to opt for any available in the Centre.

(8) So far as practicable, the education or training for skill development shall be integrated with the educational system of the country so that after their release they may continue their education or skilled work without difficulty. If needed, the inmates' stay in the Centre shall be extended till the completion of the course, if so desired by the individual inmate.

(9) Besides the academic education or training for skill development, provision shall be made and implemented for giving instructions in religious teachings in countries where this is possible at the option of the inmates concerned or in moral teachings in a compulsory and secular way.

(10) Where there are inmates from many religions accommodated in a Centre, instructions in religious teachings of each and every religion may be imparted by representatives of each religion approved by the authorities of the Centre.

(11) Provision shall be made and implemented for imparting literary and cultural education to inmates capable of profiting thereby by approved teachers or the NGOs."

RECREATION AND CULTURAL ACTIVITIES

Rule 78

(1) "There shall be facilities for recreation in every Centre and it shall be different and many consisting of as many indoor games as possible for the inmates to congregate together and release their tension.

(2) Inmates shall be encouraged to participate in cultural activities of all kinds and every Centre shall make arrangements for conducting competitions in cultural activities either in individual capacity or on group basis. Prizes and remission marks shall be awarded to the winning individuals and groups.
(3) There shall be provisions for literary activities and competitions in every Centre. Creative writings and fine arts, drawings, paint works etc. shall be encouraged.
(4) Inmates shall be allowed to participate in tournaments conducted among the inmates of other Centres in the country. There shall be inter-Centre competitions in indoor or/and outdoor games, literary or/and cultural activities. The winners shall be given prizes and remission marks.
(5) In consultation with the sports council, friendly matches shall be organized within the Centres for the inmates to compete with players outside the Centre. Prizes shall be instituted for the winning team in addition to the remission marks, if they are the inmates.
(6) Periodically, film shows, dramas, mimicry, dance, songs, concerts or other performing arts shall be arranged in the Centre's auditorium for the inmates to enjoy and to relax their tensions. Provision shall be made for the inmates to listen to radio and see television programmes. Lectures of eminent personalities on topics of interests for the inmates shall be arranged. Radio and television programmes by the inmates shall be broadcasted/telecasted for the general public to accept the talents and capabilities of the incarcerated."

SOCIAL RELATIONS AND CONTACTS WITH OUTSIDE WORLD

Rule 79

(1) "Very special and specific strategies shall be designed and implemented for the maintenance and positive improvement of homely relations between the inmate and his family as are desirable in the best interests of both and the society at large.
(2) Such strategies will include visits, correspondence and communication to and from the inmates with his family.

(3) Family is taken in its widest meaning possible and includes parents, spouse, children, kith and kin, dear and near and so on with whom and for whom the inmates desire to have human relations and exchange of homely emotions."

Rule 80

"From the beginning of an inmate's entry to a Centre, special care, attention and consideration shall be given to his life in society after his release. He shall be encouraged and assisted to maintain and establish desirable human relations with all persons and agencies outside the Centre for promoting the best interests of his family and his own rehabilitation and reintegration to the community/ society back. After-care agencies and concerned citizens may be incorporated to offer assistance to fulfil the above objectives."

AFTER CARE SERVICES

Rule 81

(1) "Services and agencies, governmental or otherwise, which assist released inmates to reintegrate themselves in the family, community and society, shall ensure, so far as possible and necessary, that released inmates be provided with

(a) appropriate documents and identification papers;
(b) have suitable home and works to go to with equitable wages;
(c) are suitably and adequately clothed having regard to the climate and season;
(d) have ways and means to have their medicines, treatment and medical care; and
(e) have fund and facilities to make an earning to live in dignity in the family, community and society under the care and concern of the agencies or services until such time they do not need their continued care, concern and support."

(2) The approved representatives of such agencies having proved integrity shall have necessary access to the Centre and to the inmates for taking up their correctional,

reformative, rehabilitative mission for reintegrating them back to their family, community and society during the period of incarceration from its beginning and shall be taken into consideration as to the life of the inmates after their release.

(3) It is inevitable that the activities of such agencies are audited and shall be centralized or co-ordinated as far as possible in order to secure the best use of their efforts recognizing the principle that the reintegration of an inmate to his family, community and society is a shared responsibility of the agencies and services with all interested in his reintegration to his family, community and society back."

INSANE AND MENTALLY ABNORMAL INMATES

Rule 82

(1) "Any incarcerated diagnosed to be insane shall be admitted to the Mental Health Hospital forthwith for treatment.

(2) Inmates who are diagnosed to suffer from mental disorders other than insanity proper shall be admitted to Mental Health Centres for specialized treatment.

(3) There shall be an Inmates' Ward attached to all Mental Health Centres under the Government. The Medical, Psychiatric, Psychiatric Social Work Services in the Mental Health Centres shall render all their services and assistance to every inmate who needs such assistance and services in all Centres of Personality Development."

Rule 83

"It is desirable that steps should be taken, by arrangement with appropriate agencies, to ensure, if necessary, the continuation of psychiatric treatment after release and the provision of social psychiatric after-care."

THE AGED AND THE INFIRM

Rule 83A(1) Laws shall be specially enacted for the release of offenders above the age of 80 years under probation of good conduct except in those cases which are coming under the category of offences against the State.

(2) Inmates in the age-group of 75-80 years of age shall be allowed to have specialists' treatment for their diseases either in a specialist institution or in Government hospitals or in the Centre for which the expenditure incurred shall be borne entirely by the inmates. In case, they are people of good character and conduct, they may be granted pre-mature release under parole conditions for treatment and reintegration to the family, community and society back.

(3) Inmates in the age-group of 70-75 years of age shall be allowed to have specialists' treatment at their expenses and depending upon each case, specialities and needs, they may be granted pre-mature release for treatment outside the Centre.

(4) Inmates who are in the age-group of 60-70 shall be granted privileges given to the inmates under Rule 83A(3) except that they will not be considered for pre-mature release in relaxation of the existing rules governing the eligibility and suitability for the granting of parole in every country.

To wind up, the prisons have never been used till recently for the development of human personality in an upright way in the right direction. They were Centres of torture, punishment, detention, cruelty, persecution, man-slaughter, penance, humiliation, harassment, sufferings, distress, tribulations, tormenting, injury, insult and thus the litany goes on. The structure of the prisons, the doors, cells, uniform, food, accommodation, life etc. are abhorring everywhere-anywhere. It took several centuries for the humanity to convert the terrestrial hells to institutions of correction. Is the humanity successful in the attempt? The U.N. Standard Minimum Rules for the Treatment of Prisoners, 1957 wanted to make the prisons centres for the treatment of the prisoners. Is it successful? Now, the United Nations want to revise the 1957 Rules and in the meantime come the Guidelines for the Management of the Centres of Personality Development. Will it be successful? Success or no success, let us proceed further with a hope that one day we will reach the destination. Yes, let us say with Sir Winston Churchill once again: **"The mood and temper of the public with regard to the treatment of crime and criminals has been always an unfailing test of the civilization of any country".**

Bibliography

AUTHORITATIVE AND AUTHENTIC BOOKS AUTHORED BY DR. JAMES VADACKUMCHERY

Acquittals in Administration of Justice, Ph.D. Thesis, Kerala University, (mimeo), Thiruvananthapuram, 1983.

Activism, Accountability and Justice (ISBN: 81-7341-4324-X), Indian Publishers' Distributors, Delhi, 2004.

Arkansayile Kuruvikal [Sparrows of Arkansas] (Malayalam) [ISBN 978-93-81318-87-4], H&C Publishing House, Thrissur, 2012.

Bankers' Safety: Methods and Techniques, (ISBN: 81-7022-937-5), (Second edition), Concept Publishing Company, Delhi, 2002.

Child Labour (Malayalam), State Literacy Mission, Thiruvananthapuram, 2000.

Crime and Society : Current Issues and Trends, (ISBN: 81-7648-024-X), A.P.H. Publishing Corporation, Delhi, 1999.

Crime, Law and Police Science, (ISBN: 81-7022-995-2), (Second edition), Concept Publishing Company, Delhi, 2003.

Crime, Police and Correction, (ISBN: 81-7024-939-2), A.P.H. Publishing Corporation, Delhi, 1998.

Criminology and Penology, Kairali Books International, Trivandrum, 1983.

Departmental Inquiries and Injustice, (ISBN: 81-7024-899-X), A.P.H. Publishing Corporation, Delhi, 1997.

Goodbye Police: Memoirs of a Criminologist, (ISBN: 81-7341-390-8), Indian Publishers' Distributors, Delhi, 2005.

Human Behaviour and Law Enforcement, (ISBN: 81-7024-688-1), Ashish Publishing House, Delhi, 1995.

Human Relations in Banking: How to get along better with people?, Santha Publishing House, Cochin, 1988.

Human Rights and the Police in India, (ISBN: 81-7024-722-5), A.P.H. Publishing Corporation, Delhi, 1996.

Human Rights Friendly Police: A Myth or Reality?, (ISBN: 81-7648-150-5), A.P.H. Publishing Corporation, Delhi, 2000.

Human Values and Police Behaviour, Bureau of Police Research and Development, Ministry of Home Affairs, Government of India, 2000.

India's Supreme Court and Police: Consensus and Conflicts, (ISBN: 81-7341-301-0), Indian Publishers' Distributors, Delhi, 2003.

Indian Police 2001: What Went Wrong Here? (ISBN: 81-7024-967-8), A.P.H. Publishing Corporation, Delhi, 1998.

Indian Police and Equal Justice Under Law, (ISBN: 81-7648-066-5), A.P.H. Publishing Corporation, Delhi, 1999.

Indian Police and Miscarriage of Justice, (ISBN: 81-7024-792-6), A.P.H. Publishing Corporation, Delhi, 1997.

Indian Police and Nexus Crime, (ISBN: 81-7835-037-8), Kalpaz Publications, Delhi, 2002.

Judiciary and Juvenile Justice, (ISBN: 81-7341-389-4), Indian Publishers' Distributors, Delhi, 2005.

Juvenile Delinquency (Malayalam), State Literacy Mission, Thiruvananthapuram, 2000.

Management Thoughts on Police Administration, (ISBN: 81-7024-914-7), A.P.H. Publishing Corporation, Delhi, 1998.

Management Thought for Justice Administration, (ISBN: 13-978-81-7268-233-0) Logos Press, Delhi, 2013.

Misguiding Philosophies and Millennium Police, (ISBN: 81-7341-278-2), Indian Publishers' Distributors, Delhi, 2003.

National Police Commission: Issues for Rethinking, (ISBN: 81-7024-826-4), A.P.H. Publishing Corporation, Delhi, 1998.

Police and the Society, Kairali Books International, Trivandrum, 1985.

Police and Human Rights(ed.), Kerala Police Officers' Association, Thiruvananthapuram, 1994.

Police and the People (Translation of the title: Public Relations at the Cutting Edge Level: Case-study materials by Prof. C.K. Muhammed Ummer), The State Institute of Language, Kerala, Thiruvananthapuram, 2000.

Police Criminology and Crimes, (ISBN: 81-7835-094-7) Kalpaz Publications, Delhi, 2002.

Police Enforcement Crimes and Injustice, (ISBN: 81-212-0471-5), Gyan Publishing House, Delhi, 2001.

Police Interrogation: DOs which the police do not DO, (ISBN: 81-7024-974-0), A.P.H. Publishing Corporation, Delhi, 1998.

Police Leadership: The Inside Story, (ISBN: 81-7648-120-3), A.P.H. Publishing Corporation, Delhi, 1999.

Police Morality, (ISBN: 81-7835-038-6), Kalpaz Publications, Delhi, 2001.

Police, Victim and Victim Justice, (ISBN: 81-7479-043-8), Kaveri Books. Delhi, 2001.

Police, Women and Gender Justice, (ISBN: 81-7648-137-8), A.P.H. Publishing Corporation, Delhi, 2000.

Policing the Largest Democracy: 50 Years and After, (ISBN: 81-7024-979-1), A.P.H. Publishing Corporation, Delhi, 1998.

Policing the Police: A Nation's Cry, (ISBN :81-7479-060-81), Kaveri Books, Delhi, 2003.

Professional Police Witness Interviewing, (ISBN: 81-7648-061-4), A.P.H. Publishing Corporation, Delhi, 1999.

Public Relations at the Cutting Edge Level: Case-study materials, National, Delhi, 1985.

Road Users' Guide (Malayalam), Assistant Motor Vehicle Inspectors'Association, Ernakulam, 1997.

Society, Police and Crimes: Tasks and Challenges, (ISBN: 81-7341-266-0), Indian Publishers' Distributors, Delhi, 2002.

Sociology of Policing India: 2000 and Beyond, (ISBN: 81-7341-279-0), Indian Publishers' Distributors, Delhi, 2003.

The Complete Reference: Methodology of Research in Criminology Law Justice and Correction (Vol. I), (ISBN: 81-7341-414-8), Indian Publishers' Distributors, Delhi, 2007.

The Complete Reference: Methodology of Research in Criminology Law Justice and Correction (Vol. II), (ISBN: 81-7341-448-0), Indian Publishers' Distributors, Delhi, 2010.

The Complete Reference: Methodology of Research in Criminology Law Justice and Correction (Vol. III), (ISBN: 81-7341-449-7), Indian Publishers' Distributors, Delhi, 2010.

The Justice Less Administered, (ISBN: 81-7341-380-0), Indian Publishers' Distributors, Delhi, 2005.

The Police and Delinquency in India, (ISBN: 81-7024-725-X), A.P.H. Publishing Corporation, Delhi, 1996.

The Police, The Accused and Criminal Injustice, (ISBN: 91-7024-80C-X), A.P.H. Publishing Corporation, Delhi, 1997.

The Police, the Court and Injustice, (ISBN: 81-7024-806-X), A.P.H. Publishing Corporation, Delhi, 1997.

The Police, The People and Criminal Justice, (ISBN: 81-7024-862-9), A.P.H. Publishing Corporation, Delhi, 1999.

The Unseen Phases of Crimes, (Malayalam), *(ISBN: 81-90-9360-1-8),* H&C Publishing House, Trissur, 2009.

Third Millennium Police: Take off Trends in India, (ISBN: 81-7648-062-2), A.P.H. Publishing Corporation, Delhi, 1999.

U.N. Universal Declaration of Human Rights and Criminal Justice: The Total Revision, Concept Publishing Company (P) Ltd., New Delhi, 2012.

United Nations and Indian Mysticism: Parallels on Human Rights and Police, (ISBN: 81-7022-664-2), Concept Publishing Company, New Delhi, 2002.

Values and God's Commandments, (Malayalam) Catechetical Centre Thalassery, 1995.

Why I am not a policeman, (ISBN: 81-7479-042-X) Kaveri Books Delhi, 2001.

Wounded Justice and the Story of Indian Police, (ISBN: 81-7479-045-4), Kaveri Books, Delhi, 2001.

Index